IF THE TOMB IS EMPTY

"If the tomb is empty, then anything is possible...What if we really believed that? Joby Martin challenges us with this question in his first book and walks us through the Scriptures to point us to the life-changing truth of Jesus on the cross."
—Matt Carter, lead pastor of Sagemont Church, Houston, Texas, and author of *The Long Walk Home*

"Joby Martin gives powerful examples in his own life and throughout Scripture where God intervened in the lives of ordinary people like you and me. He points us to the life-changing Gospel of Jesus Christ and the resurrection because it's the empty tomb that changes everything. With the same passion Joby preaches, his first book will inspire you. Every Christian should read it."
—Phil Hopper, lead pastor of Abundant Life, and author of *Defeating the Enemy* and *The Weapons of Our Warfare*

"There is no greater event, no greater story than the one Joby has based this book, his life, and his ministry on—the empty tomb. When you finish, you will gain a paradigm-shifting outlook on life."   —Bryan Loritts, author of *The Dad Difference*

"Joby Martin has a penned a Scripture-rich, no-nonsense approach to the tenets of our faith. Don't wait, dive into this book and prayerfully discover the eternal joy that awaits for those who would believe that the tomb is empty."   —Shane Everett, Shane & Shane

"No matter where you are on the journey—doubter, wanderer, seasoned believer—you need this powerful book. Joby Martin starts where you are and invites you to consider the claims and heart of the Gospel by tracing its threads throughout Scripture with fresh and profound insights. The message of Christ's death, burial, and resurrection is more relevant and needed today than ever before and can change everything about your life. Read this to deepen your own spiritual pilgrimage and to equip yourself to share God's truth in more compelling and inspiring ways."

—Dr. Wess Stafford, president emeritus, Compassion International, and author of *Too Small to Ignore* and *Just a Minute*

"Joby Martin's message in his first book, *If the Tomb Is Empty*, is compelling. I've been a leader in the church for a long time and yet it challenged me at a heart level about the power of the Gospel to change lives and make the impossible possible."

—Dan Reiland, executive pastor of 12Stone Church, and author of *Confident Leader*

"When Joby preaches…I listen! Now, when Joby writes…I read it! So thrilled for the powerful message connected to Jesus that anything is possible. I'm a big Joby fan and you will be too after reading *If the Tomb Is Empty*."

—Doug Fields, speaker, author, and pastor

"Joby Martin's message in his first book, *If the Tomb Is Empty*, is one that we all need to hear now more than ever, that the good news of the Gospel of Jesus Christ can change everything."

—Larry Moody, president of In the Game Ministries

"Illogical? Perhaps. Astounding? It can be nothing short of it. Inviting? Always. The declaration that Jesus traded places with us in order to gift us the right to become children of God is quite literally history-altering news. The knowledge that He did not stay in the tomb, but rose triumphant with the keys to hell, death, and the grave in His hands still causes me to tremble. And yet, with freshness folded into the story, my friend Joby reignites passion and pleasure in this message for anyone willing to journey with him in his first book—*If the Tomb Is Empty*. You will not regret becoming newly or freshly acquainted with the greatest news you have ever heard."

—Léonce B. Crump Jr., founder, Renovation Church, and author of *Renovate: Changing Who You Are by Loving Where You Are*

IF THE TOMB IS EMPTY

Why the Resurrection Means
Anything Is Possible

JOBY MARTIN

WITH CHARLES MARTIN

FOREWORD BY TIM TEBOW

New York   Nashville

FaithWords
Hachette Book Group
1290 Avenue of the Americas, New York, NY 10104
faithwords.com
twitter.com/faithwords

First Edition: February 2022

FaithWords is a division of Hachette Book Group, Inc.
The FaithWords name and logo are trademarks of Hachette Book Group, Inc.

The publisher is not responsible for websites (or their content) that are not owned by the publisher.

The Hachette Speakers Bureau provides a wide range of authors for speaking events. To find out more, go to www.hachettespeakersbureau.com or call (866) 376-6591.

Library of Congress Cataloging-in-Publication Data

Names: Martin, Joby, author. | Martin, Charles, 1969- author.
Title: If the tomb is empty : why the resurrection means anything is
    possible / Joby Martin and Charles Martin.
Description: First edition. | New York : FaithWords, [2022] | Summary: "The   Son of God was crucified, died and buried. Doornail dead. He lay in the tomb for three days. Until God the Father, through the Spirit, raised Him to life and He walked out shining like the sun. The Son of God lives and reigns, right this second. In a culture in which history is erased or rewritten at will, the existence of an empty tomb matters. Why? Because if the tomb is empty - then anything is possible. In his first book, Joby Martin, pastor of Church of Eleven22, one of the fastest growing churches in the country, dives deep into scripture and traces the story of salvation by highlighting the seven mountains throughout scripture where God manifests himself. As he describes each encounter with God, Martin shows us how the interaction on each mountain laid the groundwork for the sacrifice of Christ on Calvary, and shows what God revealed about Himself in the process. He illuminates even familiar passages, unveiling how God's plan for Christ's sacrifice is threaded throughout scripture, and shows why Christ's resurrection - impossible, unbelievable - means that nothing is too hard for our God. Ultimately, he asks readers, Do you live every day of your life as if the tomb is empty...or as though Jesus is still hanging on that cross? Written with New York Times bestselling author Charles Martin-a member and elder of Joby's church-If the Tomb is Empty is an insightful and spiritually rich yet accessible examination of what the miracle of Christ's resurrection means for all of us"-- Provided by publisher.
Identifiers: LCCN 2021041420 | ISBN 9781546001508 (hardcover) | ISBN
    9781546001546 (ebook)
Subjects: LCSH: Jesus Christ--Resurrection. | Mountains--Religious
    aspects--Christianity.
Classification: LCC BT482 .M37 2022 | DDC 232/.5--dc23
LC record available at https://lccn.loc.gov/2021041420

ISBNs: 9781546001508 (hardcover), 9781546001546 (ebook)

Printed in the United States of America

LSC-C

Printing 1, 2021

For Gretchen, JP, and Reagan Capri.
And Coach Bull Lee.
I wouldn't be here without you.

A NOTE ON THE TEXT

Almost all direct Scripture quotes in this book come from the English Standard Version. In some cases I've simply paraphrased instead of quoting directly from a published translation; in these cases, the Scripture will be set in italics.

That I may know him and the power of his resurrection.

—Paul

CONTENTS

FOREWORD

By Tim Tebow

Proverbs 11:14 says, "Where there is no guidance the people fall, but in an abundance of counselors there is victory" (NASB). Over the years, I have asked several pastors around the country to speak life into me and give me wise counsel as I consider important decisions. One of those men is Pastor Joby Martin from my hometown of Jacksonville, Florida. Thankfully, he looked past the fact that I'm a Gator and he's a Bulldog fan, and he agreed. We tend to talk a lot about Jesus and a little about college football. We've grown so close since that time, and there are not many big decisions I make without first calling him to seek wisdom and discernment.

Pastor Joby has a gift for taking complicated sections of Scripture and breaking them down in a way that is authentic to God's Word. He also continually helps me see how Scripture is even more applicable to my life and the lives of those around me. God uses Joby to help me understand His Word and speak to me through it. Not only that, but as I have spent time with him and his family, I have learned he is the real deal. He loves his wife, Gretchen, and he considers it one of the highest honors of his life to get to be the father of his children, JP and Reagan. Joby loves the Lord with everything he has, and he is so passionate about his calling to preach the Gospel with authority and clarity. Joby is one of the best communicators I know. Whether he delivers eye-opening insight, captivating life stories, or hilarious one-liners, or draws you in with his unapologetically southern accent, he tells the truth with great love.

Out of that love, he leads this movement called The Church of Eleven22. (The name probably has you wondering, and you can read more about that inside these pages.) By intently listening to and boldly answering God's call on his life, Joby has been a vessel whom God has used to build a thriving ministry, which has helped thousands discover and deepen their relationship with Jesus Christ.

I'm so excited Joby accepted the mission to write *If the Tomb Is Empty*. What a powerful reminder that because of that truth, anything is possible. My hope as you read these pages is that you will understand how God meets us in our everyday lives—whether on the mountaintop or in the valley. No matter where your foot lands, He has already been there.

In my own life, I've found this to be true. I've known the highs of great success and the lows of dark valleys. I'm grateful for the successes God has blessed me with because they've given me a platform to give all the glory to Him. I'm also grateful for the lows in my life because they've given me a testimony to point to God's faithfulness in the hard times. But one thing that is unchanged and not dependent upon my circumstances, emotions, successes, or failures is the Good News of the Gospel of Jesus Christ. He is with us and He is for us, always.

From the first page to the last, Joby walks you through the story of God's amazing plan to redeem a bunch of rebels like us and bring us to Himself. Not only that, but by the time you reach the last chapter, you'll know—maybe for the first time, maybe as a much-needed reminder—the unimaginable remedy to our brokenness, that God paid for our sin debt with the life of His Son. I'm so grateful the story doesn't end at the cross, and that we don't follow or strive to be like a dead prophet or moral teacher. Because three days later, God raised His Son Jesus to life, and today we worship the living Savior who takes away sin of the world!

The tomb is empty.

That is evidence that Jesus *is* who He says He is, that His Word is true, and that what might be impossible in your own ability is possible with and through Him.

If the Tomb Is Empty is a beautiful reminder of the empty-tomb, gospel-centered, Jesus-resurrected reality that for God so loved even me that He sent His only Son on a rescue mission to save me from my sin—and you from yours. Whether you have already given your life to Christ and have been walking with Him for a long time or you don't even know what trusting Him as your Savior means, this message is for you.

IF THE TOMB IS EMPTY

PROLOGUE

So there I was…
  (That's how I start every good story.)

Standing on the Mount of Olives. The Garden of Gethsemane below me, my favorite place on the planet to pray. The tips of the ancient olive trees rising up above the walls. Directly in front of me stands the Golden (or Beautiful) Gate, sealed shut since the Crusaders lost the city a thousand years ago. Some silly religious folks think that the stone and mortar will keep Christ the King from entering the city upon His return. To my right, the Lions' Gate. Some think Stephen was dragged through that gate and stoned in the valley below me. To my left spreads the City of David, an archaeological playland these days. In my mind, I imagine the rooftop upon which David spied Bathsheba. It's easy to see as you walk around how power and this perspective could get a man in serious trouble. Below the garden, the brook Kidron snakes through the valley that, since the days of Josiah, has been the most famous burial site around. Tens upon tens of thousands of graves spread left to right as far as the eye can see, buried here beneath the towering shadow of Hezekiah's eastern wall. And there, beyond the wall, sitting on the hill, rise the Temple Mount and the Old City of Jerusalem.

This is THE mountain of God.

The place where His name is written forever. Even the aerial view of the three valleys out of which the mountain rises looks like the twenty-second letter of the Hebrew alphabet ("shin") that spells His name. This is the place where Abram broke bread with Melchizedek after the battle with the four kings and raised his hand in covenant with God Most High. And later in his life, this is the place where he bound his son Isaac, the son of his love, placed him on an altar, and raised a knife to kill him. This is where David danced as he brought the ark into Jerusalem, telling Michal, *I will become even more undignified than this.* Singing what we call Psalm 24: "Lift up your heads, O gates! And lift them up, O ancient doors, that the King of glory may come in. Who is this King of glory? The LORD of Hosts, he is the King of glory."

This is the place where the plague stopped at the threshing floor of Ornan the Jebusite, where Nathan told David, *You are the man* and David paid the penalty for his sin. This is where both good and bad kings ruled and Solomon built a temple unequaled in all human history. Where Hezekiah and Nehemiah rebuilt the walls, Josiah tore down the high places, and the conquering Babylonians led a nation into captivity, leaving this city in ruins.

And this is the place where Jesus showed up as a twelve-year-old boy and taught in the temple, saying, "Did you not know that I must be in my Father's house?" This is where He walked, taught, healed, laughed, loved, drove out the tax gatherers, broke bread, and taught us to pray.

On this mountain, Jesus paraded in on a donkey while crowds shouted, "Hosanna to the Son of David! Blessed is he who comes in the name of the Lord!" *Hosanna* means "Lord, save us." The *us* was priority to that crowd. This is the place where if those people fell silent, even the rocks would cry out. And it is here that Jesus wept. Because He knew what was coming.

On this mountain, Jesus' blood vessels burst, His sweat turned to blood, and He took the first sip of the Father's cup of wrath as one of His best friends betrayed Him with a kiss. Where self-righteous and jealous murderers arrested Him and paraded Him before a kangaroo court, where they struck Him in the face, plucked out His beard, beat Him with rods, and ripped chunks of flesh off His back and sides with a cat-o'-nine-tails. Here they drove a crown of thorns into His skull, the same type of tree from which the ark of the covenant was constructed, and then forced Him to carry a criminal's cross outside the gate where they burn the trash.

Here on these Herodian stones, Jesus became unrecognizable as a man.

Just a few hundred yards from where I now stand, in what is today a busy bus station, they drove nails through His hands and feet and hung Him on a cross on a well-traveled road where people spat and laughed, and a soldier shoved a spear into His chest.

This is the spot where the blood and water flowed.

Here the Father forsook Him, here the veil tore in two—and the people of God were no longer separated from the presence of God. Here the sky turned black in midday, and here, Jesus, the sinless, righteous, spotless Son of God, who did not think equality with God something to be grasped but willingly humbled Himself and came on a rescue mission for a bunch of rebels like us, poured out His soul to the death. The Lamb of God who has come to take away the sin of the entire world. Clearing forever our debt ledger. Paying a price you and I could not pay in ten thousand lifetimes.

This is the mountain where Jesus died. Where He painted the mercy seat with His very own blood. Where His brokenhearted friends, who had watched Him heal the sick and raise the dead, pulled His limp, cold, naked, shredded, bloodless, lifeless body down, and some brave soul closed His eyes. This is where they carried Him to a borrowed tomb, and the soldiers sealed Him behind heavy stone. This is where His friends wept and knew sorrow unlike any they'd ever known.

I would imagine that those who followed Jesus were incredulous as they stared at His lifeless body on the cross. I'm convinced they asked, "God, have You completely lost control? Can't You see what's going on down here?" Little did they know this was His plan to save the entire world. This is why the writer of Hebrews says, *He upholds all things by the Word of His power.* And this is why Paul tells the Romans, *For those who love God all things work together for good, for those who are called according to His purpose* (8:28).

On this mountain, the Son of God was killed, and those who witnessed His death took His body down and laid it to rest in a tomb. They thought that was the end. Forever. All hope lost. Because once you're dead, you're dead. Who can defeat death?

But the story doesn't end there. Not by a long shot.

Because this is where, three days later, He rose from the dead and walked out shining like the sun. Tomb empty. The keys of death and hell hanging from His belt. On this mountain, the tomb is empty.

Which changes everything. For everyone who would believe it. Forever.

This is where they intended to prepare the body only to find the stone rolled away, His body gone, and an angel asking, "Why do you seek the living among the dead?"

On this mountain, He alone did what no one else could. He bought us back. Redeemed us from the curse. And cut a new covenant based on better promises. This is the birthplace of hope.

Here, Mary screamed at the top of her lungs, I have seen the Lord! Here, Thomas believed. Here, to their great surprise, Jesus appeared when they were meeting behind locked doors, breathed on them the very ruach[1] of God, and said, *Receive Holy breath. If you forgive the sins of any, they are forgiven them.*

This is where when they did not believe it was Him, He chastised them for their unbelief and hardness of heart. This is where He opened for them the Scriptures, explaining how everything that had been written before in the law, prophets, and psalms revealed Him, and how He alone is the perfect manifestation of that revelation.

And this is where He broke bread. Again.

This is where He appeared to over five hundred believers. In the very place where many saw Him crucified and dead. And somewhere not too far from where I now stand, He stepped onto the Father's chariot and ascended to heaven—where He remains seated to this day.

Down there to my left, on the day of Pentecost, standing on the southern steps of the temple, Peter was used by God in a mighty way. He did not let his multiple past mistakes define him, but God used the very thing that got him in the most trouble—his mouth— and gave what might be the second-best sermon ever given. Second only to the one given on the Mount. And when he'd finished, the Spirit of God was poured out, fulfilling the Scriptures in Proverbs, Joel, Isaiah, Ezekiel, and Zechariah that promised, "I will pour out my Spirit on all flesh." And on that day, here on this mountain, three thousand were added to the number.

This is that mountain.

And lastly, somewhere close to where I now stand, on a date known only by the Father, this mountain will split in two and Jesus will return as He left—to judge the quick and the dead. That's you and me and all those who came before us.

The most significant history in the history of history occurred

---

1   The Hebrew word *ruach* means "breath, wind, or spirit." The Greek equivalent in the New Testament is *pneuma*.

within a half mile of where I now stand. On this storied mountain. On this bloodstained hill. It is here that Jesus rendered an irrevocable, undeniable, and eternal defeat to satan. Here, in possibly the most illogical thing I've ever heard, the very Son of God gave you and me the right to become children of God. The Son of God became a man, that men and women could become sons and daughters of God. Transferring us from the kingdom of darkness into the kingdom of the Son of God's love, and in so doing, took from us the spirit of slavery and in its place gave us the Spirit of sonship, teaching us to speak one of the most beautiful words ever spoken by human lips—"Abba."

Today, when you stand on Calvary, you're literally standing in one of the busiest bus stops on planet earth, which offends all our artistic sentimentalism. But as you sit there among the noise and horns and fumes and heat, you think, *This may be a good picture of the Crucifixion, because it was a grimy place with people coming and going.* Nothing about the Crucifixion of Jesus was picturesque. It was dirty and gross, because that's what sin is, and yet God the Father chose this mountain upon which to crush it.

In stark contrast, if you walk out of the bus station some sixty-five steps to your left, you're in the most peaceful place you've ever been in your entire life: a garden where they once crushed grapes. Off to one side of the garden, cut into a rock wall, is an empty tomb. I know. I've been there. Why does this matter? Because the Son of God was dead when they put Him there, and three days later, He walked out. He rose again and walked out of that stone grave. Alive. And He was seen by over five hundred people over the course of forty days. And right this second, the Son of God lives. While this mountain holds the tomb, the tomb couldn't hold Him. (In all honesty, we don't know for sure if this was His tomb or not, but I tend to think it was.)

The reason any of what I'm about to say matters is because that tomb is empty. Paul said, *I want to know Christ and the power of His resurrection* (Phil. 3:10). Why? What's the big deal?

> *"If Christ has not been raised, then our preaching is in vain and your faith is in vain ... And if Christ has not been raised, your faith is futile and you are still in your sins ... If in Christ we have hope in this life only, we are of all people most to be pitied. But in fact Christ has been raised from the dead, the firstfruits of those who have fallen asleep. For as by a man came death, by a man has come also the resurrection of the dead. For as in Adam all die, so also in Christ shall all be made alive."* (1 Corinthians 15:14, 17, 19–22)

The heart of Paul's answer rests in this phrase: *if Christ has not been raised, your faith is futile and you are still in your sins.* Think about the ramifications of that. Can anything be worse? Name one thing. You can't. Now ask yourself the reverse: If Christ is alive, can anything be better?

You see that phrase *made alive*? Don't miss it. He's talking about us. The fact that Jesus walked out alive matters for everyone who would believe it. Forever. My question for you is this: If Christ is alive and the tomb is empty, what does this mean for you? Like, really? In total. What does the empty tomb mean for you? For me?

The answer tells a lot about you and what you believe. So, let me press you. This is a gut check. Do you live every day of your life as if the tomb is empty ... or as though Jesus is still hanging on that cross?

Think before you answer.

* * *

Let me bring it closer to home. Here are some questions we're going to work through in these pages:

1. Do you believe His promise to you?
2. Who tells you who you are: you...or Jesus?
3. Why are you still holding on to that idol?
4. Do you really want to be blessed?
5. How will you stand against the enemy?
6. Do you want to be healed?
7. What is finished?

If you believe that tomb on Calvary was empty, it should change how you answer these questions. Spoiler alert: the empty tomb changes everything, about everything, for everyone who would believe it.

In eternity past when God spoke, He made this mountain on which I now stand—Calvary. And for reasons only He knows, He said, "I already know what's going to happen between this sea and this river, between this people and this people. But here, on this map dot of earth, I'm going to do a thing that's never before been done and will never be done again. I'm going to drive an eternal stake in the ground and demonstrate, once and for all, the love of My Son, Jesus Christ."

Calvary is the epicenter of the earth. All of life—past, present, future—revolves around this mountain.

This is the mountain of God. The God of Abraham, Isaac, and Jacob, and God's Son, Jesus.

This mountain on which I'm standing is our destination. We're coming back here. But to show why this mountain matters, we need to walk over six really important mountains in Scripture before we return here. Why? Because the events that occurred on those other mountains point to this one. They lay the groundwork and tell us the story of why this one matters.

So with that in mind, I want to start with Abraham and Isaac on Mount Moriah; then move to Moses and Mount Sinai; to

Elijah on Mount Carmel; to Jesus on the Mount of Beatitudes; to Jesus tempted by satan on a very high mountain; to Peter, James, and John with Jesus, Moses, and Elijah on the Mount of Transfiguration; and finally return to the mountain where it all started, Calvary. I want to take a journey together up these seven storied mountains from the Scriptures. Specific mountains used by God for His purposes, because for some reason, God uses these mountains to manifest Himself.

Let's pause and think about what a mountain looks like. It's a high point, surrounded by shorter peaks and valleys. It's a good picture of our lives. In between now and the day of Jesus' return, you and I will stand on mountaintops, valleys, and countless hillsides in between. We will know unmatched joy and unrivaled sorrow. I can't really tell you why. Only that we will. It seems like God demonstrates His glory on the mountaintop and His love and mercy in the valley. Maybe that's why it's only when we go up and down and up and down that we get a more complete picture of Him. We all love the peak, but the valley is usually not far behind. Plus, you can't stay on the mountaintop. Nobody can. They're small, and there's no water. That's in the valley. So are all the people. Funny how that works. And as much as we yearn for the mountaintop, truth is we spend most of our time either coming down, hiking up, or in the valley between.

*   *   *

No matter where you find yourself—whether you're a new believer, a seasoned servant of the faith, or maybe you don't know what you are—join me. Walk with me through the events that occurred on these seven mountains, because each one leads right back to the rock beneath our feet and then our final destination, which is just up that hill—the cross of Jesus Christ and the empty tomb—and what it means for you and me.

Because...if the tomb is empty, anything is possible.

Pray with Me

Our good and gracious heavenly Father, I come to You humbly as Your servant yet boldly as Your son. I pray for every man, woman, and student who will take this journey from Mount Moriah to Mount Calvary. God, I lift up the one that has yet to trust You with their life and eternity. God, I pray that You will open their eyes to the deceitfulness of rebellion. I pray that the ache of the soul that this world cannot remedy would grow so acute that we would realize that You and You alone satisfy. God, I pray that You would soften the heart of the religious. I pray that we would be awakened to the reality that even our righteous activity is like filthy rags to You. God, would You mold us and shape us to always know that You are with us on the mountaintop and You are with us in the valley? God, I pray for the believer who will take this journey. Would You bless us not just with knowledge about You and Your works but a deeper knowledge of YOU? God, I pray that You will take fallible words and curious minds and do exceedingly more than any of us could ever hope or imagine. Lord, I pray that we would begin to see ourselves the way You see us: holy and blameless, sons and daughters, righteous and redeemed. God, I pray that this journey from mountain to mountain would lead us into a deeper relationship with Jesus Christ. Emmanuel, I pray that just as You met Your people on these mountains, You would meet us in undeniable ways through these pages. I pray this in the good, strong name of Jesus Christ our King. Amen.

CHAPTER 1

Mount Moriah—Do You Live as Though You Can Save Yourself?

E arly in the summer of my fourteenth year, I began wrestling with some deep questions I couldn't answer. Things weren't awesome in my house, and given the uncertainty, I didn't really know who I was. My parents weren't getting along and the tension was thick. They loved me and my brother really well. They just didn't know how to love each other. So, to fit in, I started drinking. One thing led to another and the police got involved. Shortly thereafter, a kid my age began bullying my little brother. When he didn't quit, the rage I'd swallowed and tried to drown came out my fists. Again, the police got involved. To keep me from picking up trash on the side of a South Carolina highway in a county blue jumpsuit, my football coach, Bull Lee, stepped in and "suggested" the antidote to my wretched black-hearted ways was honest, hot, sweaty, and not-so-glamorous work. The powers that be agreed, and so I found myself a not-so-willing landscape artist at a Christian camp.

Having grown up in the South, I knew about Jesus and I knew the rules: we don't drink, cuss, or chew or go with girls who do. I was good. I'd checked that box. I was a Christian. Born into it. Just like NASCAR and SEC football.

Mowing the grass led to attending the camp, and on the last night, after we'd sung "I Am a C" and "Friends Are Friends Forever," many of the camp counselors dressed in sheets and, with almost unintelligible Southern accents, reenacted the death and resurrection of Jesus, ending with "Why do you seek the livin' among the dead?"

As corny as it was, and even though I'd heard the story dozens of times, I saw the cross for the first time. For what it was. Propitiation. A payment that satisfies. Somehow, I knew that I knew that I knew that an exchange had occurred. When Jesus, God made man, climbed up on that cross, He offered me something I didn't deserve and took from me what I did. For reasons that made sense only to Him, He wrapped Himself in my sin— and not only that, but He took upon Himself all the consequences of it—and then with His very own blood, He paid my debt ledger and satisfied the wrath of God. A debt I couldn't pay in a thousand lifetimes. I believed that when Jesus pushed up on His nail-pierced feet and said, "*Tetelestai,*" it is finished, that somehow it counted for me.

Somewhere up front, Coach Lee issued "the call." "Who wants to put their faith in Jesus?" We'll talk more about this in chapter 2, but that phrase "faith IN Jesus" started to mean something for the first time. We sang "Just as I Am" about thirteen times while he waited. "Anybody else?"

There was no way I was walking up there. No way. Not in front of all my friends. They knew what I'd done. Then Coach Lee said, "I believe there is ONE MORE."

Next thing I knew, I'd walked up there and was hugging Coach Lee. All in. For the first time, I believed that what Jesus had done on that tree somehow counted for me. I can't tell you I understood everything it meant, but right then and there I put my whole trust and faith in Jesus. As opposed to me. Which was a good thing, given the track record for my summer and the downward trajectory my life was taking.

I didn't know it at the time, but I'd just made Romans 10:9 true in my life. I was "saved." I'd confessed with my mouth that Jesus is Lord and believed in my heart that God had raised Him from the dead. This was a revelation to me and the emotional high was unlike any I'd known.

I didn't want to leave camp, which was strange, given that I hadn't wanted to go in the first place. Everybody hugged; we cried. Al Gore had not yet invented the internet, so we all lied to each other and said, "I promise I'll write." We shared addresses, and just before I left, one of the counselors at the camp, a student at Clemson, gave me a Bible in which she had highlighted several verses.

I never wanted to come down from the high of that mountain, but my grandmother, Myrt, came to pick me up and we headed home for the start of my freshman year in high school. Two hours from home, I thought, *Everything's going to be better now.* I just knew it.

The problem I was about to bump into was I had to go home, and I wasn't quite sure what I was going to get when I got there. We drove in the driveway and shared with my parents that I had asked Jesus into my heart. They said they were excited for me, but they seemed a bit distracted. A few weeks later I walked into the house to a note from my mom that said, *I can't stay here anymore. Please tell your brother. I love you, Mom.* At this point in my life, I don't blame her at all for her decision. But at the time, I was in a bad way.

I held the note in one hand and my new Bible in the other, shaking both at the ceiling. "But this isn't how this goes. I just got saved. Life's supposed to be better. I mean, I met Jesus. Isn't everything going to be better now?"

So I came home to an empty house and had to tell my

eleven-year-old brother, who had no box for this. Complicating matters, my dad worked in North Carolina and only came home on the weekends, so we had to figure out how we got to school, what to eat, how to do laundry…

Further, we couldn't let anybody know that this was our situation, because we weren't sure what they'd do to or with us, but we were pretty sure we wouldn't like it. And to make matters worse, we lived in the country, and the bus didn't make it to our house. So, at fourteen, I "borrowed" my father's truck and drove my brother to middle school, dropped him off in the carpool line, and then drove to high school and went to class. Every morning.

Life was a nonsensical blur, and I just remember having to grow up fast. A couple of weeks in, I sat down on my bed and probably yelled at God for the first time: "All right, Lord, I'm giving You one chance. And if You ever leave me, I ain't doing this." I felt like my whole world was cracking down the middle, because when your parents don't love each other, it's crushing to a teenager.

I'm forty-seven today, and next to my salvation, this was the most defining moment in my life. I reached over, grabbed that Bible, and just stuck my fingers in, playing Bible roulette. In my heart, I was crying out, *Lord, what does this book have to say to me?* Unbeknownst to me, the girl from Clemson had put a bookmark and highlighted Jeremiah 29:11. And that's the first thing I read: "For I know the plans I have for you," declares the Lord, "plans to prosper you and not to harm you, plans to give you hope and a future" (NIV). I've heard several sermons from preachers who are exponentially smarter than I am say that that verse is often taken out of context and isn't meant for us today. Well, I can tell you, it meant everything to me that day sitting on my bed as a fourteen-year-old.

And I can tell you thirty-three years later, Jeremiah was telling the truth.

After I got saved as a teenager, I got involved with Fellowship of Christian Athletes (FCA) and a bunch of organizations like that. Maybe that's where the preacher thing started. We were all supposed to know how to share our faith and lead people to Christ, so I thought I'd try it out.

When I was in high school, this real pretty foreign exchange student came to our school, and since my ministry in high school was to lead cute girls to Jesus, I took her out to dinner. I didn't have any money and she ordered the filet, and I told the server, "I'll have a salad." She was from West Berlin and had absolutely no understanding of the Bible whatsoever, so I figured I'd lead her to Christ at dinner. I wove the conversation to Jesus and I asked her questions. She responded, while enjoying her steak, "I've kind of heard of Him, but I don't get it."

"What don't you get?"

"I mean... what's the big deal?"

And there it was. The softball pitch. I thought to myself, *I am taking this thing deep left center over the bleachers.* She didn't know the difference between the Old and New Testament, so I, in my infinite knowledge as a seventeen-year-old theologian, backed up to the beginning. "Okay, so in the beginning there was nothing and then God created light and there was still nothing but you could see it and then He made some people and they were naked and that was cool. Then there was a snake and they ate and then put on some fig leaves and then there was an ark and a temple and dead lambs everywhere and then Jesus came, died on the cross, and was resurrected on the third day and then He went to heaven. Oh, and He's coming back on a horse."

Her eyes narrowed. "You actually believe that?"

"Yeah. You want to come?"

While she polished off her steak, I remember thinking, *I do kinda sound like a crazy man. Maybe I need to start working on my delivery.*

In FCA, and every other youth group I went to, it seemed like everybody shared a testimony which from the moment they met Jesus, everything was up and to the right from there. Life was good. Problems fixed. But that wasn't my experience, and as I looked at my own life, I thought maybe I wasn't doing this faith thing right. In my life, there was a lot of difficult stuff. I knew far more valleys than mountaintops. Then the Lord led me deeper into His Word, and what I saw in Scripture encouraged me that just because I surrendered to the lordship of Jesus didn't mean life was forever easy street. In fact, many of my heroes in Scripture knew suffering.

One of the first places He led me to was this story of Abraham.

*   *   *

In Genesis 12, God does something that He never explains. He just decides to do it. He chooses Abraham. And He doesn't choose him because Abraham is awesome. He's not. God sovereignly chooses whom He graces or blesses. When He finds Abram, He says, "Abram"—who will eventually become Abraham—"I'm going to make you the father of many nations."

There's just one problem with this. Abraham is seventy-five years old, and he and his wife Sarai—who will become Sarah—have no kids. From Abram's perspective, it's a little late in the game for God to be tapping him on the shoulder and propping up his hopes because Sarai's almost as old as he is. But what Abram will soon learn is that God's not bound by time or time-lines, and what is impossible with man is possible with God. To accomplish His purposes through Abram, God makes an everlasting covenant with Abram. He says, *Through you, I am going to bless the whole world. Whoever blesses you is blessed and whoever curses you is cursed. I'm going to make you the father of many nations, and through you I'm going to create a nation. But first, I want to move you from here to a place I'll show you, so pack up your stuff* (Gen. 12:1–3).

At this point, Abram goes to Sarai and says, *Hey, babe, I've been talking to God today. And He told us to move.*

And she asks the one question every wife would ask. *Where?*

And Abram says, *He said He'd show us when we get there.*

The amazing thing about Sarai is that she went with him. I can hardly get my family to get in my truck if I don't tell them exactly where we are going and how long we'll be there. We talk a lot about Abram's faith, and we should, but remember, Sarai went with him. And he didn't even know where he was going.

At this point, they don't know much about God and how He works. Regardless, Abram says, "We're packing up our stuff and going to a place that the Lord will show us." Then the Bible says Abram put his faith in God. And his faith is counted to him as righteousness—not his right activity, but his trust or belief in God. Later in the New Testament, Abraham will be defined as a man who was a friend of God because of his faith.

Years pass with only a promise but no pregnancy. Which begs the question, Have you ever thought God is on a little different time schedule than you? Am I the only one? Our problem is that God's timing and our timing are not the same. All throughout Scripture, God never gets in a hurry. Which makes me wonder why we're always in such a hurry. He spoke everything into existence, but He took six days to do it. Why? I don't know. He could have done it with just one word. And yet, for whatever reason, God is on His own time frame for His own purpose and His own glory.

Not only is there no son for Abram and Sarai, but things are not all that great at home. On two occasions, when Abraham and Sarah move into a new country, the king of that country sees Sarah—who, even though she's up in age, is still very beautiful—and wants to make her his wife. To protect himself, Abraham offers his wife and says, "She's not my wife. She's my sister. You can have her." Think about this—Abram is a liar who sacrifices his wife to save his own skin. Today, we call a man who does this to a woman a "pimp." There's a lot here, but again, it's not what Abram did that made him righteous in the sight of God. It's what he believed. More on that in a minute.

And before you look down your nose at Abram, keep in mind that we're no different. Starting with me and starting early in my life. When I was growing up, we built a barn with a tin roof in my backyard. Dad worked out of town during the week, so on Monday, he said, "Son, whatever you do, don't get up on the barn." Then he said it again to make sure I heard him the first time. To make sure there was no doubt. "Don't get up on the barn."

To which I immediately thought, *Daddy, it had not even occurred to me to get up there, but now that you mention it, I have to. I can see what fun you're talking about and I have to. Besides, you just told me not to.*

So, when he drove out the drive, I pulled the trampoline up next to the barn and turned myself into human popcorn. When he got home, he said, "Were you on the barn?"

I shook my head. "No way."

He didn't buy it. "You're lying to me."

"Dad, are you calling me a liar?"

He pointed. "No, the dents in the tin roof are." So I took the beating. Meaning? I'm a liar. And you're a liar. It's in our nature.

Ten years after the move to Canaan, when Abram is eighty-five and they've been waiting on God with no result, Sarah and Abraham devise a plan. *We can't wait on God anymore. We've got to take matters into our own hands,* she says. *Abraham, why don't you sleep with our servant Hagar?* In that day and age, sleeping with your servant was totally common (the law hadn't yet been given) and, in many instances, expected. They had just one problem. That wasn't how God said to do it. God's plan has always been one man and one woman in the covenant of marriage. If you read the Old Testament and come away thinking that polygamy is a good thing, then you need to reread it. It always caused a disaster. Despite this, they took matters into their own hands to help God out and created problems that we're still battling in the Middle East today. Which is a really good reminder—in our flesh, we will always produce an Ishmael, while waiting on God will always birth Isaac.

In Romans 9, Paul describes the futile effort. It's called works-based righteousness, and it occurs when we don't trust God to do for us what we need Him to do, so we try to do it in our own power.

I don't care how shady you think you are. You're JV compared to shady, sinful, wretched, selfish, lying Abraham, who pimped out his wife to save his own skin. And yet God didn't give up on him. In His mercy, God didn't squish him, proving that our faithlessness does not void God's faithfulness.

Fourteen years later, some twenty-four years after the promise, when Abram is the ripe, old age of ninety-nine, God shows up and says, *Abram, I haven't forgotten you. And I'm going to keep my promise because I am who I say I am. I always keep my promises and you will have a son.*

Notice, nothing in their lives agrees with this. If anything, conditions have worsened. As proven by the fact that when they hear this, both Sarai and Abram laugh out loud. But God is not subject to our conditions, and a year later, Isaac—whose name means "laughter"—is born.

Then in chapter 22, it says an amazing thing: "After these

things…" (v. 1). What are "these things"? The call of God on Abram's life, God's irrevocable blessing, the covenant with God, Abram's faith being counted as righteousness, Sarai giving birth to the promised son, and Abraham's[2] making peace with Hagar and Ishmael. All is well. You would think everything would be easy street. But how many of you know that following Jesus does not promise you smooth sailing from here on out?

Look at what happens in 22:1: "After these things God tested Abraham."

God *tested* Abraham. I hate tests.

Some of you might argue, "Why? He's old. Hasn't he earned a break?" Not according to God, because the pain Abraham is going to walk through comes through the very hands of God. At His instigation. By definition, a follower is one who continually takes steps. No matter how long you have been following, God always has another step of faith for you to take. In our culture today, there is a version of church that claims to be Christianity when it's not. Flip through the channels and you can find somebody selling a gospel that says if you love God, then He owes you health, wealth, and happiness. It's called the "prosperity gospel," and the problem with it, historically, is what we call the Bible. It's just not true to Scripture, and it certainly wasn't true in the life of Abraham. And ultimately, it didn't work out for Jesus. The writer of Hebrews says, "He [Jesus] learned obedience through what he suffered" (5:8). And if the Father did that to His own Son, what do you think He intends with you? Now, does He still heal disease? Absolutely. Is He a good Father who gives good gifts to His children? Every day. But these are not His focus. His focus is His glory, and He's much

---

2   If you're unfamiliar with the story, God changed Abram's name to Abraham in Genesis 17.

more concerned with your holiness than with your happiness or cash in the bank.

Paul told the Ephesians that God "has blessed us in Christ with every spiritual blessing in the heavenly places" (1:3). And I thank God that He has. That said, there are those today who've perverted what this means. Tickling your ears with what you want to hear rather than what His Word actually says. Straight up, let me tell you what this does not mean: an empty tomb does not mean cash, prizes, and easy street for you. The prosperity gospel is a lie from the pit of hell.

Hebrews says, "For the Lord disciplines the one he loves, and chastises every son whom he receives. It is for discipline that you have to endure. God is treating you as sons. For what son is there whom his father does not discipline? If you are left without discipline, in which all have participated, then you are illegitimate children and not sons" (12:6–8). How many of you know that it's God's mercy and His grace that He would love us enough to take the circumstances of our lives and use them to chisel away anything in our lives that doesn't look like Jesus? Sometimes we find ourselves in places of immense pain, whether by our own doing or something somebody else did to us. Ultimately, God's in charge of it all. Nothing has happened to you that hasn't been sifted through His sovereign hand. And yet when it does, we say, "How could you, God?" And He says, *Because I love you, because you are My son, because you are My daughter.*

I grew up in a disciplined day, in a disciplined house. My daddy loved my brother and me, and he must've loved us a lot, because he would wear us out. Sometimes he would wear us out just in case. Like, he'd be gone for a while, and when he'd return, he'd say, "All right, line it up. I'm sure there was some shady stuff happening while I was out." And he was right. In fact, he would come in sometimes and he would open with this unfair, open-ended question: "Boy, is there something I need to know about?" And I would think, *There's probably three things you need to know about, but I don't know which one you already know about. So why don't you go first and we'll deal with this on a case-by-case basis, okay?* I may be exaggerating a bit, but you get the picture. When I look back on the way I was brought up, I don't see it as punishment. It was coaching and correcting and disciplining. He was okay with me experiencing a little pain as a kid or a young man so that I could avoid a whole lot of pain later in life.

How good is our Father that He would love you enough to walk you through some pain now so that you can ultimately know and trust Him better? There have been so many times in my life where things are not going my way and I hold out my hand and say, "Dear God, help me, save me." And He takes me by the hand, but instead of plucking me out of the muck and the mire, He loves me enough to drag me down through it. Sometimes to the point I thought I would suffocate and die. And when He gets me there, I'm desperate for Him like a drowning man is desperate for air.

Everybody I know who walks closely with the Lord says that God prunes us. Like it's the norm. Jesus said, "I am the true vine, and my Father is the vinedresser. Every branch in me that does not bear fruit he takes away, and every branch that does bear fruit he prunes" (John 15:1–2). Have you ever pruned a rosebush? To do it right, you cut off everything that's pretty. Everything about which the rosebush might brag. And you take it down to the larger stems and trunk. Leaving the bush bare. Nubs.

And then you wait until spring. And what emerges is more beautiful than what came before.

God prunes those He loves. Including Abraham and you and me.

God uses painful experiences to teach us and grow us and draw us closer to Him. And He does this far more often in times of pain than in times of comfort. God does His best work when we are most desperate for Him. C. S. Lewis says that pain is God's megaphone to arouse a deaf world.[3] And in these next few verses, God is going to call Abraham to do a thing that is going to put him in a desperate situation where the only thing he can hold on to is the promise of God.

After these things God tested Abraham. J. I. Packer says it this way: "And still He seeks the fellowship of His people and He sends them both sorrows and joys in order to detach their love from other things and attach it to Himself."[4] And so God tests Abraham. And He says to him, "Abraham?"

And Abraham says, "Here I am."

In the Bible, we often read that God speaks to people. Out loud. I've had people ask, "Does God speak to you?" And I say, "For sure." And they say, "He speaks out loud?" And I say, "For sure. You want to hear the voice of God, read your Bible out loud. And you are hearing God speak out loud." Admittedly, it doesn't often happen for me as it did for Abraham, but the reality is that God is still speaking to His people. It's just the white noise of this world is so loud in our ears that we've drowned out the very voice of God.

But Abraham is able to hear Him crystal clear, and God's going to ask Abraham to do something that makes no sense to him whatsoever. For Abraham, the next words out of God's mouth are going to be inconceivable. He doesn't have a category in his mind in which to hold this.

Verse 2: And God said, "Take your son, your only son." Underline those words—we're coming back to them. "Your only son Isaac, whom you love." Underline "your only son." "And go to

---

3   C. S. Lewis, *The Problem of Pain* (Quebec: Samizdat University Press, 2016), 58.
4   J. I. Packer, *Knowing God* (Downers Grove: InterVarsity Press, 1993), 79.

the land of Moriah." Circle that. "And offer…" Underline *offer*. "Offer him there as a burnt offering on one of the mountains of which I shall tell you." Now, let's read it as a whole: "Take your son, your only son Isaac, whom you love, and go to the land of Moriah, and offer him there as a burnt offering on one of the mountains of which I shall tell you." Now, when we read that, we think, *Who could do that? Who could take the thing that they love more than anything else and do what God says?*

My question for you is this: Is Jesus the one thing that drives everything?

Is He first? Before all things? And don't just rush on to the next sentence. Ask yourself the question. If you're a Christian, then by definition you should want to be able to say yes to this in your very soul. You've denied yourself, picked up your cross, and followed Him. But the truth is that stuff creeps in. All the time. And if we're not careful, we can take good gifts from God—like the thing we love most in this world—and treat them like they're our gods. This is what the Bible calls idolatry. And God hates it. God will not fuel and fund your idolatry. He will not be a means to your end. He does not cuddle with or make excuses for idols. He smashes them.

Let me ask the question this way: If you say you're a Christian, and you've surrendered your life to Christ, where is He not? What part of you have you not surrendered?

God shouldn't just be first on your list but the paper on which you would write your list, so that everything you do glorifies Him. So let me ask you, have you taken a gift—it could be your job, it could be a dream, it could be a relationship—and elevated it beyond the Giver of the gift? Are you worshiping the gift itself, afraid to give it up?

God, in a test to Abraham, says, Bring your son, your only son, the one that you love—you're going to take him to Moriah. You're going to offer him as a burnt offering. And then in verse 3, look at what Abraham does: "Abraham rose early."

Now, that's obedience.

I don't know about you, but when I feel like God is leading me to do something that's going to be very difficult for me, I have to pray about it for a while. And I am pro prayer, unless you're using prayer as an excuse to not be obedient to God.

Abraham, without delay, rises early in the morning, sits on his donkey, and takes two of his young men with him. And his son Isaac. Then he cuts the wood for the burnt offering and goes to the place where God had told him. Verse 4 says "on the third day." That's kind of important. "Abraham lifted up his eyes and saw the place from afar. Then Abraham said to his young men, 'Stay here with the donkey; I and the boy will go over there and worship and come again to you.'"

Don't miss this. This is the faith of Abraham. Not only is he willing to obey God, but hold nothing back. He knew that anything God had given him, he could trust God with. And anything not given him by God he didn't need anyway. The same is true for us.

Somehow, Abraham is going to trust God with his son. His only son, the one whom he loves more than his own life. But look at what he says. Really, in Hebrew, he is saying, We will go and we will be back. Even though he knows God has called him to give his son as a burnt offering, as a sacrifice, to offer him up, somehow Abraham has the faith to understand that God is who He says He is, and He always keeps His promises. And God promised that Abraham would be a blessing to all the world through his son Isaac. At this point, Abraham does not know exactly how He's going to pull this off, but he knows that even when he does not understand the mind of God, he can trust the heart of God because He is a good, good Father, and He loves to give good blessings to His kids.

Even when he does not understand the mind of God, he can trust the heart of God.

If you want to better understand your Bible, you can always interpret the Scriptures with the Scripture. Use the Bible as commentary unto itself. In Galatians 3:8, Paul tells us that God "preached the gospel beforehand to Abraham." And if you look in Hebrews 11:17–19, the writer tells us that Abraham had faith in the resurrected Christ (see also Romans 4) even if he killed his own son, God was able to raise him from the dead.

What we know by name, Abraham believed by faith—that God was sending a Messiah for the salvation of all. Hebrews 11 and Romans 4 let us know that somehow Abraham trusted God and the power of His resurrection all the way back then. In that moment, Abraham is believing—even when his circumstances give him no cause to believe—"God, I will be obedient to You, and I will do what You say, because I know that You are who You say You are and You always keep Your promises. And even if I go through with this, You are the God of the living and You can bring back my son."

So Abraham says to his servants, "Look here, boys, stay with the donkey, me and the boy are going up there, and I fully intend to do everything God has told me to do. And me and the boy are coming back safe and sound."

Had I been standing there, I would have asked him, "How is that going to work, Abraham?"

I imagine he would have responded, "I have no idea. I'm just telling you what I know. I put my trust in God that He is who He says He is and He always keeps His promises."

So then Abraham takes the wood for the burnt offering, and he lays it on Isaac, his son. And he takes in his hand the fire and the knife. Pause there—this is a picture of what's to come. The son carries the wood. The father carries the instrument of death and fire for the sacrifice. Do you see what God is setting up?

And so they go, both of them together, and Isaac says to Abraham, "Father."

And Abraham says, "Here I am, my son."

And Isaac says, "Behold, the fire and the wood, but where is the lamb for a burnt offering?"

When I was younger and I would hear this story, I always thought Isaac was fresh out of Pull-Ups. In my mind, little baby Isaac waddled up the mountain. But this is not the case. Most theologians and commentators say Isaac was seventeen or eighteen years old. Strong enough to carry the wood, and he had the cognitive reasoning to look and ask questions.

As Abraham wraps the ropes around his wrists, Isaac asks, *Dad, what are you doing?*

And, probably with tears pouring off his face, Abraham says, "God will provide for himself the lamb for a burnt offering, my son."

Not only is Abraham trusting that God is who He says He is and that He always keeps His promises, but Isaac is trusting in his dad. Verse 9: "When they came to the place of which God had told him, Abraham built the altar there and laid the wood in order and bound Isaac his son and laid him on the altar, on top of the wood."

You hear those words, "God will provide for himself the lamb for a burnt offering, my son"? Remember those. The Hebrew word for *burnt offering* is *olah* (pronounced "o-law"), and from it we get the word *holocaust*.

I believe Isaac volunteered to lay himself on the altar. Why? For starters, he's like 17 or 18 years old. And his dad is about 117, 118 years old. Have you wrestled a 118-year-old man lately? I have not but I assume doing so is not that tough. Isaac could have outrun him. He could have overpowered him. And yet he allows his dad to bind him and lay him on the altar. And the reason I believe this is because this is exactly what Jesus did.

Verse 10. "Then Abraham reached out his hand and took the knife to slaughter his son." Verse 11. "But the angel of the LORD called to him from heaven and said, 'Abraham, Abraham!' And he said, 'Here I am.' Verses 12 and 13. "He said, 'Do not lay your hand on the boy or do anything to him, for now I know that you fear God, seeing you have not withheld your son, your only son, from me.' And Abraham lifted up his eyes and looked, and behold, behind him was a ram, caught in a thicket by his horns."

This is a miracle.

You see that phrase, *caught in a thicket by his thorns*? I hunt deer a lot. I've walked to my stand a thousand times and never once have I seen a ten-point caught in a bunch of thorns or briars. This is a miracle of God. Here, on this mountain, in that moment in time, a male lamb is stuck with his head in a bunch of thorns.

In effect, God says, "Wait a minute—use this ram instead of your son." So Abraham takes the ram, sacrifices it, and offers it up as a burnt offering. Verse 14: *And so Abraham called the name of the place, the LORD will provide, Jehovah-jireh. And it is said, to this day, on the mountain of the LORD, it shall be provided.*

Don't miss these words either—*on the mountain of the LORD it shall be provided.*

"Then the Angel of the Lord called Abraham a second time from heaven and said,

"'By myself, I have sworn, declares the Lord, because you have done this and not withheld your son, your only son, I will surely bless you, and I will surely multiply your offspring as the stars of the heaven and as the sand that is on the seashore. Your offspring shall possess the gate of his enemies and in your offspring shall all the nations of the earth be blessed, because you have obeyed my voice.'" (vv. 15–18)

There is no way Abraham could have imagined what God was asking him to do, to sacrifice his own son. There's also no way that he could fully understand what God Almighty was talking about right here.

This is messianic prophecy spoken by God some fifteen hundred years before Jesus: *Abraham, one day, this boy of yours is going to have a couple kids, and one of his kids is going to have twelve kids, and those twelve boys will become twelve tribes. And then one day those tribes will become a nation, and out of that nation will come the Messiah for the entire world. And because of Him, the very ends of the earth will be blessed.*

Remember when Abraham says, And on this mountain, the Lord shall provide a lamb? Remember where he's standing when he says that. On Mount Moriah. The word *Moriah* means "foreseen by God." You can't make this stuff up. I mean, really—think about it.

The real point of Genesis 22, and the point of the entire Bible, is the gospel of Jesus Christ to the glory of God. The point of Genesis 22 can actually be found in your New Testament. The most famous Christian verse ever. The point is John 3:16. Even if you're new to Bible study, you've probably heard this one. "For God so loved the world, that he gave his only Son, that whoever believes in him shall not perish, but have eternal life." But don't stop there. Keep going:

"For God did not send his Son into the world to condemn the world, but in order that the world might be saved through him. Whoever believes in him is not condemned, but whoever does not believe is condemned already, because he has not believed in the name of the only Son of God. And this is the judgment: the light has come into the world, and people loved the darkness rather than the light because their works were evil." (vv. 17–19)

Sometimes this story of Abraham and Isaac is taught like this: be careful if you tell God you love Him a lot, because He might come in and make you give Him something that you really love. That's how I heard this as a kid. You couldn't let God know that you like things too much, because, at any minute, He might show up to your room and say, "All right, hand it over." As a result, I was terrified of God and I didn't trust Him very much. Terrified that He'd make me go to Africa and not play football.

Jesus refers to God as heavenly Father 189 times in the New Testament. Is there a father reading this book who would close these pages, walk into his kid's room, and say, "Give me all your stuff. Actually, give me all of my stuff, because you don't have any stuff. It's all my stuff, anyway. It's just in your room right now"? And then carry it all out into the front yard, dump it in a pile, and set it on fire? You could, but that's not the point.

Every good father, every good dad, will come and take away anything from their kid that is not good for that kid. This is the discipline of the Lord. Any kind of idols that we make in our life, he wants us to smash those things so they don't shatter us.

The very real story of Abraham and Isaac is not to show us what He's going to take from us. It's really to demonstrate His love for us. God gave for us what was most important to Him. His Son, Jesus Christ.

*   *   *

Let's look again at John 3, where Jesus says, "For God so loved the world, that he gave his only Son, that whoever believes in him shall not perish, but have eternal life." Jesus is having a conversation with this guy named Nicodemus here. A Pharisee. Nicodemus would have been an expert in Genesis 22. In fact, he would have been an expert in the entire Old Testament. He went to school his entire life to memorize what we call the Old Testament so that when the Messiah showed up, he could be the very first one to recognize Him.

The word *Pharisee* means "separated one," which is exactly what happened to Nicodemus when he was young. When Nicodemus went to school for the very first time, what we would call kinder-garten, he studied the Torah—the first five books of the Bible. And he didn't just read it; he memorized every word. I don't know how many Bible verses you've memorized, but Nicodemus memorized all twenty-three thousand of them. This was a requirement to be a Pharisee.

In John 3, Nicodemus goes to see Jesus at night and he says, *Surely You must be of God, because if You're not of God, You couldn't do these miracles.* And Jesus, seeing this Pharisee, this expert in the law, goes right to the top shelf and says, "Truly, truly, I say unless one is born again, he cannot see the kingdom of God." Which goes right over Nicodemus' head. He has no idea what Jesus is talking about. Which is crazy. He spent his entire life memorizing the law so that he could recognize the Messiah, and just like every other Pharisee, Nicodemus had fallen in love with the law and not the Lawgiver.

Nicodemus is so close to the presence of God he can smell the breath of God and yet he doesn't recognize Him for who He is. Jesus shows up to one of the most learned men in all of Israel and He says, *It's not about memorizing the law, you need a new life. You've got to be born again.* And then Nicodemus totally mis-understands what Jesus is saying. He has no clue. He asks, "How can that be? Would a man enter into his mother's womb a second time?" And Jesus shakes his head. "What in the name of Me are you talking about?"

Jesus, the master teacher, is going to use some rabbi tricks. Rabbis would talk to each other by using Bible verses to explain other

Bible verses. It's theological jiu jitsu. Also, rabbis were famous for teaching in threes. They would teach one point in three different stories to give people more handles to grab on to. Like in Luke chapter 15 when Jesus is trying to describe who God is, He tells the story about the lost coin, the story about the lost sheep, and the story about the lost son—we call it the prodigal son.

And in Matthew 24:3, when the disciples say, "What's the end of the world going to be like?" He tells three stories all to describe it: the parable of the virgins, or the party; the parable of the talents; and the parable of the sheep and goats. With Nicodemus, He's going to use three illustrations from the Old Testament to show Nicodemus who he's talking to. Jesus is going to talk about Moses, Abraham, and light.

He says, "Okay, I'm over your head, so let's bring this down to Pharisee kindergarten level." You remember Moses? You might not be super familiar with this story, but in the Old Testament, Moses is leading the nation of Israel. They're wandering around in the desert, and they wake up one day and there are poisonous snakes in the camp. Everybody gets bitten and everybody is poisoned from the inside out, and people are dying. Moses can't really do anything about it from the outside. Ointment on the outside isn't going to cure the snake bitten-ness on the inside. So God tells Moses, *Hey, fashion a fiery serpent, or a bronze serpent, and lift it up. And anybody that will fix their eyes on the serpent that is high and lifted up will be cured.*

And then Jesus says, *Nick, I'm like that. I'm going to be high and lifted up, and God is going to make Him who is without sin to be sin, that all of you would be made the righteousness of God.*

Nicodemus says, *Of course I know that story. I teach it all the time. That's what I do.*

And then right on the heels of that, Jesus says, "For God so loved the world." Now He's moving on to the second story, to Abraham, and the technique that He's going to use, in Greek, is called *proto logos*. Proto logos. First words.

Part of what rabbis studied were first words. Or, the first time a word was used in the Old Testament. So when Jesus says, "For God so loved the world," Nicodemus would know that the first time the word *love* is used like that in the Bible, it is used to describe Abraham's love for his son Isaac. A father's love for his son. *For God so loved the world, that he gave* ... Literally, that word *gave* would be "offered." That He offered His only Son. The ESV translation says *His one and only Son*. It's a tough translation. The Greek word is *mono genus*, like one gene. It literally means "of the same essence." So "one and only" is not close enough. I have a "one and only" motorcycle, but it is not my mono genus motorcycle.

The King James will call Jesus God's *only begotten Son*, because Jesus is not created, but God begets God. So He says, *For God so loved the world that He gives His one and only begotten Son.* At this point, all the lights on Nicodemus' dashboard are going off. He is automatically transported back to Genesis 22, and he's beginning to see all the things in the story of the sacrifice of Isaac that parallel Jesus. That pointed Nicodemus to the fact that Jesus is the Messiah, that Abraham offered his one and only son, that God is going to offer His one and only Son, that Isaac carried the wood for the sacrifice at the mountain, and Jesus is going to carry the cross on His back, up the mountain.

Nicodemus also knew that where he stood that night, Mount Moriah, is where Solomon built the temple. And he knew that for the last thousand years, every single year, on the Day of Atonement, lamb after lamb after lamb after lamb had been slaughtered for the covering of sin. I don't know when Nicodemus put all the pieces together, but I imagine that if he watched Jesus stumble out of the city with the cross on his back—and I tend to think he did—and then press up on his nail-pierced feet and cry out, "*Tetelestai*," or "It is finished," the puzzle became crystal clear.

Today, we don't call that mountain Moriah, we call it Mount Calvary. In that same place, the Lord provides not just another Lamb of God to cover over the sin of the Jewish people for a year, but the Lamb of God has come to take away the sin of the entire world.

Nicodemus would have understood that just as Isaac had to trust his father, Jesus would be sweating blood in a garden and would choose to say, *Father, if there be any other way, let this cup pass from Me. Not My will, but Your will be done.* Abraham indicates that God would provide a lamb, a male sheep with his horns caught in the briars. And Jesus, the Lamb of God, would wear a crown of thorns and die as a substitutionary sacrifice. Remember Abraham's words. *On this place, the Lord will provide.*

And He did.

Two thousand years ago on that very mountain, Jesus is led to sacrifice in our place. Jesus is saying to Nicodemus, *All that stuff happening in Genesis 22…I'm Him. That's Me. I am the Lamb who has come for the sacrifice of all people. For God so loved the world that He gave, He offered, He sacrificed His one and only Son, and listen, Nicodemus, and whoever believes in Him—* That's a big word, *whoever*, because probably at that point Nicodemus is thinking, *I don't have to believe in You, because I got the whole Bible memorized. I think I got this.*

And Jesus is saying, *No matter how religious you are, you've got to believe. And no matter how rebellious you are, you've got to believe. Whoever believes in Me will not perish but will have everlasting life.* See these words, *for God so loved?* That word *so* is an amplifier. Demonstrating the depth of the love of God. That though none of us deserve it, Christ died for us. For God so loved the world that He gave. That He offered.

There had to be an offering.

Every single one of us, by nature and nurture, are sinners down to our very core. And I know you may be offended by me calling you that, but that's because you're a sinner, and you're prideful, and you think you're awesome, and you're not. You're a sinner. Me too. Think about this. Forget God's law a minute. You can't even keep your own law. Have you ever promised yourself, *I'm never going to yell at my kids like that again*?

Sinner, because you did it again.

Have you ever promised, *I'm not going to drink that*?

And you drank it.

Or, *I'm not going to say that*?

And you said it.

If we can't even keep our own made-up commandments, how in the world would we ever keep the commandments of a holy, perfect God? We'll talk more about this in the next chapter, but the bottom line is we can't and never have.

Some look at the cross and ask, "Why? What was all that for?"

For God. Because He is holy and just, all sin must be paid for. For God to overlook sin would mean, at His very character in nature, that He was unjust and unholy. So sin must be paid for. And so in Jesus Christ, God is just and the justifier. While God requires the payment for sin, He, in His mercy, makes the ultimate payment in His Son, Jesus Christ.

Consider that a moment. Put yourself in Abraham's shoes. Could you raise the knife? And yet this is exactly what God requires of us.

There are two ways that sin can be paid for. In the Bible, the word for payment is *atonement*. *Atonement* is just a Bible word that means "to make payment." So the first way to pay is to self-atone. You can say, "God, forget you; I got this." And then you can go do whatever you want, live however you want, and be the lord of your own life. And doing so will cost you all of eternity to pay for your sin. For, Scripture says, the wages of sin is death and eternal separation from God. We would call that hell.

Option number two is you can take the substitutionary atonement. This means you take what Jesus did in your place as your payment. If you have doubts about this, look at what Jesus says: *For God so loved the world that he gave his one and only son, that whoever—*

Stop right there. Did you know that if you fall into the "whoever" category, you could be saved? No matter how good you think you are, you could be saved. No matter how bad you think you've been, you can be saved. Because it's not by your works that you were saved, it's by Christ's life, death, and resurrection that you can be saved. *That whoever believes in him.*

You see that word *believe*? I find it a little frustrating that we continuously translate this Greek word into *belief*. The Greek word is *pisteuō*. When we read that, we think if we "believe that" God is who He says He is, and that Jesus died on the cross, then we're good. Our problem is that there's a big difference between "believing *that*" and "believing *in*."

When I was a kid, my dad would take me to the Dillon public pool. He'd look at me and say, "Get on the diving board and jump off into the water with me." And strangely, I would start to climb the ladder. For those of you not from Dillon, South Carolina—which is most of you, since its population is just over five thousand—this is how we were taught to swim. This was swimming lesson number one. It was very Darwinian. If you didn't make it, then you weren't supposed to live anyway.

So, I climbed to the top of the board and then walked to the edge and looked down to, sure enough, find my dad in the water. He was saying, "Come on, buddy. Jump. I got you." Now, at that point there was a line forming behind me and great fear and trepidation in me. Because I knew if I turned around and climbed down, I'd never hear the end of it. At the edge of the diving board, I'm looking down into the water. And at that point, I believed that the man in the water was in fact my dad. I recognized it. Magnum P.I. mustache. LP shorts. Cigarette hanging out of his mouth—in the pool. And I could hear his voice and I knew his voice because he lived at my house. I also knew that he came with that lady over there. That's my mom. The lady drinking TaB. Covered in baby oil.

Evidently, I needed coaxing, because he kept saying, "Come on, buddy. I got you." Now, at this point, while still on the board, I "believe that" this was my dad. But I had not yet "*pisteuō*'d" in Dad as evidenced by the fact that I had yet to leave the board. This is what Jesus is talking about to Nicodemus. Nicodemus is recognizing that Jesus is who He says He is, but he has not yet taken that leap of faith. At some point, you've got to make a decision. You have got to ask yourself, *Do I believe He's telling the truth, and do I trust Him with my life? Do I trust that He is who He says He is and He's going to keep His promises?* Because the undeniable fact was this—if I stepped foot off that diving board into that water, I would sink like a rock and drown because I could not keep myself afloat. I didn't know how to do that yet.

So, THE question was, would he catch me and keep me alive? The problem with this was that there was one and only one way to know. So, I did it. I just decided that, at the end of the day, he's my dad. I trust him. So, I took that step off and *pisteuō*'d in my father. And because he was a good dad and he loved me, he caught me. This is what Jesus is talking about. This is what Genesis 22 is all about.

Let me ask you, have you ever taken that leap of faith? Have you ever trusted Jesus as your Savior? Have you ever "believed in" Him? *Pisteuō*'d in Him? Put the weight of your life into the arms of your heavenly Father believing that He is who He says He is? I know that the Holy Spirit is doing something in some of you and you hear your heavenly Father beckoning from the water, "Come up. Come on."

If you're like me, that kid standing on that board, then sixty seconds feels like six weeks and you have ten thousand questions. I know you don't know what you're going to tell your mom and your friends when you turn this page, but if you haven't "believed in," then this is the most important page you've ever read. My invitation is this: Come on. Jump. Jesus has got you. He's never lost anyone in the water. That's what salvation is. That's what it means to put your faith in Jesus Christ.

I love Christmas. And I've had some really good Christmases. My family was into Christmas. We'd watch the movies. From *Rudolph* to *Charlie Brown*. We decorated, went to see Santa. Every year, the day after Thanksgiving, we would pull out the Christmas tree. Some of you put up the Christmas tree, but we would just pull it out because we love Christmas so much. We never even took it down. We had a fake tree and we just slid it into what became known as the Christmas closet. The morning after Thanksgiving, we'd slide that mug out and put it in the corner.

And it was easy to figure out which side went in the corner. It was the part with no decorations. Why would you decorate the backside? That just don't make sense. Then we'd plug it in and evaluate what we're working with this year. As in, which half of the lights were going to turn on? And we weren't looking for the dead ones to know which to take off the tree. We just needed to know where to add the new strands. By the time I was in seventh grade, our little tree weighed eight hundred pounds. Total setup from closet to corner to lit and tinseled took five minutes. Many of my family members kept up their lights year-round. I remember going to my uncle Phillip's one time in June. We were going fishing and the chain-link fence in front of his house was still wrapped and twinkling with Christmas lights.

I asked my dad, "Daddy, why's Uncle Phillip got his Christmas lights on?" He just shook his head. "Boy, you can't hide money."

And Santa Claus was good to us. One year, I got a car. That was cool. Another year I got a motorcycle—which I cranked in my grandmother's house at 4 a.m. But one of my favorite gifts, maybe tops of all time, was around first grade. I woke up early and came tiptoeing into the living room about quarter to four, looked around the corner, and boom. I don't know how Santa works at your house. I think he must have different modes depending on whose house he's at and possibly the weather or how much time he has, but at our house, the wrapped presents were from people and the unwrapped ones were from Santa. Santa just chunked them down the chimney. Dumped them in a pile. Turning the corner that morning, I spied some stuff, so I woke up my brother and my folks and we started opening presents. Off to one side was this one little box and it was literally shaking. Rocking back and forth. I began thinking, *Oh my goodness, I got a gremlin*. For those of you not familiar with gremlins, they were these little demonic things sold in the eighties. Caused trouble. Not good. And had bad reactions to microwaves. Finally, we got to that box and I popped the top off of it. And...there was a puppy.

A beagle puppy. And she was sitting there shaking, big eyes staring up at me, begging me to lift her out of that dark cell. She didn't smell that good but man was she cute. Russ, my brother, had a wiggly box too. So he popped the top off of it and there was another beagle puppy. A boy. Daddy said, "All right, what do you want to name them?" So I looked at her for a little while and I said, "Daisy Duke." Daisy Duke was the cousin of Bo and Luke Duke. They were traveling evangelists in the eighties. Had a delivery service. In truth, I thought if the real Daisy Duke ever found out that I named my puppy after her, she'd fall madly in love with me and we'd get married. That was my plan. But it didn't work out.

Russ named his dog the Incredible Hulk. Not because he wanted to marry him but because he was tough. The Incredible Hulk and Daisy Duke were rabbit-hunting dogs to their core. In fact, they didn't even spend that night in our home. The rest of our Christmas gifts that day were two-by-fours and plywood. We spent Christmas afternoon building doghouses. Why? Because dogs don't sleep in the house. I know some of you aren't into this, but that's the way it was.

Second grade rolls around and the Incredible Hulk and Daisy Duke have turned into fine hunting dogs. One morning, we're tracking through the woods and it's cold. I'm talking ice-cold. I'm carrying my .410. While I'm at it, I want to say that you parents should all get your kids dogs and shotguns for Christmas. Then go spend time in the woods. Hang out. Talk. Like, with your mouths and not your thumbs. Kids spell *love* "t-i-m-e."

Walking through the woods, Hulk and Daisy were doing their thing and my dad was talking to the dogs. I had no idea what he was saying. Couldn't understand a word. Maybe he was speaking in tongues. It's a South Carolina dog-whispering thing. We reached this creek and in my mind, it was like a huge river, but you know how your mind works. It was probably six or eight feet wide. Daisy, who was afraid of nothing but who had also never really seen ice, given that we lived in South Carolina, walked right out on the creek. Which was frozen. Ice. But again, this wasn't like Minnesota ice where you can drive on the stuff. It's South Carolina. Just barely frozen. Dad hollered something unintelligible, which when translated meant, "Daisy, that is dangerous and you should come over here with us."

Meanwhile, the Incredible Hulk found a little downed tree and he hopped up on the tree and crossed to the other side of the creek. Daisy was not so lucky. Seconds later, I heard the ice break under her feet. And boom...she was gone. As in disappeared from the face of the earth. Mind you, this is a little creek, so it's got some flow to it. Once through the hole, the current caught her and she couldn't just pop right back out the hole. She was gone. Bobbing. Clawing at the underside of the ice. Staring at me with those big eyes.

I didn't know what to do. I was freaking out. Folks, this is the condition of every single one of us. Every single one of us, whether we realize it or not. Every single one of us has rejected the law, the loving law of our heavenly Father, who is our Master. And we say, "Forget You. I got this." And when the ice breaks, we ain't got this. Every sin we fall into is prepackaged with a "got you." And when it gets you, you get to the point where you go, "Uh-oh, I need help."

So, Daisy broke through the ice and I couldn't save her. The end.

I'm kidding. That would be the worst story ever.

Why am I kidding? Because my father was with me. And he knew what he was doing.

The Incredible Hulk was standing on the other side of the creek barking. And barking. No help whatsoever. It sounded like, "You shouldn't have done that. You shouldn't have done that. You shouldn't have done that. You shouldn't have done that. You shouldn't have done that." Honestly, for many of us, "You shouldn't have done that" was our church experience growing up. Somehow we got to that place in our life where we thought, *Uh-oh. It's true. I'm a sinner in need of a savior.* So what did we do? We did what our mama told us. We went to church. And when we showed up to church, most of us heard somebody standing up front saying, "Well, you shouldn't have done that. And you shouldn't have done that. And you shouldn't have done that. And you shouldn't have done that." While we sit there and scratch our heads. "Yeah, I know that. That's why I'm sitting here. But what now? I thought you had the answer." I don't think 'You shouldn't have done that' is the gospel." The gospel is not "God's good. You're bad. Try harder, see you next week." Yelling that week after week does little more than run people off. They get that six days a week. They don't need one more.

But standing there watching Daisy drown, I wasn't very helpful either. Plus, the ice was magnifying her eyes so they looked like saucers. I was standing helplessly on the other side of the creek and all I could offer her was my great affection. I wanted her to get help. I just didn't know what to do.

I just stood there frozen. Which is also an apt picture of many churches today. People have great affection toward other people, but it takes a lot of love to look at somebody in the face and say, "You are not a mistaker that just needs to do better. You're a sinner that needs a savior." In fact, if somebody gave you this book and said, "You should read this," and you actually cracked these pages, the underlying message they are trying to tell you is this: "I know we're just golfing buddies, but I really love you."

Me yelling at Daisy did nothing. She knew she'd messed up. That's how she landed in the water. The fact that the ice was blocking her exit was ample evidence that she was in a bad way of her own making. So yelling at her was useless. And just hopping forward didn't do any good because she'd just slide by me—under the ice. But thank God my dad was standing ten yards downstream. When he saw all the commotion, he glanced down at the ice and saw Daisy coming toward him. Scratching. Clawing. Scratching. Clawing. Here's the thing you need to understand. No matter how hard she tried, she could not break through that thing that was keeping her from air, which equaled life. But my dad, with a 12-gauge in his hand, busted through the ice. Making a hole. And when she came by, he timed it, jabbed his hand down into the water—glove, sleeve, watch, and all—grabbed her by the back of the neck, and pulled her out of what certainly would have been her own death. Then he sat her down right next to him.

My brother and I were jumping around. Screaming. We couldn't believe it. Dad saved Daisy. Unbelievable. But then it got crazier.

We had a '71 Chevy, and when it got real cold, some of the pleather would stab me a little bit from where it was cracked and peeling. So to make it more comfortable, we laid down a quilt to sit on. Anybody else have those seat covers growing up? When we got to the truck, Daddy took the blanket seat cover and wrapped it around Daisy. And—get a load of this—he put her inside the cab. And...turned on the heat. This may not be a big deal for you all, but at my house, hunting dogs rode in the back of the truck. In the box. And they never—and I do mean never—slept in the house. I leaned over to Russ. "Brother, you better get your heart right. Jesus is coming back. This is a sign of the end times."

From that day forward, Daisy became Dad's dog. She still liked me when I had treats, but she was his dog. Why? Because somehow, intuitively, she knew she was dead. Without hope. And by his goodness and grace, he broke through the thing that was killing her and rescued her.

That is the gospel.

Every single one of us, in our own rejection of God, has said, "I got this." And then by the power of the Holy Spirit, He sometimes lets the scales fall off of our eyes and we realize, "Oh no, I ain't got this. No matter how much I scratch and claw and try, I just can't undo this thing that I have done. Even if I was perfect from this day forward and promise I'll never go walk on the ice again."

What are you going to do about your past? What can you do? In your own strength, nothing. You can't get you out of the ice. That train has left the station. But God, being rich in mercy because of His great love for us, busts through sin and death and snatches you out by the back of the neck. He pays the price, and for anyone who believes that when He died on the cross, when He said, "It is finished," somehow that counted for them. That somehow, He, by His very own death and blood, had put an end—once and for all—to my willful defiance of Him and separation from Him. That He bridged the gap. Reached through the ice. Redeemed me. And not only that, but He has wrapped me up and taken me home as His very own son or daughter of the Most High King. If you've never surrendered to the lordship of Jesus, then you have a problem, and it's greater than your circumstances. It's a soul-level problem. You need God to do for you what you can't do for you. And maybe right now for the very first time you would believe. You don't have to have it all figured out. You just need to believe that when Jesus died on the cross, somehow that counted for you. And if you're ready to admit that you need a savior and that you believe that Christ is that Savior, then you just confess. You say, "Father, here I am, save me."

Pray with Me

Father, here I am. Save me. I surrender my life to the lordship of Christ. Jesus, I believe that You are the Son of God, the only way to God, that You died on the cross for my sins and rose again from the dead. And somehow, Your payment on the cross counts for me. Please forgive all my sin, and I receive that forgiveness now. I admit it. I'm a sinner in need of a savior. I believe in You. I confess You as my Lord.

Now just let me pray over you:

Our good and gracious heavenly Father, I thank You for Your Son, Jesus. I thank You that He came to take our place. I thank You that Jesus did not come merely as a teacher, a religious leader, or even as an example for us to follow. God, I thank You that what we need is not to turn over a new leaf, but we need a brand-new life. God, I thank You that it is by grace through faith that we are saved and not by our works. God, I thank You that whosoever would put their trust in the saving work of Christ is forever forgiven and adopted into the family of God. God, I pray against the lies of the enemy right now that are infiltrating the minds of men and women that are being drawn to You. God, I thank You that when You pushed up on Your nail-pierced feet and declared, "It is finished," it counted for me. And that it counted for anyone who would believe or trust in You. God, I praise You that at the cross, the pressure of performance and pretending are finished. I thank You that because Jesus is the payment that satisfies the debt requirement for our sin, You are not dissatisfied in Your sons and daughters. Holy Spirit, would You come in this very instant and seal the hearts of men and women that are crying out to Jesus for their eternal salvation? WE love You because You loved us first, and I pray this in the name of Jesus. Amen.

If you just prayed to receive Christ, would you please contact me at my church, The Church of Eleven22? Either email or call me at:

Joby.Martin@coe22.com
904-685-6722

I am not asking this of you so we can count you as a number and take some sort of weird satisfaction in adding you to a head count, but so we can encourage you and get you connected with a body. With a local church. Christians were not meant to walk alone but in community. In fact, the enemy would really like for you to try and go it alone. So please, contact us and let us help you start this journey.

CHAPTER 2

Mount Sinai—Who Tells You Who You Are: You . . . or Jesus?

Whe you turn the page from Genesis to Exodus, four hundred years elapse in the lives of the Israelites. By the time you get to the end of the book of Genesis, you've been reading about a guy named Joseph with a Technicolor dreamcoat. If you're a little bit older than me, you'll understand this reference. Joseph leads a rough life. He's sold into slavery by his brothers, then falsely accused, imprisoned, and left to rot, but by the sovereign hand of God, he's brought out of prison and ends up as the second-in-command in all Egypt—the deliverer of the people of God. A famine in Canaan, Joseph's homeland, drives his people to Egypt, and because of Joseph's position, they are allowed to stay. But eventually, they become so numerous that Pharaoh grows worried about holding on to his power, and he begins enslaving them.

Now, follow me to Exodus—the second book of the Bible. If you're new to the Bible, go to Genesis and *In the beginning* and turn right one book. Exodus is so named because God's people—those promised people that came from Isaac's seed—are exiting slavery. Which is a great picture of us, but we'll get to that.

By the beginning of Exodus, four hundred years have passed, and we have no record of God doing anything in that time. Let that sink in. His chosen people, the seed of Abraham, are living as slaves to people who worship false gods. Does that make sense to you? Think back to God's promise to Abraham: "I'm going to give you the promised land…" But apparently, the way to the promised land goes through slavery in the land of Egypt. Now, think about those generations of slaves calling out to God. For what do you think they were asking? Have you ever prayed and asked God to hurry up?

In the first few chapters of Exodus, we find Pharaoh oppressing God's people. Definitely not a mountaintop for them. You've heard me say it and I'll say it again: God often does some of His best work in the valleys of our lives. What Israel thought was imprisonment and punishment was actually preparation for who God intended them to become. Remember that.

Worried about a threat to his throne, Pharaoh is killing all the Israelite boys two years and under, so the mother of Moses puts him in a basket and sends him downriver. Miraculously, someone from Pharaoh's house picks him up and says, "We'll raise him." And then they hire Moses' mom as the nanny, so Moses grows up in Pharaoh's house. This will matter more when, later in his life, he stands before Pharaoh, because he alone will be uniquely qualified to understand the royal culture, customs, body language, and so forth. But long before he becomes the deliverer of God's people, Moses bumps into a problem. He sees an Egyptian beating up an Israelite, so he kills the Egyptian and buries his body in the desert in an attempt to cover his sin.

I recently received a letter from an inmate. I pastor a church that has opened campuses inside prisons around Florida, and this man had attended one of our services inside a prison. The letter read, *I surrendered my life to Jesus, but how in the world could God accept somebody like me based on what I've done?* It's a great question. Maybe THE question. The answer is simple: "Brother,

God accepts you based on what His Son, Jesus Christ, has done on your behalf, okay? There is no one too far gone from the hand of God to be saved."

So maybe you have a tattered past and some sin in your history, I don't care what you've done, nothing disqualifies you from the love of God or being used mightily by God. (If you're having trouble with this, let me lead you to Romans 8:3 through the end of the chapter. Memorize it. It's speaking to all of us who call Him "Lord.") This was true with Moses. With David. With Peter. And with you and me. Scripture says, *His arm is not so short that it cannot save.* The Joby Martin translation says, "No one is ever—and I do mean ever—too far gone from the hand of God." This is why I praise God that Facebook didn't exist when I was in high school. If it did, you wouldn't be reading this book. My past too is very tattered.

So Moses kills a guy, gets busted, fears for his life, and takes off. He ends up in Midian, marries a woman named Zipporah, and becomes a shepherd. Tending his father-in-law's sheep. A far cry from the plush palace in which he was raised. One day, he leads the flock to *the back of the desert* to a mountain called Horeb, also known as "the mountain of God," and the angel of the Lord appears to him in a burning bush. Given the intense sunlight and the reflective properties of sand and rock, bushes burn all the time in the desert. That wasn't a big deal. What surprised Moses was that it was not consumed. So he goes to check it out. And a voice speaks from the bush: "Moses, take off your shoes for you are standing on holy ground." If I'm Moses, I think, *It's holy? Did it just get holy? I've been walking around here for forty years and I've never known this?*

Moses takes off his shoes and God speaks to him and says, "Go to Pharaoh and bring my people out of slavery." And so he does—after God answers all of Moses' excuses. But Pharaoh isn't going to just lie down, because the Egyptian economy and his power are built primarily on the backs of the slaves of Israel. So, to prove His power and to show that they are completely powerless against Him, God afflicts Pharaoh and the Egyptians with ten plagues. This is strategic on God's part, as each one of those plagues specifically targets an Egyptian god: Hapi, the god of the Nile; Heket, the goddess of fertility; Geb, the god of the earth; Khepri, the god of creation; Hathor, the goddess of love; Isis, the goddess of medicine; Nut, the goddess of the sky; Seth, the god of storms; and Ra, the sun god.

The tenth god is Pharaoh himself, or so he thinks. He considers himself the ultimate power in all the earth. To show him that he's not, God tells Moses to tell the people of Israel to sacrifice a perfect spotless lamb and spread the blood onto the doorpost of their homes because an angel of death is coming through at midnight and the firstborn of every home not painted with the blood of the lamb will be killed. But, the angel of death will "pass over" any home painted with the blood of the lamb.

What the nation of Israel doesn't understand is that this sacrifice points to Jesus.

The Israelites do as they're told, the angel of death passes through, and every firstborn Egyptian son is killed. Including Pharaoh's son. So he lets them go. Israel leaves, but fickle Pharaoh quickly changes his mind, and when the Israelites make it to the Red Sea, they turn around to find the Egyptian army barreling down on them. Moses scratches his head because things don't look good. He's got an impossible sea in front of him and the most powerful army in the history of the world behind him.

But God is not surprised, and what is impossible with men is possible with God, so He splits the Red Sea, and God's people walk through on dry ground and in the shadow of a ten-story wall of water. Yet when the Egyptian army enters, God releases the waters, which crash down on the army. No more army.

Having escaped Pharaoh and his army, you would think the people of Israel are just days from the promised land. *Finally. We made it. The worst is behind us.* And if you look at a map, you'll see that they were really close. Literally. But God's not interested in the shortest route, as evidenced by the fact that Mount Sinai is farther away from the promised land than where they started. In South Carolina, we call this "going around your elbow to get to your thumb."

Many of you were told that when you put your faith in Jesus, your life would get awesome. Easy street. All your problems solved. Problem was, it didn't and they weren't. For some of you, things got worse. Terrible, even. But as we're about to see, God does some of His best work in the terrible. God sees what we can't and won't, and because He loves us with a love we can't fathom, He wants to strip away everything we cling to so that we would know that all we really need is Him. That He alone gives us everything we need. And if we don't have it, it's probably because He knows we don't need it.

And so God leads His people into a desert that, for them, is going to be worse than their homes in Egypt. In fact, they're going to wish they were back in Egypt. And God does this on purpose.

Then in Exodus 19, the Bible says the Lord called to Moses out of the mountain, saying, "Thus you shall say to the house of Jacob, and tell the people of Israel: 'You yourselves have seen what I did to the Egyptians, and how I bore you on eagles' wings and brought you to myself'" (vv. 3–4).

Stop right there. You should underline that in your Bible. That's the point. The point of everything. The reason for re-demption. To bring us to Himself. Remember this. We're coming back to it at the end of this book, but in order to get there, we've got to go through the law.

God reminds Moses what He did to the Egyptians and that the Israelites had nothing to do with their own liberation. What they experienced was not a prison escape. Not a revolt. *You did nothing to earn this. This was a gift from Me to you that I bore you on eagles' wings. And I brought you to Myself.* " 'Now therefore, if you will indeed obey my voice and keep my covenant, you shall be my treasured possession among all peoples, for all the earth is mine; and you shall be to me a kingdom of priests and a holy nation.' These are the words that you shall speak to the people of Israel" (vv. 5–6).

The order here is important: grace first, then salvation. Notice it's NOT works first, then salvation. God saves them not because of anything they've done but just because He saves them. And if they'll obey Him, He'll bless them beyond imagination. The singular requirement is obedience. Through the rest of chapter 19, God lays down the ground rules: "I'm going to descend on this mountain, like a hurricane, like a tempest, like a fire." So, Moses climbs the mountain and disappears into the mist. From the valley floor, the Israelites can only see a cloud and lightning flashes and hear crashes of thunder. As a result, they're frightened and they say to Moses, "Can you ask God to quit talking to us? We think it'd be best if you just talked to Him and then us. That'd be much better. We can't even look at Him or we'll burn up and die." Which is true. So God draws a line on the mountain and says, "Make sure no one crosses this line because the only one that can cross this line and come up this mountain is the one that I consecrate and make holy—i.e., you. And if anybody—your kids, your sons, your daughters, your dogs, whatever—crosses this line, they will be stricken. Dead immediately."

God wants to transform a nation of slaves into a kingdom of

priests, so He walks them out into the desert for what will be forty years. And it is here, as the Israelites wander the desert, that God does something He's never done before—He gives the law.

On Mount Sinai. He literally speaks the Ten Commandments to Moses.

Some churches view the rescue of Israel through a legalistic lens that sees God meeting His people in Egypt, giving them the Ten Commandments, and saying, "If you obey, then I will rescue you." The unspoken inference is this: obedience determines identity. But it didn't happen this way. The rescue preceded the law. The nation of Israel was first accepted by His grace and only then did obedience follow.

In the kingdom of heaven, identity always precedes activity and only God gets to tell you who you are. Not the other way around. And while the law was impossible to obey, the law was not the problem. The law was perfect. Still is. It's a tutor. A diagnostic. Like an X-ray, it projects the problem onto the screen, and the problem is us. And not only are we the problem, but we can't fix us. The law leads us to a simple understanding and only one conclusion— we are in need of One to save us from ourselves.

But without the law, we can't know that.

Hence, the Ten Commandments. Actually, in Jewish law there are over six hundred laws, but we're going to focus on the first ten because of what they say about us and what they say about God.

Basically, the Ten Commandments are the diagnosis that we are sick, and only Jesus is the cure to that sickness from the inside out. This is the covenant established (or cut) at Mount Sinai.

And the Ten Commandments are not just rules for living. They represent a covenant that God is making with His people. In order for us to know how to relate to and with Him, He gives us the Ten Commandments. In these commandments, God reveals His

---

character and His nature. You and I cannot rightly and fully know Jesus if we don't rightly and fully know the backdrop of the Old Testament out of which Jesus steps.

Hence, the law.

For the last four centuries, the Israelites have lived in Egypt. Slaves. They've been beaten, mistreated, unloved, and the only gods they know are the Egyptian gods, which were all soundly defeated in the Exodus. But God doesn't see slaves. He sees a kingdom of priests in the making. A people holy to Him. He also understands that the first step in their transformation is to know how to interact both with Him and with one another. And lesson number one is obedience. If they will just obey, it will change everything about everything. This is why the writer of Hebrews, speaking of Jesus, says, "Although he was a son, he learned obedience through what he suffered" (5:8). And just as the Passover lamb is a type of Jesus and points to Jesus, so does the suffering in the desert.

And so God calls Moses and says, "This is what it looks like to live in a right relationship with Me." Ultimately, the Ten Commandments are both a map and a mirror. They're a map to show us how we ought to live before a holy and righteous God, and a mirror that diagnoses the problem that we can't. And the diagnosis is not good. We're oh for ten. Once we study them, we begin to understand—"Oh, I'm lost and I can't get myself unlost. I need a guide." Those of us who know our Bibles hear this and want to jump to Romans 3, which is directly addressing the law when it says, *No one by works of the law will ever be made righteous, but a righteousness has been manifested apart from the law through faith in Jesus Christ.* Trust me—I'm with you and I thank God for this, but why is this such great news? Keep reading.

The commandments are binoculars, or X-ray vision, for me to examine myself and point out all the wrong things I'm doing—or, said another way, the things that separate me from God. Which is not His wish because, remember, He has brought us to Himself. And if I will look closely, they become a mirror that reflects the sin that is in my heart. Which He wants to cleanse me of.

Many evangelicals give the law a bad rap, but the Bible does not give the law a bad rap. In Psalm 1, David says, *Blessed is this man who does not walk in the way of the wicked, or sit in the seat of the mocker, or stand in the way the sinner, but his delight is in the law of the Lord and on this law he meditates day and night.* I pray this over my kids all the time. Jesus would have grown up with the law and He would have delighted in it. And if Jesus did, why wouldn't we?

So, let's dive in. When I was a youth pastor at Vinton Baptist Church many years ago, a young kid taught me how to remember the Ten Commandments with hand signals, and as a result, I've never forgotten them. Corny? Maybe. But in the years since, I've taught them to several thousand people and many remember them, and so I'm going to attempt to teach you. Don't laugh—they work.

Number one. Chapter 20, verse 2. And God said, "I am the LORD your God, who brought you out of the land of Egypt, out of the house of slavery." Don't miss the grace of God here. He hasn't given them the law yet. And yet He's already saved them. Rescued them. Redeemed them. He's speaking both of whose they are and who they are. Notice what He didn't do: He did not show up in Egypt and say, "I've heard your cry; here are the Ten Commandments. I'll be back for a midterm. If you can pull off, like, a B+, then I'll come and redeem you." Nothing could be further from the truth. Based on nothing that they have done except to cry out to God for Him to save them, He saves them, redeems them, and says, *I am your God. And out of Egypt, I have saved you. Out of the house of slavery.* And don't miss what we often do. It's amazing:

Obeying the law is not a prerequisite to knowing God, but the follow-through of what it looks like for those of us who do. Jesus says it this way: "For out of the abundance of the heart, the mouth speaks" and "If you love me, you will keep my commandments" (Matt. 12:34; John 14:15).

We find the first commandment in verse 3: "You shall have no other gods before me." So here we go. Back to kindergarten. Remember those hand signals I told you about? Lift up one of your hands, make a fist, now hold up one finger. Just your index finger. That's the one next to your thumb. So, hold it up. This represents the first commandment. Why? Because there's only one God. That's where He starts. One God. Signified for us by one finger. When God starts with the command to have no other gods, I think He's addressing this childish thing in us that thinks the world revolves around us. He's throwing that on its head. It doesn't. Everything, and everyone, revolves around Him. Period.

I hope and pray every single one of you will have this kind of Copernicus moment where you realize you are not the center of the universe. We're the earth. He's the sun. Not vice versa. So God begins with this—there is one God, and it's not you.

Verses 4–6:

"You shall not make for yourself a carved image, or any likeness of anything that is in heaven above, or that is in the earth beneath, or that is in the water under the earth. You shall not bow down to them or serve them, for I the Lord your God am a jealous God, visiting the iniquity of the fathers on the children to the third and the fourth generation of those who hate me, but showing steadfast love to thousands of those who love me and keep my commandments."

So, commandment number two. Turn your hand horizontal and cut out the idols like scissors. Like rock, paper, scissors. Today, we don't really have carved images. We're much more progressive than that. Instead of the carved image, we worship the image in the mirror. Us. The first letter of John tells us that we should not love the world or anything in it, but all the world has to offer is the lust of the eyes, the lust of the flesh, and the pride of life.

That said, don't think we don't have our idols. We do. We worship consumerism, our careers, and we worship greed over generosity. And we worship what our house looks like infinitely more than the ministry we could be doing in it. We worship the idol of likes and followers and the approval of our peers, which is the idol of perception. And possibly our biggest idol is comfort. If nothing else, we want to be comfortable. Our lives are centered around obtaining it. So, while we would never bow down to a carved image, we still bow to our idols. To help you remember, God says, "Cut it out." Again, the scissor motion.

Commandment three. God says, "You shall not take the name of the LORD your God in vain, for the LORD will not hold him guiltless who takes his name in vain." You've got to be a little creative to remember number three. Make a fist again and hold your middle three fingers up. It should look like a *w*. The *w* stands for "Watch your mouth. Don't use the Lord's name in vain." This doesn't just mean don't say bad words with God's name in it. You shouldn't, but it means more than that. It means to take His name seriously and to not just use it to exploit others for your own benefit. Don't be flippant with it. God is not some eternal cosmic butler to get you what you want when you want it. He's not a dog we've trained to fetch or sit or lie down. Here, God is saying, "Don't do that. Watch your mouth. Don't use My name in vain." This is why when Jesus teaches His friends to pray, He starts with, "Our Father in heaven, hallowed be your name." I'm not quite sure, but I think His reason has something to do with holiness and

Jesus' command to be holy as He is holy and let no unwholesome word come out of our mouths. It's what comes out of us that defiles us.

Verses 8–11. Commandment number four:

"Remember the Sabbath day, to keep it holy. Six days you shall labor, and do all your work, but the seventh day is a Sabbath to the LORD your God. On it you shall not do any work, you, or your son, or your daughter, your male servant, or your female servant, or your livestock, or the sojourner who is within your gates. For in six days the LORD made heaven and earth, the sea, and all that is in them, and rested on the seventh day. Therefore the LORD blessed the Sabbath day and made it holy."

In a normal month, there are four Sundays. Occasionally we get a fifth, but it's the exception and not the norm. So, back to our hand motions. Tuck your thumb and hold up four fingers. Honor the Sabbath, keep it holy.

God created us to live in rhythm with Him and His model is to work really hard six days, from sunup to sundown. And then rest on the seventh, trusting that you are going to rest in Him and that He will fill in the gaps. Some call this the Chick-fil-A model but it started with God. And remember—the Israelites lived in an agricultural society where if they didn't work, they died. Knowing this about them and wanting them to learn to trust Him, God said, "Trust Me." Think about it this way: Adam and Eve were created on the sixth day, and on day seven, the very first day of their lives, they rested. From what? I have no idea. But they did. They didn't rest from work. They rested for work. They reconnected with Him. When Jesus arrives, He frees us to define what Sabbath is in our own life. He allows you to learn what it is that helps you be in rhythm with Him—to refuel, reconnect, and recharge so that you can do all that He has called you to do. To fulfill the Great Commission all week long.

Speaking of Chick-fil-A, let's be honest—it's aggravating, is it not? How many times have you driven by and you're like, *No line! Sweet!* and then you pull into the drive-thru and all the lights are off. *Oh, it's Sunday. You Christians!* I'm kidding. My family and I are huge Chick-fil-A fans. But think about the decision they made before they saw the blessing from it. Everybody thought they were crazy when they said, "We're going to close on Sundays." Do you know how difficult it is to make a profit in the food business? Their critics said, "That'll never work." And yet God blessed them and continues to bless them. Sabbath matters, and yet for some reason we think we know better.

If you notice here, the first four commandments are all about our relationship vertically with God. Commandments five through ten focus on our horizontal relationships with one another. Most rabbis and theologians call the fourth commandment the hinge commandment, because if you don't get this one right, then you won't be full enough of the love of God to then love one another. So let me ask you, do you Sabbath? And before you answer or start making excuses, let me point out the obvious—it's still one of the commandments and it's part of the rhythm of God that He's modeled for us so that we find our rest in Him. It's meant to bring us back to Him and remind us of the first commandment. There's only one God, and you're not Him.

The hinge of sabbath rest has brought us here. The fifth commandment. Straighten five fingers. Now salute. *Yes, sir.* Why do we salute? Because we are honoring someone. So, the fifth commandment is "Honor your father and your mother, that your days may be long in the land that the LORD your God is giving you." By the way, this is the first commandment with a promise. My daddy used to say, "Boy, the Bible says I brought you into this world and I can take you out." And I was like, "I think that's *The Cosby Show*, but I know what you mean." The reality here is that regardless of how you feel about it or whether you like it or not, God always works in and through authority. No matter how good or terrible your parents are or were, God anointed them as the leaders over you. And that authority has nothing to do with how they treated you.

Just focus on the first word—*honor*. There's a big difference between honor and respect. Respect is earned. Honor is given. Some of you are thinking, *I can't honor my parents because they're not very honorable*. Doesn't matter. Paul told us in Romans to honor everyone. And the emperor of Rome would later murder Christians, and yet Paul would tell us, *Yes, we should honor him even while he's not very respectable, because honor and respect are two different things*. Respect is earned, and honor is a decision we willfully make. Also, I've looked at the fine print here, and there's no expiration date on this one. As long as you've got them, you honor them. I'm not downplaying that for some of you, this one is really tough. Some of you have parents who have done bad things to you. I get it. I'm also not saying be a doormat. Don't hear that. But I am pointing you to the Word and reminding you that this is a command, and like the Israelites, we can choose to obey it or not.

Number six: "You shall not murder." This one's easy and it uses both hands. Turn your left hand sideways and make a fake pistol. Now pull the trigger. Bang! Your right hand falls down. Don't murder. This is the command where many of us take a deep breath. Phew! When we start feeling pretty good about our performance. *Finally, I nailed one. I've never murdered anybody*. By the way, if you're grading yourself, how're you doing? Have you ever worshiped another god, ever used the Lord's name in vain, ever worked twenty-one days in a row, ever dishonored your parents? The answer for all of us is the same—we're not doing very well. We're oh for a thousand. But if you ask most people, their honest assessment of themselves is, "I'm a good person."

Really? Compared to what? The nightly news? The problem is, God doesn't grade on a curve. He grades on perfection. He says, *Be holy because I am holy.* For some of you, this is equivalent to the place in your college career where you evaluated your grade and the amount of the semester you had left and you realized, *Uh-oh, I need 173 on the next two tests to be able to pull a C.* It's not mathematically possible. So you tap out.

Take a look at your inventory. Is anybody crushing it? Anybody thinking to themselves, *This is seriously not even hard. Let's get to the hard ones. Can we get to Leviticus where it gets into detail?* Let me remind you that even if you crush it from here, 50 percent is still failing. Despite that, we get to number six and think, *Finally! I have not murdered anybody.* But before you get too puffed up, remember that Jesus says this in the Sermon on the Mount: *You've heard that it was said, thou shalt not murder. But I say to you, if you've ever hated your brother in your heart, or even said to him, 'You fool' that you have committed murder in your heart.*

Am I the only one guilty of that one?

I'm not proud of what I'm about to tell you, and you should never do this, but the Bible says to confess your sins to one another, so here goes. Some years back, Gretchen and I were driving in my truck and we were having what I like to call "robust fellowship." I wasn't getting the answer or agreement I wanted so, like a child, I got mad and hit the steering wheel.

And because God is a just God, the horn stuck. On. As in blowing constantly. Loudly. And to make matters worse, Gretchen started laughing. So, we drove home—with the horn blowing the whole way. Which by that point sounded to me like, "Murderer!" We pulled up to a light and everyone around me was looking at me with these angry looks and my wife was laughing and I wasn't thinking warm, fuzzy thoughts.

While I'm offering honest confession, here's another example of which I'm not too proud. My son, JP, was playing in a flag football game and I was his coach. This young kid, probably nineteen or twenty years old, was one of the referees. Note: in flag football, you're not supposed to touch each other. Hence, flags. So, JP was playing quarterback, he dropped back, threw the ball, and a kid on defense ran him over. Flattened him. So, I used my grown-up voice. "Hey! Where's the roughing-the-passer call?" No kidding, the kid ref turned and said, "I wasn't watching." Are you kidding? And as loud as I could, I said, "You have one job!" And from one of the parents on the opposing team's sideline, I heard a lady say, "Hey, Pastor Joby."

Both in the truck and on that field, I was not thinking kind, loving, pastoral thoughts. And in God's kingdom, He calls this murder.

Number seven. Verse 14. Hold up both hands. Left hand, extend all five fingers. Right hand, make a fist, then hold up two little rabbit ears. Like V for victory. Together they total seven fingers. "You shall not commit adultery." And as you say that, the right hand slowly disappears behind your back like the Easter bunny, suggesting something done in secret.

As He did with commandment number six, Jesus raises the bar here also. He says, *You've heard that it was said, thou shall not commit adultery. But if you've ever lusted after a woman in your heart...* (Matt. 5:27–28). He says those aren't just pictures. They're a pathway. They'll kill you. And the result will kill your marriage. Jesus is saying that according to God, sex is only for married people. And according to God, marriage is one man, one woman, one lifetime. Now listen, the Supreme Court can't redefine marriage, because it never defined it to begin with. God defined it.

In both commandments five and seven, God is assembling a

people and this is how He requires we live together. And the integrity of marriage and the family are fundamental to being the people of God. And so He says, *"You shall not commit adultery."*

Number eight. Hold both hands up. Extend five fingers on your left hand and three on your right while sort of tucking your pinkie finger down with your thumb. In some countries, if you get caught stealing, they'll cut off your pinkie. So, use your left like a sword and cut the pinkie off your right. "Thou shalt not steal." It's pretty cut-and-dried.

Here's how God defines stealing: taking something that's not yours. And that means anything. Including files. And for the record, file sharing is stealing, and I don't care how easy it is. Stealing is usually easy.

Number nine. Hold your hands out again. Same fingers. Five on the left and three on the right while tucking the pinkie behind the thumb. Again, cut off the pinkie but only fake it this time. Tell everyone it's gone when it's not. Now pop the pinkie back up. That's lying. Or, in biblical language, "bearing false witness."

In eight we cut the pinkie off for stealing, and in nine we pop it back up for lying. Verse 16: "You shall not bear false witness against your neighbor." Let me tell you something that maybe no one has ever told you: you're a liar. And if you say you're not, you're still a liar. I've had people legitimately get offended by this and come to me and say, "I'm not a liar. I just struggle with telling the truth." My response is, "Well, that's not your only struggle."

Don't believe me? How many times have you said, "I have read the terms and conditions" and clicked Accept? No, you didn't. None of us have. You're a liar, and it's not just silly stuff like this. And little white lies are just as much lies as big fat ones.

Last one. Number ten. Hold up both hands and extend all ten fingers. Now reach out and grab something that's not yours. "Thou shalt not covet." In this last one, God gives a little more commentary. He says, "You shall not covet your neighbor's house; you shall not covet your neighbor's wife, or his male servant, or his female servant, or his ox, or his donkey, or anything that is your neighbor's." Now again, you may say, "Well, I don't covet." If you've ever watched HGTV, you're a sinner and a liar.

Now, here's the thing. Wives, if you're honest, most of you don't covet the house. You just covet the husband that was more handy than the one you picked. You wish you had disposable income and a husband who knew how to do all that stuff. And maybe those granite countertops. And guys, we're just as bad. Golf clubs, cars, just stuff, we're all guilty. Especially in this Amazon culture when anything you want is one click away.

Verse 18: "Now when all the people saw the thunder and the flashes of lightning and the sound of the trumpet and the mountain smoking, the people were afraid and trembled, and they stood far off." Why? Because they'd just heard the voice of God speak the Ten Commandments and they understood not only the requirements of the covenant, but also what came next. Making the covenant. Or "cutting" the covenant. Because that's what they did. And without cutting, without blood, there was no covenant. So they would take a lamb, ox, goat, or something, and they'd kill it and literally cut the animal in half. And the two people making the covenant would walk in between the two halves of the animal. This established the covenant. The implication between the two parties was, "If you don't keep your part of the covenant, then the carnage you see around is what I'll do to you." This was understood. And so the people shook because they knew they were about to make a covenant with God and their chances of keeping it weren't great.

As they thought through the implications, they were trembling and standing at a distance. So they said to Moses, "You speak to us, and we will listen; but do not let God speak to us, lest we die." And Moses said to the people, "Do not fear, for God has come to test you, that the fear of him may be before you, that you may not sin." The people stood far off, while Moses drew near to the thick darkness where God was."

They knew before the covenant was cut that they couldn't keep up their end. Because if any one person broke any one commandment, the covenant would be broken. So the people asked, "What do we do? Because if this is God's standard to be in right relationship with Him, then we can't be." Well, fear not—God had an answer for that as well, and the next thing He did was describe how to make sacrifices on an altar to cover over their sin. Notice again the goodness of God to provide the remedy before the sin. You see a picture of this in your bathroom every day. Under the mirror is a sink and while the mirror exposes the problem, the sink addresses it.

We find out in Galatians 3, in Hebrews, and in the book of Romans that God gave the law so that we would be aware of what wretched, black-hearted sinners we are. Let me ask you this: How do you know if you're speeding? You compare your speedometer to the speed limit. Without a limit, there's no such thing as speeding. If the sign just said DRIVE CAREFULLY, then some of you would drive 45 mph and some 145 mph. And how you "feel" would determine whether you were safe or not.

In the commandments, God says, "These are My standards. My limits." And if we look at them closely, we can see that we're in trouble. So, a holy, perfect, and mighty God, existing in the form of a storm and clouds and lightning on top of a mountain, says, "You are My people and I am your God and this is what it looks like to be My people." And all the people look at that standard and they say, "There's no way. If we step one foot on this mountain, we are toast."

The good news of the gospel of Jesus Christ is that Jesus came down that mountain and became flesh. A man. And He lived the perfect life, fulfilling every one of these laws that we may know God, not as fire on the mountain or a cosmic judge, but as heavenly Father. This is what Romans 3 is all about. Martin Luther said that the paragraph that follows Romans 3:20 is the most important paragraph ever written. And I agree. Paul says, "For by works of the law no human being will be justified in his sight, since through the law comes knowledge of sin." That word *justified* is a legal term. The best way to remember it is this—because of what Christ has done for us, I'm justified—just-as-if-I'd never sinned.

Paul is telling us that we come to know our sin through the law and because of this, once we are confronted with our own stuff, none of us are good enough to stand before the almighty God. Look at it this way: Our daughter, Reagan Capri, is the toughest Martin in the house. She doesn't cry. She cries watching animal movies but not when she falls down and scrapes her knees. A couple of years ago, she was in one of those concussion cubes. You know—those little trampoline places where everyone bounces around like popcorn. Bodies flying everywhere. I think these places are sponsored by all of these new pop-up emergency care places. A few minutes later, she walks up to me holding her arm and says, "Dad, I heard it pop." Not good. So we get in the car, drive to the hospital, and they take an X-ray of it. I still have the X-ray and I hate it because you can clearly see her elbow was broken right at the growth plate. Snapped. But that's all the power it has—the X-ray has zero power to do anything, to heal or fix her. It's just a picture. All the X-ray can do is point out that there's a problem.

This is the law in our lives. The X-ray can't unbreak her arm. I can wrap the X-ray around her arm, even take ten thousand more pictures of it, and it would not heal her arm. This is why Paul says that through the law comes knowledge of sin. This is why the Israelites stood at the bottom of the mountain, heard the law, looked at themselves, and said, "No way. We'll never pull this off."

Romans 3:21. "But now the righteousness of God has been manifested apart from the law." When the Bible uses the word *righteousness*, it doesn't mean right activity. It means right identity or right standing with God.

You should be asking yourself by now, *So, if God laid out this law that none of us can ever fulfill, how in the world can we be right with God?* Good question. And it is *the* question Paul is answering in Romans. He is saying that you and I need what the reformers will later call an "alien righteousness." A righteousness that doesn't come from us. For the answer, Paul points to the Scriptures—the law and prophets—and says to the church in Rome that everything in the Old Testament all points to one thing, and that one thing is the person and work of Jesus. May we never unhitch from the Old Testament.

Noah stepping into the ark to save mankind points to Jesus as the greater ark. The Passover lamb that was slain points to Jesus. The whole sacrificial system of the temple all points to the Lamb of God who comes to take away the sin of the entire world. Paul argues that God gave us the old covenant, the Old Testament, so that we could and would recognize the manifestation of the new when the righteousness of God shows up in the person of Jesus. Paul ends verse 21 by saying, "The Law and the Prophets bear witness to it." Meaning Jesus. Then, verse 22: "The righteousness of God through faith in Jesus Christ for all who believe." To the early church, this was mind-blowing.

Remember my story of diving off the board into the arms of my dad? That's what this is. Your heavenly Father is standing in the deep end, or maybe on the deep end, saying, "Come on, jump." That's what this is. This righteousness of God through faith in Jesus is when we don't trust in our own good behavior and our own commandment-keeping, but we trust in the finished work of Jesus Christ. That what He accomplished on the cross somehow counted for me. This means that no matter how good you think you are, you still need to believe in Jesus for the forgiveness of your sin. And no matter how bad you think you've been, you can still be part of the "all who believe" if you believe and trust that Jesus' life, death, and resurrection make you righteous before God. In Jesus, there is no distinction. Why? Verse 23. "For all have sinned and fall short of the glory of God."

The word *sin* is an archery term. It means "to miss the mark." If the bullseye is the holiness, perfection, and justice of God, then every single one of us has missed the mark. Most of us have missed the entire target. It's like this: If you were in an archery competition and you had to hit three bullseyes to go on to round two, and your first arrow fell short, didn't even hit the target, just stuck in the ground, then it "missed the mark." Undeterred, you nock a second arrow and split the bullseye. Nock another and Robin Hood that arrow. Two perfect, one not so much. Do you get to move on?

No. Why? Because perfection required one perfect bullseye followed by two Robin Hoods. Which you failed to shoot. So, even from that day forward, for the rest of your life, if you can pull off perfection, you are still judged by the one that sailed into the dirt.

It follows you everywhere. Can't erase it. That one errant arrow will forever stand between you and a perfect score—which is required to stand in the presence of God—so what are you going to do about it? *For all have sinned and fall short of the glory of God.* But we are "justified," or made just-as-if-I'd never sinned (or just-as-if-I'd never missed the mark), by His unmerited grace, which we cannot earn. Ten thousand perfect shots don't erase the reality and memory of the one. God, in His mercy, gave us the Ten Commandments so that we will know how far we've gone astray and that we can't rescue ourselves. When we read them, our singular response should be, "I need Jesus. Period."

Have you ever clipped a coupon? Think about that transaction. You walk to your mailbox and, wonder of wonders, find a mailer inside with umpteen coupons. They are free and cost you nothing. So, you clip the one for the free ham, go to Publix, get your ham, and set it on the belt. The cashier says, "Twenty-three bucks." But you shake your head. "No, I don't think so. I have a coupon." We literally call this "redeeming your coupon." And what does it cost you? Nothing. You receive the ham as a gift. It costs the manufacturer full price. And it cost the pig everything. You? Nothing.

This is the redemption that is in Christ Jesus. Verse 25: "Whom God put forward as a propitiation by his blood, to be received by faith." Propitiation means "a payment that satisfies." What's being satisfied? The wrath of God.

Jesus on the cross is our propitiation. He alone is the payment that satisfies the justice and the holiness of God. The reason we don't have to be afraid of the wrath and terror of God like the Israelites were at the base of the mountain is because God emptied His wrath on the head of His Son, Jesus. On the cross, Jesus fully paid the price for all of our sin. He "bore" our sin and He is the payment that satisfies. A. W. Tozer says the most important thing about you is what you think about when you think about God.[5] And most of you think God is just frustrated with you because you're a liar and a cheat and a murderer.

Our natural response to the image of ourselves in the mirror is to try harder. Clean ourselves up. But that's not the gospel. The gospel is that Jesus is the propitiation for our sin. The payment that fully satisfies the wrath of God, fully satisfies the righteousness of God, and fully satisfies the justice of God. Therefore, if you are in Christ and His righteousness has been counted or imputed to you,

---

5   A. W. Tozer, *The Knowledge of the Holy* (Indo-European Publishing, 2018), 4.

then when God sees you, He sees His Son, Jesus Christ, and He credits Jesus' payment to your debt. Jesus Christ is the payment that satisfies. This means it is impossible for God to be dissatisfied with you. Because He is completely satisfied with His Son. Even when we fail, we can run to God, rather than from Him.

In 2012, I planted a church called Eleven22. I'll tell you more about it in a later chapter, but when we first planted the church, a lot of church experts told me that I shouldn't use theological terms like *pisteuō* and *propitiation*. They said people didn't understand those terms and I would confuse people. But I think if you can order a venti caramel macchiato, you can understand a little Greek and some theological terms.

The short definition of *propitiation* is "the payment that satisfies," and Jesus is that and does that for us. And if this is true, and it is, then God can't be dissatisfied in you because disappointment has to do with surprise. And He's never been surprised by your actions, by your failing.

We first see God's provision for His people's failures in the temple. Inside the Holy of Holies sat the ark of the covenant, and sitting on the ark of the covenant is the mercy seat. It's the throne of God. It is here that He tells us, "There I will meet with you." Below it, inside the ark, is the broken law of God. This very law we've been talking about. One way to think about it is that as God looks down from heaven onto His throne, His seat, He sees His broken law. And while God is love, He has to be stirred to anger and the broken law of God stirs His anger. His wrath. I said this before: the punishment is determined not just by what you do, but who you do it against. And a sin against an almighty, eternal God requires an everlasting punishment. The Greek word for mercy seat is *hilastērion*. And literally it means "propitiation." In Leviticus 16, God required that every year on the Day of Atonement, the people of God would come and confess their sins to the high priest. The high priest would then transfer the confessions of the people to the head of a goat, which they would take to the edge of town and cast out into the wilderness. The people would then watch their sins depart from them, as far as the east is from the west. Then the high priest would consecrate himself, shed the blood of a perfect spotless lamb, catch it in a bowl, and walk into the Holy of Holies. Then he would paint the mercy seat, covering the *hilastērion* with the blood of the spotless lamb. And the picture is this—when God looks from heaven and sees this, now He does not see His broken law; He sees the blood of the lamb. And so when John the Baptist said, "Behold, the Lamb of God, who takes away the sin of the world!" he was talking about this. Jesus is the fulfillment of Leviticus 16. He did not say, *Here's another lamb who has come to cover the sin of the Jewish people for one more year,* but *The lamb who's come to take away the sin of all the people.* Propitiation. If you keep reading, you'll find God says this in the next chapter: "For the life of the flesh is in the blood, and I have given it for you on the altar to make atonement for your souls, for it is the blood that makes atonement by the life" (Lev. 17:11).

People have asked me, "How come God doesn't just forgive all sin?" Because all sin must be paid for. Let's say you borrowed my truck, wrecked it, and then disappeared, saying nothing to me. There's no forgiveness between us because you haven't asked for it. Now, let's say you stole it, wrecked it, and then brought me the keys, saying, "I'm sorry, please forgive me." To that I would say, "Don't worry about it. I forgive you." While it's true that I really did forgive you, somebody still has to pay to repair the truck because the truck is still broken. And that somebody is me. My forgiveness has brought us back into right relationship with each other but it hasn't fixed the truck. Payment does. This is overly simplistic, but you get the idea. What is implied is that forgiveness from God includes payment. God is saying, *When I forgive you, I will make the payment and fix you.*

When people hear this, they usually ask, "Okay, but why did Jesus have to die? Why kill His own Son? I don't understand."

Great question. Remember, payment for sin is not just determined by what you do but who you do it against. And when we sin, even when we sin against one another, we sin ultimately against an almighty God. Paul answers it this way: *God puts forth Jesus as a propitiation by his blood to be received by faith. This was to show God's righteousness because of his divine forbearance He had passed over former sins. It was to show His righteousness at the present time so that He might be just and the justifier of the one who has faith in Jesus.* (Rom. 3:25–26).

In other words, because of God's justice, all sin must be paid for, because for God to just say, "Don't worry about it," would make God unjust. God Himself would be a hypocrite and unholy and imperfect. Because of God's mercy, payment was delayed. This is how Moses gets saved. This is how Abraham gets saved. This is how David gets saved. The wages of sin is death and because of God's mercy, because of His divine forbearance, He passed over former sins until the Lamb comes to be slain on the cross for the forgiveness of all sin. And that Lamb is His Son.

This can be tough to wrap your head around, but God is both just and the justifier. It means that at the cross of Jesus Christ, the love of God and the justice of God intersect in the gospel of Jesus Christ. Think about it this way—the vertical beam of the cross of Jesus represents God's justice poured out on the sin of all humanity. The horizontal beam demonstrates His love for His people. And in the middle, His love and justice meet in the body of Jesus who "bore our sins in his body on the tree" (1 Pet. 2:24).

Romans 3 ends this way: "Do we then overthrow the law by this faith?" In other words, because we put our faith in Jesus, does this mean that the law does not apply to us anymore? Paul says, "By no means! On the contrary, we uphold the law." In other words, the condition for our acceptance has already been met. We, too, can become children of God because of what Christ accomplished on our behalf. Therefore, knowing what He saved us from and who He's taking us to—His Father—we obey. That's our response. How can you not? Here's the point.

The Ten Commandments—the law—are the diagnosis, the X-ray, the MRI. It is the scan of your soul to say something is broken and needs to be fixed. When Jesus pushed up on His nail-pierced feet, the last thing that He said was these words: "It is finished." *Tetelestai.* In the first century, when loans were paid off, banks would stamp one word on the paperwork: *tetelestai.* Signifying *it is finished.* Final payment has been made.

Many of you think God is standing up there with a clipboard, watching you through a raised eyebrow, checking off when you do and don't live according to the Ten Commandments. If you're good enough, maybe He'll let you in. Your enemy would very much like you to think your Father views you this way.

Nothing could be further from the truth. And the truth is, you're three-quarters of the way through the semester, currently rocking a zero average. There's not enough time left in the semester for you to pull this thing off. Even if, from this day forward, for the rest of your life, you nail an A+, you've still missed the mark. God requires perfection. And Jesus was perfect. "For by a single offering he has perfected for all time those who are being sanctified" (Heb. 10:14). You see that *perfected for all time*? He's talking about us.

I've heard people say, "I just need a second chance at life. To turn over a new leaf." No, you don't. You'd mess that one up, too. Here's what I mean—if my eleven-year-old daughter took a calculus exam, how do you think she'd score? Not well for two reasons. First, she's a Martin, and second, she's eleven. So, if she failed the exam the first time, and I, in my mercy, gave her a second chance, she'd only fail it a second time. God is not the God of second chances. I know what people mean when they say that, but it's just illogical and inaccurate. God is the God of a new life. This is why He says, *I make all things new.* Notice He didn't say anything about second chances.

Some of you are still not convinced you're a sinner. Let me come at it another way: even if you don't hold yourself to God's standard of the Ten Commandments given on Mount Sinai, you can't even measure up to your own self-imposed standards. Nobody has lied to you more than you. Nobody has broken more promises to you than you. How many times have you said, "I'm never doing that again"? And yet here you are doing it again. Have you ever broken your own New Year's resolutions? If you can't keep your own self-imposed law, how in the world do you think that you are good enough to stand before a righteous and holy God? Let's just say for one second that God only held you accountable to the laws you decided you would live by. If that was your only standard of judgment, you'd still fail miserably. We all do. We can't even keep our substandard law, much less His holy and righteous law. Therefore we need a righteousness manifested apart from the law.

Even though I'd heard it a lot, I came to really know this the night I watched my camp counselors reenact the crucifixion. And trust me, they were in no danger of winning any Academy Awards. We watched Jesus go marching to the other side of the pond—and there wasn't even a pond in the Bible, but there was one in South Carolina. The whole thing was lit by other counselors carrying torches so we could see what was happening. And as I sat there watching Him in the firelight, I heard the hammer pound the nails into the wood. And in my mind's eye, I saw them pierce His hands. And then I watched as they hung Jesus up on the cross. Somehow, even though this was the '80s in South Carolina, I was transported to Mount Moriah. Calvary. Two thousand years ago.

When we get to the last chapter of this book, we will walk through the seven things Jesus said on the cross. For now, let me shorten it with this: He started with, "Father, forgive them, for they know not what they do." He ended with, "It is finished." When He said, *"It is finished,"* the camp counselors dropped those torches in the water, and you've never seen dark until you've stood in the backwoods of South Carolina at night. Then, a few seconds later, a single light shone on the cross—which was now empty. Jesus was no longer there. And Coach Bull Lee, my football coach, stood in front of us and just said these simple words: "For God so loved the world." Then he said, "For God so loved you," and he pointed right at me. "For God so loved you that He gave His only begotten Son, that whosoever..." And he pointed at me again. "Whosoever would believe in Him would not perish but have everlasting life." Then he said, "For any-body that's ready..." The language we would use today is this: Are you ready to surrender your life to the lordship of Christ? Coach Lee asked us if we were ready to "ask Jesus into our hearts." Even though I have some problems with that language theologically today, that night I asked and He entered.

I sat there and my heart was about to beat out of my chest. I didn't know anything about the Lord's propitiation or substitution-ary atonement or even that there was a Holy Spirit. I didn't know that by the power of God, the scales were falling off my eyes and He was ripping out my heart of stone and replacing it with a heart of flesh, His heart. I didn't know any of that. I just knew that for some reason, I believed. I believed that the thing we just watched counted for me. And then we started singing. It was a Baptist camp, so we sang "Just as I Am," which is as Baptist as you can get. And to give everybody time to wrestle with the question, we sang one verse for about forty-five minutes. We were probably on the twelfth time around—"Just as I am, without one plea. But that Thy blood was shed for me." And I'm still sitting. Not about to go up there. But Coach steps up and says, "I believe there's one more out there that needs to come and surrender to Jesus." I had my feet wrapped around the seat that I was sitting on. *I ain't getting up.* Because at the Baptist church, you couldn't get saved in your seat. You had to get saved right up there in front of everybody.

Now, I know this is not true. You can be saved in your car, on an airplane, or in cell block D. It doesn't matter to God. He'll meet you wherever you are. I was a pretty tough kid with tough skin and I thought, *Ain't no way I'm getting up there and feeling all weepy. I'm not crying in front of all these people. There's no way I'm getting out of my seat and getting up there.* Then, for reasons I cannot explain, on what was probably the thirteenth time through the song, Coach said, "One more," and the next thing I know, I levitated to the front or something and I fell into the arms of Coach Lee and prayed.

It's been over thirty years and as I write this, tears are streaming down my face. Why? Because I cannot, no matter how much time passes, get over the cross and what Jesus did there for me. It makes no sense to me whatsoever. And yet He knew all that, and He did it anyway. Later, I would come to know the truth of what Paul says in Romans. *But God*— Two of the greatest words ever written. "But God shows his love for us in that while we were still sinners, Christ died for us" (Rom. 5:8).

In that moment, when I surrendered my life to Jesus Christ, I became one of those "whosoevers." When Jesus says, "Whosoever would believe," He's talking about me. And He's talking about you. Right now.

I know we did this in chapter 1, but I've been a preacher a long time, and in my experience, this message of surrendering my life to the lordship of Jesus can take a minute to sink into our stubborn heads.

Would you like to become one of those whosoevers right now?

Then surrender. Admit you're a sinner in need of a savior and not just a mistaker in need of a life coach. Believe that when Jesus died on the cross, somehow, even though you still have ten thousand questions, that counted for you. Call on the name of the Lord—"Lord, save me." And He will.

I ended the first chapter by inviting you to put your faith, your belief, *in* Jesus. To *pisteuō* in Him. Some of you are still on the fence. Unwilling to surrender. Thinking you got this and you need neither map nor guide. And some of you need to repent for how you've judged the law as being harsh and insensitive. Which is like saying you don't like how the guardrail dented your car when the drop down the other side is a thousand feet. Jesus said, "If you love me, you will keep my commandments" (John 14:15). Well, okay, which ones? And remember, Jesus said this before any of the New Testament was written.

If you read the Ten Commandments, the crazy thing is that the verdict comes first. Before the evidence. God says, "I am your God. You're My people." Now, let's talk about what that's going to look like. In our Western culture, the evidence comes first, which brings about a verdict. Not with God. In the gospel, He says, "*Tetelestai.* It is finished. And now that it's finished, let's talk about you loving Me, loving people, and accomplishing the Great Commission."

When you get run over by the grace train of the gospel, you look different. And if you don't, you should hold up the mirror of God's Word and ask yourself, *Do I do this? Do I know Him?* Because here's the deeper question: If you're not doing what He says, is He your Lord? We'll talk more about this in a coming chapter, but when Jesus says in the Sermon on the Mount, *"Blessed are the meek,"* the Greek word we translate as *meek* is also used to describe the bit that goes in the horse's mouth. This is salvation terminology. He's saying, "Blessed is the one who has turned the reins of their life over to Me. Blessed is the one who has made Me Lord." Lordship doesn't just believe that, but trusts in.

In the same way that Coach Lee pointed at me, God is, even now, through His Holy Spirit, pointing at you. Otherwise, why read this book? If you believe "for God so loved you" that He sent Jesus, His only begotten Son, as a willing sacrifice in your place for the punishment of your sins, and in this moment, right now, you want to believe in and take that step off the diving board into the loving arms of your heavenly Father, then wherever you are—carpool line, thirty-five thousand feet, the drive-thru, or life without parole— raise your hand and:

Admit—"I am a sinner in need of a Savior."
Believe—"When Christ died on the Cross, it counted for me."
Confess—"Jesus Christ is my Lord and Savior."

If this is you, pray with me:

Pray with Me

Our good and gracious heavenly Father, I thank You for Your law. Your law is good and a gift to Your people. I thank You that as a good Father, You love and discipline Your children. God, I pray for a renewed hunger for Your Word. God, I praise You for the gospel. I praise You that by works of the law no one will be declared righteous before You. I ask that You use Your law as both a map and a mirror in our lives. Use Your law as a map to show us how to rightly live and use Your law as a mirror to remind us of how we fall short and our desperate need of a savior. I thank You that Christ did not come to abolish the law but that through His perfect life He fulfilled every word and intent. God, I thank You that the mercy seat has been covered with the shed blood of the Lamb of God once and for all. Holy Spirit, I pray that You would encourage and equip us to walk in a manner worthy of the gospel of Jesus Christ. Lord, I pray that we would strive as believers to do what is right because we serve a righteous King, and when we stumble and fall, that we would be reminded that Christ has already taken our penalty. Jesus, thank You for Your perfect and righteous life imputed unto us. May we walk in step with You, Lord. I pray this in the name of the Lamb who was slain to take away the sins of the world: Jesus. Amen.

CHAPTER 3

Mount Carmel—Why Are You Still Holding On to That Idol?

O r how long will you limp between two opinions?

From the book of Exodus, the nation of Israel wanders the desert and eventually makes it into the promised land, but by the time we reach the book of 1 Kings, the nation is in a bad place. Remember the first commandment? Make a fist with your right hand; now hold up one finger. "You shall have no other gods."

Israel has violated this commandment in more ways than they can count. Not only have they sinned, but their kings have sinned as well, and while some kings were good and followed Yahweh, most were bad. And few were worse than Ahab. As king of Israel, Ahab had been born into the worship of Jehovah. He knows what God expects; he even named his children Ahaziah, which means "owned by Jehovah," and Jehoram, which means "Jehovah is exalted." So, he's without excuse, but he doesn't care and he certainly doesn't obey, so Israel is covered up in idol worship. And not just one idol. Hundreds. Ahab is doing everything God said not to do.

That said, he had help, and it came in the form of his wife, Jezebel—whose name means "worshiper of Baal." That alone should tell you Ahab was disobedient from the moment he asked her to marry him. Many theologians suggest the last decision Ahab made was saying, "I do," because Jezebel took the reins and became the de facto ruler of Israel, leading the nation down a path of idol worship unlike any they'd seen before. They even started building temples to false gods like Baal and Asherah.

This does not bode well for Ahab and the people of Israel. What's worse, we have no evidence from Scripture that Ahab ever returned to God.

So God sends the prophet Elijah—whose name means "the Lord is God"—to tell Ahab that no rain will fall for three years. This is the worst news he could receive in an agrarian culture. No crops means no money and the people will starve and Ahab will have a difficult time ruling because they will blame him. But rather than repent, Ahab blames Elijah and calls him the "troubler of Israel." Ahab realizes that God is saying, "I am going to take away everything that makes you comfortable." He does that with us as well. Just like He loved the nation of Israel, He loves us enough to strip away anything comfortable, anything that we rely on rather than Him, so that we look to Him and Him alone. This is what God is doing. God is setting the stage for Ahab and all of Israel to make a decision on what god they are going to follow. Why? Because it is His intention that *they become a holy nation and kingdom of priests.* But currently they are priesting for false gods. And God Most High has had enough.

Elijah prays, God turns off the rain to an entire country, and drought soon follows, which makes Elijah popular with no one. To provide for and protect him, God tells Elijah to hide by the brook Cherith, which is east of the Jordan. When he does, ravens bring him bread and meat morning and evening—the first Grubhub. Eventually, the brook runs dry. Have you ever had a brook dry up on you? It happens. Ministries have seasons and sometimes they come to an end—sometimes through no fault of your own. One day all is well and God is providing everything you want and need.

And the next day the brook dries up. So Elijah turns to Zarephath, where he meets a widow collecting wood to cook what will be her and her son's last meal before they die—evidence that the drought has hit them hard.

And Elijah says, "I'm the man of God. Cook me some dinner."

The widow responds, "We don't have enough for ourselves."

Elijah responds, "If you cook me dinner, you'll have enough forever." Which she did. Her jar of flour and jug of oil never ran dry. But trouble seems to follow Elijah and soon the widow's boy dies, at which point the widow blames Elijah. Elijah takes the boy, lies down on him three times, prays, and God resurrects the boy. At which point the widow says, "Now I know that you are a man of God, and that the word of the LORD in your mouth is truth."

In 1 Kings 18, Elijah shows up three and a half years later. During this time Ahab and Jezebel's worship of false gods has only intensified. God tells Elijah, "Now it's time to go. We're going to have this showdown with King Ahab and all the false prophets that he's been employing." On the way there, Elijah bumps into Obadiah (Obadiah works for the king) and says, "Obadiah, go and tell Ahab it's on. I know he's been looking for me, so I'm about to meet with him." And Obadiah responds, "I'm not telling him that, because we've been looking for you for three and a half years. And as soon as I go tell Ahab I found Elijah and we go look for you and you're not there, he'll kill me." Elijah assures him, "Go tell him. I'll be there."

And so we pick it up in 1 Kings 18:17. And it says, "When Ahab saw Elijah, Ahab said to him, 'Is it you, you troubler of Israel?'" Ahab is indignant, but read between the lines. He's accusing Elijah, saying that the reason the entire nation is in this mess is solely because of the prophet. Which means there is still no repentance. He's saying, *Listen, you're the reason we're in this mess. It's your fault. You turned off the water.*

My favorite seminary professor said that my job as a pastor is to comfort the afflicted and afflict the comfortable. That's what I'm supposed to do. Which is exactly what Elijah is doing right here.

In the Old Testament, every believer did not have access to the Holy Spirit like we do in the new covenant. And so the role of the prophet in the Old Testament was to get in there and stir it up so that God's people would be convicted of sin. This is a little different than my job. I can't convict you of anything. I'm not your Holy Spirit. My job, through the power of the Word, is to stir up the Spirit of God in every believer so that He will speak to you and convict you of sin. So that you will be "troubled" to the point that you would choose the one true God and stop serving the Baals and Asherahs of this world. You need to know that as I write this, I'm praying for you. I'm praying that you would be troubled and that God will comfort you or crush you, bless you or break you, whatever you need, so that you would begin to see the idols in your life, and you would choose this day whom you would serve. And I'm praying this for me too.

Elijah responds, in verse 18, "I have not troubled Israel, but you have, and your father's house, because you have abandoned the commandments of the LORD and followed the Baals." He's saying, *Ahab, when times got tough—like this drought—you failed to turn to the one true God. Instead, you turned to the little-g gods of this world.* During this time in history, people worshiped a little-g god for every need they had. If you needed rain, there was a rain god. If you needed the flowers to grow, there was a flower god. If you needed a baby, there was a fertility god. There was a little god for all of this. And the problem with all of these little-g gods was the problem with every idol in every day and age. Idols make promises they don't have the ability to keep. Because we, in our faithlessness, give them power they don't have—and never have had. Whatever or whoever you idolize will let you down. And when they do, you'll demonize it or them.

Oftentimes, we in the twenty-first century can have what C. S. Lewis calls a generational snobbery or arrogance. We look down our nose at men and women of the past and say, "How in the world could they worship idols like that? Those little carved images were powerless."

Notice Elijah is talking to God's people. To the Israelites. They're not anti-God. And like Ahab, they know better. They turn to the temporary things of this world that let them down over and over and over. The question they and we all face in the drought is this: Is He enough for you? Period. When you've got nothing else, is He enough? John Calvin said, "For what is idolatry if not this: to worship the gift in place of the giver Himself."

Let me ask you, what do you do when God doesn't do what you want Him to do? Like, you're praying for rain, but it's not raining.

Do you turn to money for security?

Do you turn to a pill to take away the pain?

Do you turn to a bottle to help forget what's going on in your life?

Do you turn to that girl at work who's not your wife to validate you because you don't feel validated at home?

Do you turn to one more Netflix show just to avoid reality?

Do you turn to Facebook hoping someone will like you?

Turn the mirror. Ask yourself, *What is wrong with us? Their problem is our problem. Why are we so prone to wander?*

In verse 19, Elijah says, "Now therefore send and gather all Israel to me at Mount Carmel." There's our mountain. "And the 450 prophets of Baal and the 400 prophets of Asherah, who eat at Jezebel's table." Which is telling, because the one thing an idol could not do was feed itself. So to show your allegiance, you would cook dinner for it, and then you get all the leftovers.

This is why in the New Testament, they would argue about food sacrificed to idols. Here's the thing. If you were in Elijah's spot, would you do this? Could you? If you were convinced that God told you to orchestrate a showdown with 850 prophets of false gods, would you? And before you answer, you need to know what Elijah knew, which is this—Jezebel has murdered all the other prophets of Yahweh.

How much faith do you think it took for Elijah to follow God up Mount Carmel? A little or a lot? People ask me all the time, "How come God doesn't do something big in my life? Perform a big miracle in my life? How can we see all these miracles in the pages of Scripture, but none in our lives?" Maybe those are the wrong questions. What if we should be asking something else? Like, what if God's miracle for you is on the other side of a step of faith? Prosperity preachers have beat this one up pretty well so we're all gun-shy when anything smacks of works-for-miracles, and we should be, but when could the lame man walk? Before or after he picked up his mat? In Acts 3 when Peter encounters the lame man begging outside of the temple, Peter says, " 'I have no silver and gold, but what I do have I give to you. In the name of Jesus Christ of Nazareth, rise up and walk!' And he took him by the right hand and raised him up, and immediately his feet and ankles were made strong." The man's feet and ankles were not made strong at Peter's declaration. They were made strong when Peter took him by the right hand and raised him up. Peter acted in faith. Faith is acting like you actually believe God is who He says He is and that He always keeps His promises. I wonder how many miracles are still sitting on the sidewalk begging because of our lack of faith.

I do believe that, sometimes, God requires our obedience before He releases His blessing. And sometimes that outpouring of bless-ing is one step away. What if that one step releases it? Step or not, it's up to you, but I'd like to think that I would move.

What if the miracle of reconciliation in your family is not waiting for Him to sprinkle reconciliation dust on those who need it, but you picking up the phone and saying, "I forgive you," or harder yet, "Will you forgive me?" What if, along with praying for a revival, you open your mouth at work and risk the discomfort, saying, "One thing that has become obvious to me is that God can use a nobody (like me) to tell anybody that'll listen (like you) about the only-body (I know that's a made-up word but we are talking about Jesus) that wants to save everybody on the planet"? That will probably get their attention.

Stop right there. Read that again: I'm just a nobody trying to tell anybody about the Somebody who wants to save everybody.

Does that describe you? Yes, no? If not, why not? I stand on a stage weekly and do this for a living. I'm a professional Christian. But the truth is, I'd do it even if I weren't. And I'm not saying you have to be me, but if you're a believer in Jesus and He's done in you what you say He's done in you, then who knows about it? I realize we have introverts and extroverts and some of us are comfortable talking to others and some aren't, but are you trying? Jesus said, *By your words you will be judged and by your words you will be condemned.* Judging by your words, how would you judge you?

Shortly after Gretchen and I married, I took a job as a youth pastor. We hadn't been there very long when Dr. Bill Ross, my boss, surprised us by saying, "I'm taking a church in Athens, Georgia. We've got twenty-five thousand college kids across the street from our church. I want you to help me reach them."

I turned to Gretchen—and note, we'd only been married three months—and said, "You want to move?" So help me, she said, "I'm with you," and then she actually quoted Ruth: "Your people will be my people. And your God, my God. Where they bury you, they'll bury me. I'm with you." Gretchen is a gift unlike any other. You wouldn't be reading this book without her in my life.

I turned to Bill. "We're in. Let's do it."

We move to Athens, one thing leads to another, and I'm teaching a couple hundred college kids at the Baptist student union and running a Bible study with a hundred kids out of our twelve-hundred-square-foot home. Crazy.

But as I preached Jesus, the folks above me were coming down on me and wouldn't let me preach because I was too Jesus-y. Too right-wing. Too fundamentalist. It wasn't Dr. Ross, but the powers that be at that church. Because again, I believe the Bible. Every word. Things like Elijah was an actual person who really did call down fire from heaven. And Jesus was and is the Son of God. Again, it all came back to the life, death, and resurrection of Jesus, and I wasn't about to compromise on that. Still won't.

Period.

But I had so many negative people speaking to me that I actually began to wonder if I had what it takes to do ministry. Maybe I was out. Along in here, I got two job offers that I seriously considered because, despite the numbers of people I was ministering to, I was getting hammered on all sides. One offer was from a guy who used to be a pastor. A great guy. I love him. Love his family. He ran a coaching network and was really successful. He was also really liberal. But he came to me with a job offer and he basically said, "Just do this thing you're doing. Don't change your style. Just leave all the Jesus stuff out of it. You motivate people and help them be the best they can be and all that kind of stuff." Some of his clients were huge companies that we've all heard of, and part of what he sold me on was the thought that I'd be able to give Gretchen the life she'd always wanted. Or, maybe, the life I always thought she wanted, the life it would make me feel good to be able to give her. To make her feel like she married somebody rather than a nobody from Dillon, South Carolina.

The self-doubt was raging and I was seriously considering this.

While this was going on, another guy, a friend of mine from the gym at the University of Georgia, owned a funeral home and graveyard service. He offered to hire me and pay me six figures, which was tempting, given that I was making $35,000 a year on a pastor's salary. His offer was equally tempting. He said, "It's a little town. About one person dies a week, so you'll only work maybe ten hours a week, and given what you're currently doing, you can do the pastoral care thing too. But you're also a really good salesman, so while you're caring for them, you can upsell them into the plush velvet casket or whatever."

I've never understood why we spend so much on a box in which we just return to dust. Plus, it's buried. Forever. Once it's in the ground, nobody's ever going to see it. But whatever.

Again, the monetary upside was huge compared to my present situation.

Between these two offers and my miserable situation, I legitimately considered bowing out of ministry in 2003.

Then I talked to Gretchen.

Gretchen has always been—and continues to be—this gift of discernment to me and for us. She's also the sane one in our relationship. So while I took a bunch of kids to camp that summer—what I thought was my last hurrah and my exit from ministry—Gretchen posted my resume on a youth pastor job-search thing. This was back in the day of answering machines. When I returned from camp, I had twelve messages.

Staring at that flashing light was the first time I thought, *Maybe I'm just in the wrong environment.* I didn't know it at the time, but I was in the middle of a transition where I went from believing that to trusting in. Believing in.

We visited some really big churches, like huge megachurches where they asked me to be a student teaching pastor, but I never really found my fit. Then we received this one call from Beach United Methodist Church in Jacksonville Beach, Florida. Mind you, I'm not a Methodist. I'd never even been inside a Methodist church. And I didn't agree with a lot of their ecclesiology and their national theology. But they were three blocks from the beach, and Gretchen and I couldn't afford a vacation, so I said, "G, this'll be like a time-share thing. I'll interview, they'll put us up, and we'll just stretch this thing through the weekend. Spend a few days in the sun."

We arrived, and because I already had a job, I felt like I could interview them. And so I said, "You pass a dozen churches to get here, why do you come to this one?" One by one, people started sharing their testimonies, and what I discovered was that this was a Methodist church where God was moving and they were teaching the Bible. People were getting saved. God was being honored in the obedience of the leadership. Addictions were being broken. Traditions were giving way to new methods to reach people at the beaches. The senior pastor spent every morning in the Word and then acted like it all day. These people believed what I believed. Maybe I'd found my people.

But I didn't know what Gretchen was thinking, so as we walked out of the interview, Gretchen hung her arm inside mine and whispered, "We're coming here, aren't we?"

I nodded. "I think so."

We arrived in 2003 and grew the ministry from a couple dozen to a few hundred. They put me to work doing all the things everyone else said I could never do. You remember the story of when I jumped into my father's arms in the pool? When I grew up, Gretchen and I jumped into the Father's arms in the sea we call ministry. I didn't plan this. I just said, "Yes, Lord. Send me." Then I stepped. Or better yet, we did.

For us, this was a step of faith. A big one. We didn't know these people and we really had no idea how this would work out. We could not see then what we know now. We just had to trust Him. Were we uncertain? Sure. Did we have doubts and questions? Absolutely. But I refuse to be ruled by the tyranny of fear. And the opposite of faith is not doubt—it's fear. So let me turn the mirror. What step are you afraid to take? Often, the thing preventing us from stepping, the thing feeding our fear, is an idol we are unwilling to lay down.

I'm praying as you read this that the Spirit of God would do a thing in you that you would not be able to explain. That He would make clear to you and me our idols and that we'd willingly throw them away and pursue the one and only God. This is what I know to be true—what is impossible with man is possible with God, and He can snap His fingers and wham! Problem solved. He's done it before, and I believe He can and will again. But what if He's trying to do a thing in you, which is refine your faith, and He needs you to step to start the refining and bring about the miracle? I don't think you can call yourself a Jesus follower if you don't take a step.

Because that's what He did with Elijah. He called him to climb Mount Carmel. Which made no sense whatsoever because Mount Carmel was the epicenter of pagan worship and just outside Jezebel's house. Calling Elijah to pick a fight with demon worshipers on top of Carmel was like God giving away home field advantage and several touchdowns before kickoff.

But God doesn't mind being the visiting team. He'll play anyone, anytime, anywhere. Because no matter who we are and how lost we are, He pursues His people into the darkest pagan places to capture and redeem their hearts. Scripture says, *He rules in the midst of His enemies*, and He's about to prove it. So Elijah tells Ahab, *Call Baal and bring all your best players.* By the way, Baal was not one god—it was a title. He represented a bunch of gods. And Asherah was the mother god. So essentially, Elijah is saying, *Go get your mama and daddy gods and meet me at Mount Carmel.*

Verses 20–21: "So Ahab sent to all the people of Israel and gathered the prophets together at Mount Carmel. And Elijah came near to all the people and said, 'How long will you go limping between two different opinions?'" Underline those words. This is the key question that I hope and pray you would have the guts to deal with in your life. Let me ask you. Directly. "'How long will YOU go on limping between two different opinions? If the LORD is God, follow him; but if Baal, then follow him.' And the people did not answer him a word."

Elijah's not talking to people that are anti-God or anti-Jehovah. He's talking to church people—who come to church several times a month and know the songs and when to raise their hands at the right time. They know how to send a tweet with fire, fire, hands up, hands up—all that stuff. These are people who sponsor Compassion kids and sign up to go on mission trips. Elijah is talking about good old church people here, because they treated God like you would treat a buffet. I'll take that and I'll leave that.

These people aren't anti-God or anti-Jehovah. They appreciate their salvation and deliverance from Egypt. And they appreciate the promises. But now it's real because they need crops to grow, and what does God know about crops? Other gods do that. So they worship Baal because he makes it rain. And they worship Asherah because she makes babies. Fact is, they are us. We do this all the time. In our modern Christianity, we believe Jesus on Sunday. We raise our hands, hype our emotions, and shout "Amen," but come Tuesday, when the God thing isn't working for you in your dating life, you start swiping all over the place. Looking for comfort and assurance in a bottle or bong or someone's opinion of your two-dimensional false self that you post online instead of trusting Him. This is what we do. Over and over and over. We are just like the people who say, "Okay, God, listen—I hear that hell is hot and forever is a long time, so I'll trust You for this salvation thing, but You don't get to tell me what to do sexually or what to do with my money. Those are off-limits." This is the group of people he's talking to, which means, He is talking to us.

Jesus says, "No one can serve two masters, for either he will hate the one and love the other, or he will be devoted to the one and despise the other" (Matt. 6:24). In our church, people show up in this condition every week. We've got one foot in the God camp and one foot in our own camp. It's like stepping out of a boat. We put one foot on the dock and keep one foot on the boat. That moment is not the time for indecision. Because very soon, those two things are headed in different directions. And by definition, you will either make a decision or you will be torn in two.

This is what Elijah is saying. "How long will you limp between two decisions?"

Elijah says, "If the LORD is God, follow him; but if Baal, then follow him." So if money is your god, then serve it with everything you're made of and quit blaming your idolatry of money on your family. You neglect your family to make more money, and the excuse you give is that you want to provide nice things for your family. They don't buy it, so just admit it: "You guys are all right, but you're slowing me down because I've got to have more money for me." Or if comfort is your idol, then just serve it. Don't even get dressed—just wear pj's, get a big screen, Netflix. Just serve it with everything you're made of. If love and romance are your idols, then just serve them. Abuse whoever you need to get what you want. It's all about you anyway. If approval is your god, then just take a selfie every minute and put all the filters on it, and everybody will like you. Worship that idol. Which is you.

But if Jesus Christ is who He says He is and you believe that He is the Christ, the Son of the living God, who came to do for you and me what we could not do for ourselves, then serve Him and serve Him only. The truth is we are all prone to wander. This is why He calls us sheep. And I'm the worst of all of us. On Sunday, we have our eyes clearly fixed on Him, but come midweek, things are blurry and some other shiny stuff has caught our attention. Which is not uncommon among the people of God. Paul chewed out the Galatians for this very thing: "Foolish Galatians! Who has bewitched you? It was before your eyes that Jesus Christ was publicly portrayed as crucified" (Gal. 3:1). They'd lost their vision of the cross, even though they'd personally seen Him on it and heard Him speak the word, "*Tetelestai.*"

C. S. Lewis says in *Mere Christianity,*

I am trying here to prevent anyone from saying the really foolish things that people often say about Jesus. That I'm ready to accept Jesus as a great moral teacher, but I do not accept his claim to be God. That is the one thing we must not say. A man who was merely a man and said the sort of things that Jesus said would not be a great moral teacher. He would either be a lunatic, on the level with a man who says he's a poached egg, or he would be the devil of hell. You must make your choice. Either this man was and is the Son of God or else a madman or something worse. You can shut him up for a fool, you can spit at him and kill him as a demon, or you can fall at his feet and call him Lord and God. But let us not come with any patronizing nonsense about his being a great human teacher. He has not left that open to us. He did not intend to.[6]

---

6   C. S. Lewis, *Mere Christianity* (London: Macmillan Publishing, 1952), 31.

Elijah is saying to Ahab what the nation of Israel heard generations before in the words of Joshua: *Choose you this day who you
will serve. If it's God, then serve Him. If not, then serve another.
But choose.* Jesus says something very similar in Revelation 3 to
the church at Laodicea—a church where everybody looked great
on the inside of the church. Their problem was that Jesus was on
the outside, knocking on the door, saying, "Hey, you ought to let
Me in church." Then He said, "Here's your problem. I know your
deeds. You're neither hot nor cold. You're lukewarm and it makes
Me sick. I'm going to spit you out of My mouth." This is what is
happening between Elijah and Ahab.

But sometimes God has to confront His people with the futility
of their own foolish choices, which means a showdown is coming.
Verse 22: *And Elijah says to the people, "I, even I only, am left a
prophet of the Lord, Ahab, because your wife killed all my coworkers.
But Baal's prophets are 450 men."* Then he sets up the rules of
engagement. Verses 23–24: He says, "Let two bulls be given to us."
By the way, the symbol of Baal was a bull. So Elijah was poking at
Ahab a little bit here. "And let them choose one bull for themselves
and cut it in pieces and lay it on the wood, but put no fire to it.
And I will prepare the other bull and lay it on the wood and put
no fire to it. And you call upon the name of your god, and I will
call upon the name of the LORD, and the God who answers by fire,
he is God." And the Israelites finally speak up. "And all the people
answered, 'It is well spoken.'" The reason they're saying this is because Baal was the god of lightning. He's the god of thunderstorms.
And so they're thinking, *You dummy. This is like the Brer Rabbit
thing. Don't throw me in that briar patch. You just set up this big
event where our god is in charge of lightning, and what's your puny
God in charge of? Lamb killing and singing?* Again, they're thinking
they've got home field advantage and Elijah is playing perfectly into
their hands.

Verses 25–26:

Then Elijah said to the prophets of Baal, "Choose for yourself one bull and prepare it first, for you are many, and call upon the name of your god, but put no fire to it." And they took the bull that was given them, and they prepared it and called upon the name of Baal from morning until noon, saying, "O Baal, answer us!" But there was no voice, and no one answered. And they limped around the altar that they had made.

Notice the terminology here. They limp around. This is a pagan worship dance, and they are totally into it because they believe Baal has some power to do what they're asking.

Verse 27. I love that this is in the Bible. It makes me feel better about being a human. Check out what Elijah does at noon. Elijah mocks them. He openly makes fun of them and their foolishness. "At noon Elijah mocked them, saying, 'Cry aloud, for he is a god. Either he is musing, or he is relieving himself, or he is on a journey, or perhaps he is asleep and must be awakened.'" In today's culture, the prophets of Baal would be like, "Oh my, you hurt my feelings. I need a safe place." Not all viewpoints and cultures are equal. There are some that are just dumb, but there are some that are dangerous and destructive and they deserve to be mocked.

Elijah is sitting there in his lawn chair while they're building this altar to Baal. When I think of him, he's got a big *Duck Dynasty* beard and he's mocking them. Here's what he's saying: *Maybe he's in the toilet doing paperwork and he doesn't have time for you right now.* Now notice what happens.

There's no answer.

Even though they're crying out to their god with all the intensity they can muster, he's not answering. And do you know why he's not answering? Because he's not there—there is no Baal. Baal is a made-up thing. He's nothing. And if you are worshiping nothing, then in return, you will only get nothing.

You should highlight that.

The opinion shapers in our culture spend billions of dollars a day to convince us to put our hope in the little-*g* idols the world has to offer. To put our trust in them, our faith in them. The argument is that this thing—whatever it is—will do for you what you've always hoped and dreamed. But it can't and never will satisfy. It will let us down over and over and over. And the reason it lets us down is it cannot do what it promises. Idols always break their promises.

You should highlight that too.

The Bible says, *There is one name under heaven whereby we must be saved* (Acts 4:12). 1 Kings 8:60 says, *That all the people of the earth may know that the Lord is God, that there is none else.* Jesus says in John 17:3, *This is eternal life that they know the only true God and Jesus Christ, whom you have sent.* And the Shema says, *Hear O Israel, The Lord our God, the Lord is One...* This is a prayer these people would have known and memorized and prayed thousands of times over, and it reminds us that the Lord our God, the Lord is one (Deut. 6:4). And yet every single one of us has a tendency to look to our idols with affection and cry out to them to do something for us. And yet they remain silent because they are powerless to provide for us.

Every single one of us looks to our stuff for ultimate satisfaction. It can't and never will satisfy, but despite this, we go back to it over and over again. This is what I lovingly describe as taking one more lap around the cul-de-sac of stupidity. I think I first heard my friend Matt Chandler use this phrase. It's called the cul-de-sac of stupidity not because stuff is stupid. But because we're stupid. Me too. We go back to the same stuff when it did nothing the first time. A new house, new car, granite countertops—this is the shiny stuff at which we stare and to which we give our attention rather than focusing on Jesus. And most of this stuff ends up either on the street or at the thrift store. Some of us look to find security in a bank account. Literally, we log on daily, and if the number is greater than a certain figure, we feel secure. If not, we're anxious. Insecure.

Here's the thing—there's nothing wrong with money. The Bible says you should steward it well. You should be really generous and you should plan in such a way that you accrue enough to bless your children's children. But the problem arises when you look for a number on a screen to do something in your soul. That number can't provide what you need. Don't believe me? One call from the doctor and all the security's gone.

Or maybe you look for your self-worth in the opinions of other people, but no matter how many likes or comments and compliments you get, nothing fills your need for affirmation. Why? Because you were created in the image of God, with a God-shaped box in the center of your chest. Only He can fill it.

If you are a girl, let me be real specific. This is why you've had three boyfriends in the last six months, you willingly gave yourself to all of them, and now you feel more alone than you did before. Why? Because no matter what they tell you—and they'll tell you whatever you want to hear, provided you give them what they want—they can't give you what you're looking for. Until you enter into a covenant with one man before God, no physical intimacy will ever fill your emptiness.

On the flip side, guys—you thought you could play the field, take what you want, strip emotion out of it, treat her like a commodity, and that'd make you more of a man. But if you're honest, you now feel like more of a little boy. Having stolen what wasn't yours. Until you're willing to lay down your life for somebody and quit taking and start sacrificing, you're not ready to be with one of God's daughters. We read this story of Elijah and the prophets of Baal, running around and screaming, and yet we do the same thing.

Now, here's the crazy part. Baal doesn't say anything. Doesn't respond. Doesn't show up. So the prophets put their heads together and think, *Let's just turn up the volume. That'll work. Let's do more of the same dumb stuff.* If you know me, you know I'm talking about us more than them. We are them. They are us. "And they cried aloud and cut themselves after their custom with swords and lances, until the blood gushed out upon them. And as midday passed, they raved on"—literally in Hebrew, *raved* means "strenuous dancing"—*"until the time of the offering of the oblation"*—which is just the regular offering time—"but there was no voice. No one answered. No one paid attention" (1 Kings 18:28–29). In the meantime, Elijah is laughing at them. "What are you all doing? Your god's on the throne—not in heaven, but in the men's room. And that's why he's not answering."

Today, we live in a politically correct world that would call this bigotry. *Who are you to tell me what I should and shouldn't do?* This is just the enemy's attempt to silence the truth. He can't compete with it, like he couldn't compete on Mount Carmel, so he's hoping to mute it by making you afraid to speak up. Our framers knew what they were doing when they made a priority of protecting our freedom of speech and religious freedom. A Christian looks through a worldview framed by the words of Jesus. Anything outside that is contrary to His will. Said another way, it's wrong. Or, as Paul says, *Anything not of faith is sin.* Our world accuses us of bigotry when we look at somebody else with a different worldview and say, "That path you're on, those decisions you're making—faith in anyone other than Jesus Christ will lead you straight to hell." Most of the time, these words come from a place of love. And we do have an enemy that twists our words in the ears of the hearer. This is not to say our thoughts couldn't sometimes be communicated better. They should be, and those hearing them deserve better. And I know people have abused this. A lot. And said a lot of dumb things to the lost and broken. But how will they hear if we don't risk discomfort and tell them?

Today we live in a world that says, "If you believe in something intently and intensely, that's all that matters." It's not true. No matter how hard you believe in something, that does not make it true. There is no "your" truth. The quickest way to neuter the word *truth* of its meaning is to add *my* in front of it. There's just truth. And the reality is that every religion outside of the gospel calls people to do what these people are doing on Mount Carmel. They say, *Dance harder. Dance harder. Dance harder. Perform. Perform. Perform. And if you perform well enough, then maybe you'll be acceptable to this little*-g *god.* Every other religion will call you to mutilate or cut yourself (figuratively), which is called works-based righteousness. False gods always require more dancing and more performance to stand in their presence. To be called one of their own. And it's never enough. And I'm not just talking about major religions and cults—I'm talking about every secular god too. There will never be enough money. There will never be enough promotions. There will never be enough attention. All of those things say, "Just keep dancing." And it causes you to cut out time with your family or mutilate your marriage vows or break the promises you've made.

God is the opposite of this.

The gospel tells us that God sends Jesus, His only begotten Son, to put away the performance trap because God incarnate, Jesus Christ, performed perfectly on our behalf. Once and for all. He fulfilled the law, which we could not. He was tempted in every way that you and I are, and yet He went to the cross in our place, pushed up on His nail-pierced feet, and said, "It is finished. I have done for you what you can never do for yourself." When Isaiah prophesied that Jesus would become unrecognizable as a man, that means Jesus was mutilated for us. There is no measuring stick that gauges our performance in the gospel of Jesus because Jesus snapped it in two when He stepped out of the tomb.

And if the tomb is empty...

In Luke 9, Jesus and the disciples go into an area and they share the gospel and they're rejected. The disciples reference 1 Kings 18, saying, *Jesus, how about calling down fire of judgment from heaven on all these people who have rejected You?* When the disciples say this, they are talking about this very account on Mount Carmel right here. This Super Bowl between Elijah and the 850 prophets of Baal.

Amazingly, Jesus rebukes the disciples, telling them they've totally missed the point. Again. The disciples had no problem recognizing the power of God, they just could not recognize the humility. They got the lion, they just couldn't get the lamb. But that's the point—you don't get the lion without the lamb.

Jesus knows that the fire of God's judgment is going to come down on Him on the cross so that we can be accepted before the Father. This is the fundamental difference between the gospel and every false religion. Jesus has done the work because He knew we couldn't.

One of my friends and co-laborers in the gospel, Pastor Adam Flynt, says, "You know idols are false hope when things fall apart, because when they do, you never cry out to money, house, job. Name your idol. You cry out to God."

Tim Keller says it this way: "Jesus is the only savior in the world who if you gain him will satisfy you, and if you fail him will forgive you."[7]

So the 850 are crying out and cutting themselves. And the Bible says, *No one answered. No one paid attention.* Why? Because a false

---

7   Timothy Keller (@timkellernyc), Twitter, May 22, 2017, https://twitter.com /timkellernyc/status/866655892158152705?lang=enn.

god will never answer you. It can't. It'll just let you down. Time after time.

Verse 30. This is where everything changes. If there's a soundtrack to this movie, it gets better here. And then Elijah said to everyone, *Come near to me.* That's Hebrew for "Bro, hold my beer. Watch this." Now, if that offends, just hold on. I'm trying to put this into context. Elijah was a real man. This really happened. And he really did wave everybody closer so they could see exactly what he was doing. He didn't want them to miss it.

"And all the people came near to him. And he repaired the altar of the LORD that had been thrown down. Elijah took twelve stones, according to the number of the tribes of the sons of Jacob, to whom the word of the LORD came, saying, 'Israel shall be your name,' and with the stones he built an altar in the name of the LORD. And he made a trench about the altar, as great as would contain two seahs of seed" [that just means a bunch]. *"And he put the wood in order and cut the bull in pieces and laid it on the wood. And he said, 'Fill four jars with water and pour it on the burnt offering and on the wood.' And he said, 'Do it a second time.' And they did it a second time. And he said, 'Do it a third time.' And they did it a third time."* (vv. 30–34)

If these water pots were the same size as those used at the wedding at Cana in Galilee, then each one held between twenty and thirty gallons of water. This means Elijah doused the altar with 240 to 360 gallons of water. Meaning, it was totally saturated. And remember, this was during a three-year drought.

Those watching were shaking their heads. "Elijah, what are you doing? You've created an impossible situation here." But impossible situations perfectly position you to see God move in a way that only He can move.

Some of you are reading this right now and you're like, "Hey, man, I appreciate your Old Testament stories about the bearded guy and the fire-from-heaven stuff. But I am in an impossible marriage right now. There's no way either of us is submitting to the other out of reverence for Christ." Some of you have been praying for a prodigal son or daughter for so long. It seems impossible. You've prayed and you've prayed and you've prayed and you've sent messages and begged them to come home and yet they're still feeding pigs. Some of you look at your financial situation, which maybe wasn't even your fault. Maybe something happened to you that was outside of your control. And you're like, "If God doesn't come through in a major way, a miraculous way, right now, then I am in trouble." Some of you are in a dire health situation and you're like, "God, if you don't show up, I'm gone."

I'm trying to encourage you that when you're at the end of your rope, when you're at rock bottom, you are perfectly positioned for God to do His best work. He is a God of miracles. Oftentimes God allows us to fall flat on our back so that we will finally look up to HIM. Will He do what you want? I have no idea. I hope He does, but my ways aren't His. What I do know is this—He can. Your enemy wants to use your circumstances to convince you He can't or that, even worse, He won't.

Think about it this way—the disciples are huddled together, clutching one another, staring at a sealed tomb. Jesus lies inside. Doornail dead. And yet, when He showed up and healed the sick and raised the dead, they knew that He was the Son of God. The promised Messiah. What's more, they knew the kingdom of God was at hand. Just like He said. And yet they're standing there, staring at cold granite, and they're thinking the kingdom of God is lying in there in a dark tomb. Powerless. *What are we going to do now?*

And if they were to look at God and say, *God, what are You doing?* He would say, *I'm redeeming the world. Just hang in there for about three days. And it's going to get way, way better.*

So, to every one of you who finds yourself in an impossible situation, hang in there. The bottom of the ninth with a hanging curveball is the perfect spot for God to just jack the thing out of the state.

Every impossible situation we face is temporary, save one. Our sin. It's the only thing we can't do anything about. We are powerless to fix our sin problem. And yet, even in that situation, God does for us what we can never do for ourselves. He sent His Son, Jesus Christ, to live the perfect life, to die a sinner's death, and to take the judgment of God upon Him. Why? So that we could become the righteousness of God and be reconciled to the one true God. Or said simply, because He wants to bring us to Himself.

You think your circumstances are impossible? Not so.

If the tomb is empty, anything is possible.

If God can breathe life into His dead Son, then I promise you He can breathe life into your marriage. If God can speak into existence everything that is, He can take care of His kids. If He made you, He can heal you. Whether through pills, people, or prayer, He can. And if your sin is your impossible situation, just cry out. Cry out to Him as Lord. Whatever it is, He defeated it on the cross and He can walk you out of it.

Verse 36: "And at the time of the offering of the oblation, Elijah the prophet came near and said, 'O LORD, God of Abraham, Isaac, and Israel, let it be known this day that you are God in Israel, and that I am your servant, and that I have done all these things at your word.'" People ask me sometimes, "Should I do something crazy like this? Like meet in the break room and say, 'All right, everybody bring your reports and we'll put them in the middle and we'll call down fire.'" If God tells you to do that, then yes, you absolutely should. And if you think He did but you don't know with 100 percent certainty that it lines up perfectly with His Word, then come see an elder, because you might just be crazy, which is fine. God uses crazy people all the time.

Verse 37: "Answer me, O LORD, answer me, that these people may know that you, O LORD, are God." I like this part. I dare you to add this phrase to all of your prayer requests this week and watch how your prayer life changes. If you're praying for healing, which you should, then pray for healing, *that all may know that the Lord is God*. If you are praying for a financial breakthrough, add *that all may know You*. If you are praying for your safety, add *that all may know You*. So Elijah says, " 'Answer me, O LORD, answer me, that these people may know that you, O LORD, are God, and that you have turned their hearts back.' Then the fire of the LORD fell and consumed the burnt offering and the wood and the stones and the dust." That's right, the dust. I didn't even know it could do that. *And licked up the water that was in the trench.* Now God's just showing off. He doesn't just send enough fire to cover the situation, He sends enough to lick up the water. In our Bible, the book of Ephesians says that our God does exceedingly more than we ever hoped or imagined in the church. Exceedingly more.

Is that the God you worship? If your prayers are not intimidating to you, they very well could be insulting to God. Elijah is asking for something impossible, and when God answers the prayer, He doesn't just kind of sort of answer it over time. It's not like one little fire drip from the head of a bowl that almost roasted a pig over thirty-six hours. It consumed it all because He was just showing off and showing out. It's like when Jesus came out of the grave. You realize Jesus wasn't just sort of dead, right? Not just a little dead. Not like someone who happened to pass away in his sleep one night and then three days later, "Oh, I'm back." That's not how it happened. He was beaten, flogged, and mutilated. They stabbed a spear into His heart. They put Him in a cave and put the multiton stone in front of it. And then there was a garrison of Roman soldiers guarding the tomb. They're tough. They took over the world. And under their guard, God breathes life into His Son. Resurrects Him from the grave. And when He does, He puts death to death and then rolls the stone away. Finally, Jesus walks out with such glory that the soldiers—who, again, are men of war—panic. They lie motionless, frozen in fear as the Bright Morning Star walks out of the grave.

This is the God we serve.

Verse 39: And when all the people saw it, they fell on their faces and said, "The LORD, he is God; the LORD, he is God." You know how to say that in Hebrew? *"Eli-Jah. Eli-Jah."* That's crazy. Right?

Here's the point. A mustard seed–sized faith and an infinitely powerful promise-keeping God is infinitely more powerful than putting your faith in a temporary, promise-breaking idol. That's why Jesus says, "If you've got faith the size of a mustard seed, you could say to this mountain, 'Move,' and it's got no choice." The point is this—it's not the amount of faith you have; it's the object of your faith that matters.

In 1912, Franz Reichelt, a thirty-three-year-old Parisian dressmaker, built a flight suit for aviators that would convert to a parachute in the event they ejected during flight. Encouraged by successful test runs he conducted with dummies from his fifth-floor apartment building, he offered to test his parachute suit in person. On February 4, before family, friends, and a curious public, he climbed to a restaurant on the first platform of the Eiffel Tower. He then climbed onto a table and then a small stool, which allowed him to step onto the railing—fifty-seven meters above the earth. Teetering on the edge, he took some forty seconds to adjust his suit and gather his thoughts. Then he smiled for the cameras, said, "À bientôt" ("See you soon"), and jumped. At which point he plummeted to the earth at fifty-five feet per second before his flailing body intersected with the frozen ground, creating a twenty-centimeter crater, as later measured by local authorities. Say what you want, but Franz "believed in"—*pisteuō*'d—that suit.

Today in China they are building bridges out of glass. It's all over YouTube. Mindless entertainment. You can see right through the bridge. Straight down. Eleven hundred feet over this canyon. Just walking across this bridge has become a thing. A spectator sport, even. Because people get onto the bridge, make it halfway across, look down, and freak out. Drop to the floor. Screaming. Their family members have to physically drag them off the bridge because they are paralyzed by fear. Here's the thing. These people had just enough confidence to step from the land onto the glass bridge. That's all they had. One step. That's all they could muster up. But here's the cool part. The bridge doesn't care if that's all they have, because that's all the bridge needs. It holds them regardless. Whether the person had lots of courage or no courage doesn't matter to the bridge, because it's still standing and all it needs is for those scared and terrified people to take one step. Here's the point—their courage didn't hold them up. The bridge did. But the bridge couldn't make them step. All the bridge could do was be available and offer the invitation. "Want to get to the other side? Walk with me." Infinite faith in a faulty flying suit equals death. The tiniest amount of faith in a sturdy bridge equals life.

My encouragement to you is this—call on fire. Have big faith.

Now, watch what happens. Elijah calls down fire from heaven that consumes the offering, the wood, the dust, and the rocks. And licks up the water in the trench. Which is incredible. But he's not finished. Not by a long shot. Elijah then seizes the 850 prophets of Baal and loads them onto the long black train at the Brook Kishon—and slaughters every last one. We would all call this huge. But he doesn't stop there. He then prays for rain seven times—

and remember, it hasn't rained for three and a half years. But as he prays, a cloud appears. Elijah says to Ahab, "Hey, boss, you might want to hop on your chariot and head to the house, because you're about to get rained out." Sure enough, the sky turns black.

The Bible then says Elijah hikes up his robe and outruns the chariot. Think about that. He calls down fire, calls down rain, and outruns a horse-drawn chariot. This is the stuff that legends are made of, which is why when Jesus appears, some say He is Elijah.

But remember Elijah's first question? "How long are you going to limp between two opinions?" People who really put their faith in God don't limp around. They outrun chariots. They run and don't grow weary. They rise up on eagles' wings.

Back at the palace, things are not good. Ahab tells Jezebel that Elijah has killed all her prophets, all those who do her dirty work. Jezebel responds by sending a message to Elijah: "So may the gods do to me and more also, if I do not make your life as the life of one of them by this time tomorrow" (1 Kings 19:2). Meaning? Jezebel has just put out a hit on Elijah.

You would think after what we just read, Elijah's literal mountain-top experience, Elijah would stand up like a boss. He'd turn to Jezebel and say, "Come on and get some of this. I'll call down fire on you, you loudmouthed woman." You would think with all the weapons at his disposal, he'd find one for her.

You know what the hero does?

He asks God to take his life and when He doesn't, he runs. Verse 3 says he runs for his life and hides in a cave. Why? Because he's afraid of what she said. Her threats. Even though he just defeated everyone who works for her.

Think about the heroes in the Bible. Elijah's a coward. Moses was a murderer. Abraham pimped out his wife, twice. David was a murderer because of his adultery. Paul was a religious terrorist. Peter denied his faith three times after being warned he would.

I'm not knocking these guys. I thank God for them, but they're men. Fallen men just like us. The only hero in the Bible is Jesus.

But watch what happens in 1 Kings 19. You get another picture of the gospel. God doesn't give up on Elijah because of his lack of faith. He chases him down, meets him in the cave, and He says, *Elijah, what are you doing here?* Elijah says, *I'm afraid, I'm scared.* God says, "Go out and stand on the mount before the Lord."

So, Elijah walks to the edge of the cave where he's met by a tornado that tears rocks off the mountain, but God is not in the tornado. Then an earthquake shakes the mountain, but the Lord is not in the earthquake. "And after the earthquake, a fire, but the Lord is not in the fire." Watch what the Lord is doing. He's reminding Elijah who He is. His power on display. But watch how He interacts with Elijah.

Verse 12 says, "And after the fire the sound of a low whisper." What is needed to make a whisper? Breath. This is the *ruach* of God, the breath of God, whispering to Elijah. In one of the lowest points in his life, coming off one of the highest victories of his day, God speaks to him not in the fire, not in the earthquake, not in the wind, but in what the Bible calls a still, small voice.

I know there are a lot of you who say you love Jesus and you want to love Jesus, but you get Jesus amnesia. Don't be ashamed, you're in good company. You'll make a great disciple.

I see this every week in my church. On Sunday, we sing, praise, worship. Everybody leaves ready to call fire down on the false prophets at work. But by Tuesday you're cuddled up on a bean-bag chair wondering if there is a God. The good news is that He pursues you. Let that sink in—He pursues you. John Calvin said our hearts are idol-making factories and every single one of us has a tendency to take our eyes off the one true God and fix it on something that is telling us lies.

I dare you to step off the safe road that you're on. Step onto the bridge that frightens you. Maybe the still, small voice of God will speak to you in your darkest places. The places where you need chains to be broken. Where you need the Spirit of God to trouble you so you can do away with the idols in your world. I'm not just talking about surface idols like sex, drugs, and rock and roll. I'm talking about those deep idols like comfort and security. The stuff we lean on more than Him. Maybe God would do a miracle—not fire from heaven, but better. Maybe the grace of God would wash over you and wash those idols away. If you are unsure what that looks like, then ask yourself this: What is the step you are afraid to take?

One of my mentors, Pastor Doug Fields, used to ask me this question: What would you do for the glory of God if you knew that it wouldn't fail? And the moment you know the answer, the next question is this: Then why are you not doing that thing?

In 2008, five years after Gretchen and I moved to Jacksonville, Beach United Methodist Church was doing really well with the high school age and down and the forty-five-and-up group, so the leadership at the church decided to start a service to target the ages in between. The 18–45ers. They asked me to lead the service.

The time of that service was 11:22. If you've ever wondered why the church we eventually planted, the church that grew out of that service, is called Church of Eleven22, that's where we got our name. I wish I could say it was more thought-out than that, but I promise it's really not. I'm just not that creative and I wanted people to know when to arrive, so that's what I named the service that eventually grew into our church. Proving that God has a great sense of humor.

We never thought that service would become its own thing. We just thought we were starting another service to love on God's children. I never thought we'd grow beyond about 350 people per service, but that's fine. What if we made 350 disciples in Jacksonville? That'd change the world, I thought. We set off, and it didn't have to work, because we already had church jobs. We had been given a blank slate. We had the freedom to do church the way we thought we would do it if we were in charge. I'm not saying that's the right way to do it, because there's a lot of different flavors of church, but that was our thinking.

For a couple of months, everything was peachy. We were running three to four hundred people per service in a worship center that seated eight hundred. No problems.

Then comes Easter. And Ben William, our worship pastor, said, "I think we should fast for Lent." I'm Baptist. We don't fast and we don't anoint. We anoint biscuits with gravy and we fast from R-rated movies, but that's it. (Today in our services, we fast and anoint a lot, proving that people and things can change. Jesus did it, so we do it. I'm a big believer in both.) So, at the beginning of Lent, I stand onstage and tell everybody, "I'm fasting from meat."

That may not sound like a big deal to you, but I don't think I'd ever had a meal without meat in my whole life at that point. So I get all stirred up by my own sermon and fast from meat and I think I even threw in a single-day total fast. Water only. Well, maybe water and coffee. It's basically just dark water. If anyone ever tells you to not drink coffee, gather your things and leave. Never return. That's a cult! Next thing I know, our whole church was fasting.

On Easter Sunday, fifteen hundred people showed up. I looked at Ben. "What are all these people doing here?"

He stared at the crowd. "I have no idea."

"Me neither, but don't screw this up."

My point is this: we faced decisions and steps that we weren't too certain about. We had no idea how this thing would pan out. In truth, we had no idea what we were doing. We were just telling people about Jesus. I was just teaching the Bible verse by verse in a way that longtime believers and brand-new potential followers could understand. We knew a lot could go wrong, but the fear of what might go wrong didn't deter us from following where Jesus was leading. From what God could do.

We had no idea God would do what He did or what He has done since. None of us saw around the corner. We were, and still are, just a bunch of sold-out sinners who love the One who died to save us. It really is that simple. The church continued to grow, and soon we needed more space.

Five years later, I stood in the parking lot staring at the Walmart we now call our church building. We needed serious renovation. It looked like the end of the *Terminator 2* movie. I didn't know if anybody would show up. So I just begged God. "Lord, please let enough people come so we can have a second service." You think I'm kidding.

Now we're in our seventh campus. Two of which are legit campuses in prisons. And so many inmates are showing up we've had to go to multiple services. By the time this book is published, we will have launched three more campuses, one in another state. I'm not telling you that to tell you how great I am. Please. I'm telling you that because He is doing exceedingly abundantly more than we can imagine.

Our God is the God of the impossible. Jesus says, "If I'm lifted up, I'll draw all men to Myself." So, we lifted Him up and kept our eyes focused on Jesus.

Unlike our friend Ahab.

Circle back with me to the start of this chapter. Ahab started out as a follower of Jehovah. Gave his kids godly names. At a minimum, as king of Israel, he knows better. But something happened along the way. And that something was an evil someone and her name was Jezebel. A wicked woman. Was she an idol? Did something about Jezebel speak to some deep place in Ahab?

I don't know, but there's no sign of him ever coming back or making the turn.

Let me fill you in on a few details about Jezebel. Jezebel was the daughter of a Sidonian king. Her name was somewhat of a joke. In Phoenician, *i-zebul* means "Where is the prince?" or "Where is Baal?" but in Hebrew, *zebel* means "dung." She married Ahab, who was king of Israel from 874 to 853 BC, and from the beginning she brought Baal worship with her. So zealous was she that she began systematically killing the prophets of the Lord and ordered the murder of Naboth for refusing to sell his vineyard to Ahab. For the crime of not giving the king what he wanted, Jezebel had him stoned to death on false charges. At this point, she had become the de facto ruler of Israel while Ahab stuck out his bottom lip and pulled the covers over his head. For some reason, Ahab abdicated his authority and allowed Jezebel to take it from him. Which is exactly the way an idol works. It doesn't take you over at the outset; it wins you over and then takes you over.

She was a princess by birth and probably served as the high priestess of the local god. She elevated Baal worship to a state-supported religion and encouraged the worship of Canaanite fertility gods and goddesses. She further supported 450 prophets of Baal and 400 prophets of the goddess Asherah at her royal table. Meaning, she funded their every need herself. In practical terms, Jezebel employed court prostitutes and practiced sorcery and divination.

After marrying Jezebel, Ahab caved to her persuasion and promoted the worship of Baal in Israel. This was not good. Remember *Thou shalt have no other gods before me*? Ahab ignored this. Why? Jezebel. Ahab either couldn't or wouldn't see it, but he had been won over by Jezebel, who eventually took him over. Including his power. Ahab abdicated his position, power, and authority for Jezebel. Two chapters later, Jezebel killed the prophets of Yahweh.

Despite her ranting, Jezebel eventually suffered mutiny at the hands of her own eunuchs, who throw her out a second-story window. Lying dead on the road below, she was eaten by dogs and trampled by horses. Her remains were spread as dung over the field of Jezreel.

So what's your Jezebel? What have you allowed to win you over that has actually taken over? What is the idol that you're pressing into and crying out to? Don't know? Not sure? Trust me—God knows. Will you ask Him? Let me pose the question this way— What would you need to do in your life to be able to hear the whisper of God? Will you ask Him what in your life needs to be placed on the altar? Sacrificed? A sacrifice is simply laying down something less important for the sake of something or someone more important.

And remember, there's no bartering with an idol. God didn't just warm up the prophets of Baal. He burnt them until they were gone. What if you were to take a hammer out and smash your idol? Right now. What if you were to throw your smartphone in the ocean? Quit your job? Write the biggest check you've ever written and give it away? Some of you are wrapped up in a guy or girl you don't need to be wrapped up in and you need to walk away and you know it. But like Ahab, you like your Jezebel for what she does for you.

How many times did Ahab not listen to the still, small voice of the Lord? We don't know but I would imagine a lot.

We are no different. We need the still, small voice of the Lord, and make no mistake about it—we would do well to find the cave. There's something about the cave. You can be driven to the cave or you can go willingly. Jesus was never forced to the cave because He often put Himself in a place where He could hear the still, small voice of God. You and I would do well to learn from that, realizing that we will bow or we will bow. We will be humbled or we will be humbled. There is no option B. God will not allow you to carry your idol into His kingdom. Period. So you can crush it now at a time of your choosing, or you can wait and it will be crushed, as the Puritans said, at a time of His choosing. (John Owens said, "Be killing sin or sin will be killing you.") Either way, your idol is getting crushed. We would do well to get into the cave to hear the still, small voice of God.

What does that look like for you?

To follow someone, by definition, requires a step. Followed by another step. And another. If you are a follower of Jesus, there are steps (plural) in your future. Solomon said we plan our course, but the Lord determines our steps. What step is He asking you to take? And what fear, or what idol, is preventing you from taking it? To quote Elijah, "How long will you vacillate between the two?" One last time—in this moment, would you have the courage to admit your idols, to radically identify each one and lay them down on the altar?

My encouragement is to crush the idol and take that first step.

Pray with Me

Our good and gracious heavenly Father, please remind us in a world that constantly tries to distract us with shiny idols that You are all that we need and that You are the only one that can satisfy. God, I boldly pray that You would break us or bless us. Whatever it takes to draw us close to You. Lord, I pray that each and every person reading these pages would stop limping between what this world offers and the abundant life that You offer. I pray that they would see You as beautiful and be overwhelmed by Your goodness and grace. God, I pray for the men and women and students that You have called to take a step of faith. I pray that You would give us courage to take the next step.

May we be willing to fail but never be willing to avoid taking the chance. God, I pray that You would give us the boldness to open our mouths, to make the phone call, to start the ministry, to offer forgiveness, to write the check, to pursue reconciliation. God, I pray that You would identify the deep idols in our lives that vie for our attention. I pray that You would give us the courage and strength to stop cuddling with our idols and by the authority of Your Word and the strength of Your Spirit we would smash those idols. I thank You that You don't send down fire on us when we disobey, because Jesus took Your judgment at the cross. God, I pray that You would give us the courage to answer this question: If I could do anything for the glory of God and I knew it wouldn't fail, what would I do? And I pray You would give us the faith to do it. And I pray that You would speak to us in Your still, small voice. I pray this in Jesus' name. Amen.

CHAPTER 4

Mount of Beatitudes—Are You Chasing Blessing or the One Who Blesses?

"Seeing the crowds, he went up on the mountain." (Matthew 5:1)

Jesus has moved His ministry north, where the small fishing towns dotting the shoreline of the Sea of Galilee have become the epicenter of His ministry. In case you've never been to Galilee, after one look it's obvious why people would want to live there. It's a beautiful landscape of rolling hills, calm waters (usually), and lush vegetation. If you've gotta live somewhere, you might as well live somewhere awesome. That's why I live at the beach. Anyway, given the signs and wonders Jesus has been doing and the fact that He's healing everyone brought to Him, huge crowds have started to follow Him everywhere. Everyone wants to see what He'll do next. So, seeing the size of the crowd following Him, he goes up the mountain.

"…And when he sat down, his disciples came to him."

Matthew is one of four gospel writers, and he's writing his book to a Jewish audience. From the beginning, he wants to make it clear that Jesus is the promised Messiah. And when he talks about Jesus going up the mountain, Matthew is signaling something here Jewish readers can't possibly miss. He is drawing a clear parallel to Moses. Just as people followed Moses to the mountain where he received the law from God to give the people, Jesus has received the Word from the Father and is giving it to His people. Here on this mountain. This is why a little later in this Sermon on the Mount, Jesus is going to say, *You have heard that it was said...But I say...* That's the kind of authority Matthew wants his readers to know that Jesus is walking in.

To the Jewish audience reading Matthew, this is significant. A shot across the bow.

And then Jesus goes on to preach what we call the Sermon on the Mount, in which He gives some very tough teachings. Jesus doesn't just say, "Don't commit adultery," like the Ten Commandments said, but "Don't lust in your heart." He doesn't just say, "Don't murder," like Moses did, but "Don't be angry at your brother in your heart." If you're scratching your head thinking, *That's impossible*, you're absolutely right.

In my life in ministry, more often than not, when I hear any teaching on the Sermon on the Mount, everyone looks at it and says, "Nobody can pull this thing off." It's impossible.

But what if we have been reading the Sermon on the Mount wrong? What if the teachings of Jesus in this sermon are not so much a kingdom ethic that we strive toward in order to be a "good Christian" (by the way, there is no such thing)? But what if, instead, Jesus' kingdom teaching on everything from money to murder is evidence of what a gospel-infected life looks like, which is impossible to pull off by our own striving?

Which is why, I think, Jesus starts this sermon with the Beatitudes. (A beatitude is a blessing from God.)

"And he opened his mouth and taught them, saying:

'Blessed are the poor in spirit, for theirs is the kingdom of heaven.

'Blessed are those who mourn, for they shall be comforted.

'Blessed are the meek, for they shall inherit the earth.

'Blessed are those who hunger and thirst for righteousness, for they shall be satisfied.

'Blessed are the merciful, for they shall receive mercy.

'Blessed are the pure in heart, for they shall see God.

'Blessed are the peacemakers, for they shall be called sons of God.

'Blessed are those who are persecuted for righteousness' sake, for theirs is the kingdom of heaven.

'Blessed are you when others revile you and persecute you and utter all kinds of evil against you falsely on my account. Rejoice and be glad, for your reward is great in heaven, for so they persecuted the prophets who were before you.'" (Matthew 5:2–12)

Even if you're new to Bible study, you've probably heard these before, but in my experience, the Beatitudes are misunderstood for a number of reasons. First, the Greek word for *blessing* is *makarios*. Often it is translated or understood to mean "happy," but it doesn't mean happy because happiness has to do with circumstances, whereas *makarios* means "one who is fully satisfied." And not just fully satisfied because of favorable circumstances, but because God indwells us through Christ.

Why doesn't He mean happiness? Because God is less concerned with your happiness and far more concerned with your holiness. Happiness is found in your happenings. Joy is found in Jesus. Big difference. And I've got bad news for us as Americans. Our motto from the beginning has been life, liberty, and the pursuit of happiness, but it's not going too well. When the countries of the world were surveyed with regard to their citizens' happiness, we came in nineteenth. It's our motto, it's our thing, and yet in the whole world, there are eighteen countries happier than us. (For the record, the first few were Finland, Denmark, Norway, Iceland, and the Netherlands. So apparently wherever you'd think Anna and Elsa would live are the happy places.) So when Jesus says "makarios"—or blessed—He's talking about how we become fully satisfied in Him.

Most of the time when we talk about the Beatitudes, we think of them as if they're somehow eight separate blessings. Not connected. I think this adds to our confusion because I don't see them this way. If you ever get a chance to go to Galilee, you will most likely go to the place where they say Jesus preached the Sermon on the Mount. I would highly suggest it. It is beautiful. And on the pathway that leads to that place on the mountain, you will see eight separate headstone-looking markers. Each with one of the Beatitudes written on it. This is how most people view the Beatitudes. As if Jesus is giving a multiple-choice "blessing" for any who may be poor in spirit or pure in heart. I think we've been reading it wrong.

I think Jesus is laying out the process of salvation in these verses. Of sanctification. In a sense, He is saying, "This is what is happening to you as you become more sanctified in Me." Jesus is laying out how the gospel works in us from the moment the Spirit of God begins to reveal our own sinfulness all the way to that moment when we are face-to-face with Him. These verses are not eight disconnected impossibilities. They are building blocks—we stand on one to step to the next.

The reason Jesus starts with the Beatitudes before He rolls out the ethic of what it looks like to follow Him is to tell us that the verdict comes before the performance, to borrow a phrase from Tim Keller. Let that sink in.

In this one phrase, *"Blessed are...,"* the Judge issues the verdict before the performance. Meaning, before we've done anything to earn anything, the Judge declares us blessed. Which means we can't take credit for having done anything to earn that blessing. We can't "work" our way to blessing. We're blessed simply because He blessed us. Period.

Where else does this happen in your life? Nowhere. Almost everywhere else in our lives, performance precedes verdict. The promotion to CEO occurs after the thirty years of hard work. Not before. But the gospel doesn't read that way at all. God chooses you, graces you, and loves you, and that changes everything about you. And notice His blessing you has nothing to do with you or what you've done or earned. So read with me through the Beatitudes and then we'll unpack them one by one. And hopefully, you'll be able to see how they're really linked together.

I need you to put on your theological big-boy pants and stay with me. We'll move fast.

Step One: Poor in Spirit

"Blessed are the poor in spirit, for theirs is the kingdom of heaven."

Now, what does it mean to be poor in spirit? I don't think Jesus is talking about being financially poor here. He's talking about the place where we realize at the soul level, *Houston, there's a problem, and the problem is me.* This means we come to the realization that we are spiritually bankrupt and that the goal in life is NOT to try harder, do better, or turn over a new leaf. Remember, we are not mistakers in need of a life coach. We are sinners in need of a savior.

We need for someone else to do for us what we could never do for ourselves. Again, big difference. And because of this, we need a new life. This is what Jesus meant when He said to Nicodemus, *"You must be born again."*

Look at your own life—you've tried to be good, and you can do it for several hours or days. It depends on you. And some of you reading right now are looking at your own lives and you've got the job you've always wanted, your marriage is great, your kids are great. Yet when you lay your head on your pillow at night, you know something is busted up and broken. That you are spiritually bankrupt. And you're asking yourself, *What is missing in here?* Ecclesiastes says that God has put eternity into our hearts. Jesus is saying this: "Blessed is the man, blessed is the woman that realizes that you are bankrupt at the soul level."

If you're down and out, if you feel like life is hopeless, if you feel like God needs to do something for you because you can't get out of what you're in, then I've got good news for you. You are perfectly positioned for God to do a miracle in your life and you are on your way to becoming poor in spirit. When you begin to realize that you, on your own, by nature and nurture, are a wretched, black-hearted sinner, then you are perfectly positioned, and the kingdom of heaven is within reach. God is stirring that up in you.

Some of you are familiar with the prodigal son story that Jesus tells in Luke 15. It's about the kid who goes to his dad and says, "I'm done with you. Give me what's mine. Give me my inheritance. You're dead to me." Then he goes out and squanders his inheritance on wild and reckless living. Once broke, he finds the only job he can, which is feeding pigs—a horrible job for a first-century Jewish boy. Then one day, he's feeding the pigs and he looks at the pigs and he's jealous of the pigs. And in that very moment, the lowest point in his life, the Bible says that *he comes to his senses.*

This is where Jesus starts. The bottom. Blessed is the man

who comes to his senses because he realizes his utter depravity. Only when you start at the bottom can you take the next step. Poor in spirit is our spiritual bottom. Poor in spirit is what Isaiah recognized when he found himself in God's presence and cried out, "Woe is me! For I am lost; for I am a man of unclean lips, and I dwell in the midst of a people of unclean lips; for my eyes have seen the King, the LORD of hosts!" (Isa. 6:5). It's step one.

Step Two: Mourning

"Blessed are those who mourn, for they shall be comforted."

Jesus is not saying, "Happy are you when you cry." That doesn't make any sense at all. If you find yourself in circumstances that make you sad, where's the blessing in that? You should cry. God gave us emotions to navigate this thing called life.

But Jesus is laying out the gospel, and this naturally follows from what came before: blessed are those of you that realize you are spiritually bankrupt and begin to mourn over your sin and sinfulness. This is the conviction of the Holy Spirit. When we get a picture of who God is and how much He loves us and what He did for us on the cross, and then we look at our own rebellious activity against God and the damage that it has caused the people that we love so much, we begin to mourn and weep. Not because we got busted, but because deep in our souls, we know that we are sinners.

After His resurrection, Jesus told us that He would send the Holy Spirit to be our comforter. Why? Because when the things that break the heart of God begin to break your heart, the Holy Spirit will move into your life and give you a comfort, a peace that transcends all understanding. That was also Jesus' invitation in Matthew 11:28. He says, *Come to me, all you who are weary and heavy burdened.* Meaning, "Come to me, all you who are exhausted by trying to live rightly and prove yourself righteous before a holy and righteous Judge. Is that not exhausting? If you're worn-out at the soul level, come to Me and I will give you rest for your soul."

When God begins to convict us of our sin, we mourn. Only then do we really turn our eyes to Jesus. Only then do we say with conviction, "I need You to do something that I could never do for myself."

Step Three: Meekness

"Blessed are the meek, for they shall inherit the earth."

From poor in spirit to mourning, we step to meekness. "Blessed are the meek." I believe this is the moment of salvation. "Blessed are the meek, for they shall inherit the earth."

I don't know anybody who has said publicly, "Gee, I would love to be meek. I would love to be known for meekness. When I die, I want people to stand up at my funeral and say, 'That brother was meek.'"

Our problem is that we don't understand what the word means. It rhymes with "weak." And it's usually used in the phrase *meek and mild*, so we don't understand it, but the word *meek* in Greek means "a bit-bridled horse."

It doesn't mean "weak" at all. It means "guided strength." A big, powerful horse is not weak. He's just handed over the reins to his master. The horse yielded his will to the will of one who can direct his energies for his purposes.

Theologians call this repentance. Blessed are you when you get to the place in your life where you realize your way isn't working.

When you realize you're headed in the wrong direction. When you say, "God, I surrender my life to Your lordship. I trust You not only for the forgiveness of my sins but also to guide and direct my life. Here, take the reins. I'm not the boss of me anymore. You are."

The Bible says, "Everyone who calls on the name of the LORD shall be saved" (Joel 2:32). Calling on His name is standing in meekness and turning over the reins. It's also a good picture of repentance.

I think this is why He promised, "Blessed are the meek." The blessing ends with directional language: "for they shall inherit the earth." When we get to the last book of the Bible, Revelation, we read that everything we can now see, everything we call earth, burns up. John actually sees a new heaven and a new earth and those who are in Christ Jesus rule and reign over the new earth.

That's what this means. Everybody who surrenders their life to the lordship of Jesus Christ will one day inherit the earth. Not the broken, busted-up thing that we live on now, but this perfect new heaven, new earth. It's a directional change. But for anybody who remains the lord of their own life, you will continue in the direction that you're headed. God will give you in eternity what you ask for in this life. You reject God here and you will live a godless eternity forever. If you forever remain in charge of you, all you'll have left is you. Separated from the source of life and love. We call that place hell.

Step Four: Hungering and Thirsting for Righteousness

"Blessed are those who hunger and thirst for righteousness, for they shall be satisfied."

From poor in spirit to mourning to meekness, we step to "Blessed are those who hunger and thirst for righteousness, for they shall be satisfied." The word *righteousness* is often misunderstood. It does not mean "right activity." It means "right standing before God." And it occurs through the imputed righteousness of Christ. What God has done for us on the cross. In Romans 3:20, Paul says, "For by works of the law no human being will be justified in his sight, since through the law comes knowledge of sin." In other words, no matter how many right things you do in a row, you will not be declared righteous before God. And lots of religious people declare themselves righteous because of their right activity.

By definition, this is called self-righteousness.

And it's no good. No matter how good you think you are, walking with Christ is not about right activity—it's about right identity. Think about it. The Pharisees in Jesus' day were experts at keeping the law, and yet they were standing three feet away from God in the flesh and they missed Him. "But now the righteousness of God has been manifested apart from the law, although the Law and the Prophets bear witness to it—the righteousness of God through faith in Jesus Christ" (Rom. 3:21–22). In other words, righteousness is manifested in the person of Jesus Christ. And our righteousness means that we have a right standing before God because our identity is in Him. Now, make no bones about it—if your identity is in Jesus, your activity will change. You cannot be a fruitless Christian and be connected to the Vine. It just doesn't work that way. Now, it might not be coming along as fast as your wife and your grandma were hoping, but He promised, "He who began a good work in you will bring it to completion" (Phil. 1:6).

The Bible says, "The righteousness of God through faith in Jesus Christ for all who believe. For there is no distinction: for all have sinned and fall short of the glory of God, and are justified by his grace as a gift, through the redemption that is in Jesus Christ, whom God put forward as a propitiation by his blood" (Rom. 3:22–25).

Propitiation is a payment that satisfies the justice of God because Jesus fully absorbed God's wrath toward sin at the cross. So at our church we simply say propitiation means "a payment that satisfies." Meaning, if Jesus made the payment that satisfies, God cannot be dissatisfied in you. Because it's not about your activity; it's about your identity in Christ. When the Father sees you, He no longer sees your sin but His Son's perfect righteousness.

"Whom God put forward as a propitiation by his blood, to be received by faith. This was to show God's righteousness, because in his divine forbearance, he had passed over former sins. It was to show his righteousness at the present time, so that he might be just and the justifier of the one who has faith in Jesus." (Romans 3:25–26)

Any sin against an almighty, eternal God requires an everlasting eternal payment. Why? Because God is just, holy, and righteous, and because of this, all sin must be paid for. We recognize this in our own legal system. Punishment for a crime is determined not only by what you do but who you do it against. If you get mad and kick the wall, that's not good. If you kick your spouse, you go to jail. If you kick the president, they'll put you in federal prison. You kick your cat, and it's not even a sin. (Cats are obviously evil.) Fortunately for us, because He's merciful, He delayed the payment. That mercy is what allowed you to wake up this morning.

What if the first time you sinned He demanded payment? We'd all be greasy spots. You'd be gone. I'd be gone. But by His mercy, payment was delayed, and by His grace, He made the payment. This is what is meant by *He might be just and the justifier* (Rom. 3:26). So blessed are you who hunger and thirst for that. Not right activity. Blessed are you who hunger and thirst for that manifested righteousness. You could put Jesus' name in here. Blessed are you when you hunger and thirst for Jesus.

This is a spiritual truth that we see played out in the natural world. When you eat and eat and eat, you're never fully and finally satisfied. The more you eat, the more you want to eat. Thanksgiving is the perfect reminder of this. You gorge yourself until you're miserable. You think to yourself, *Nope, I'm done. I'm not eating again until Christmas.* But by halftime in the Detroit game, you're digging through the refrigerator. "Anybody need a turkey sandwich?" Some of you show up in yoga pants. "Listen, I learned last year. I will not be uncomfortable."

The more you feed that appetite, the bigger it grows. Jesus is saying, *Blessed are those who hunger and thirst for the understanding of the gospel and what I have done for them.* The Puritans called this vivification. The more you do the things that stir your affections for Christ, the more your appetite for Him grows.

I've got to be honest—I can't get over the gospel. And I hope you can't either. I hope you understand that the gospel is not merely that doctrine that began your relationship with Jesus but it is the eternal reality that sustains all of your life. I know how sick and twisted I am, and I can't reconcile it in my mind that He would die for me. That my relationship with Him is not measured by my activity but by His activity on the cross. That my acceptance with Him is not conditional upon whether I obey, but that He accepted me on the cross. I'm acceptable to Him before I try to be.

This way changes everything about obedience in my life. This is why when we sing songs like "How Great Thou Art," I don't even know how others really get through it, because the third verse says, "And when I think that God, His Son not sparing, sent Him to die, I scarce can take it in." This is what I'm talking about. I cannot reconcile in my mind when we sing about this thing that Jesus did.

He died for me. He died for you. "That on the cross, my burden gladly bearing, He bled and died to take away my sin." Which leads to "Then sings my soul, my Savior God, to Thee." Every time we sing this, I lose my mind! I stare out sometimes across our church and I see people worshiping like mannequins, and I wonder, *Do you realize what you're singing?*

Or when we sing that Passion song, "Worthy of Your Name." We get to the verse where we sing, "You stand by my side; You stood in my place." Are you kidding me? I can't hold back the tears. I can't hold back the worship. I just can't get over the gospel. When the gospel gets you and gets into you, I think it's this thing that grows. You're a little bit hungry and then you feed it with His Word and you find that the next day, you're a little bit hungrier. Soon, you're just gorging on the gospel.

That's why some of you are so dissatisfied. It's because you're looking to the wrong things for satisfaction. New house? New car? Those things are great but they don't satisfy your soul. The only thing that will satisfy your soul is a right standing before God. We have been created as image bearers of the almighty God. He has placed eternity in our hearts. The only thing that can satisfy the insatiable soul of the human condition is the everlasting and eternal God. C. S. Lewis says it this way: "God can not give us peace and happiness apart from Himself because it is not there. There is no such thing." Blessed are you when you hunger and thirst for that deepening relationship with Jesus, because He will satisfy you. Because the opposite of this is true too. Woe to you who hunger and thirst for the shiny things of this world. Whatever it is. Success, sex, stuff, whatever—woe to you. If you chase this stuff, you will live your entire life utterly dissatisfied.

Step Five: Mercy

"Blessed are the merciful, for they shall receive mercy."

First, let me let you off the hook. This is not a personality type that only a few of us fit. This is a description of all of us. Everyone who is poor in spirit, who mourns, who has turned over the reins of their life to Jesus, who hungers and thirsts for righteousness will, by default, be merciful. You can't help it. It's the product of Jesus in you.

Which is 180 degrees from our condition at birth. By both nature and nurture, we are sinners, not full of mercy. Paul puts it this way: *You were dead in your trespasses. You were a child of wrath* (Eph. 2). But God didn't leave us there. *But God, who is rich in mercy, saves us by grace through faith.* He doesn't just merely wipe away your sins. He also gives you the righteousness of Christ that you did not deserve. And He changes your name to His name. He adopts you. He makes you a coheir with Jesus and everything that He has. Once again, the verdict precedes the performance. He has poured out mercy on us. Period.

Now, don't miss what's beginning to happen here in the Beatitudes. It's much like the law of Moses, the Ten Commandments, in that the first few are about our vertical relationship with God and the last few are about our horizontal relationships with one another. The vertical influences the horizontal. Same is true here. When we're poor in spirit, we've mourned, become meek, hungered for righteousness, and received mercy, we begin to offer mercy. The offering flows out of the infilling. We are meant to be conduits of God's love and mercy. Not cul-de-sacs. That's what's happening here in the Beatitudes, and this changeover time is called "sanctification." It's the process by which we become more like Jesus. The Holy Spirit in us uses the Word of

God like a hammer and chisel to hammer away anything in us that doesn't look like the Son.

Step Six: Pure in Heart

"Blessed are the pure in heart, for they shall see God."

When we read about salvation in the New Testament, the text is talking about being saved from three aspects of our sin.

We have been saved from the penalty of our sin. We are being saved from the power of our sin. And one day we will be saved from the very presence of our sin.

In other words, we are justified, we are sanctified, and one day we will be glorified. All of that is called "salvation."

So Jesus says, "Blessed are the pure in heart, for they shall see God." By the way, here's how we know that He can't be talking about a personality type—as in, some of us are, and some of us aren't. Let me ask you this—are you pure in heart? The moment you say, "I'm pure in heart," you're prideful and you've just ceased to be pure. So who, then, is pure in heart? If you've surrendered your life to the lordship of Jesus Christ, you are. And you will see God. And you were made for this.

Let's go back to the beginning. One God in three persons: God the Father, God the Son, and God the Holy Spirit. Out of an overflow of God's love, God creates humankind for God's glory. The Bible says that He speaks everything into existence with merely a word. But when it comes to image bearers, He does it differently. God forms Adam from the ground (*adamah*, which is where we get *Adam*, means "dirt" or "earth"). But the Bible says that he is not yet a living creature. Then the Bible tells us that God breathes the *ruach* of life into the nostrils of Adam. *Ruach* can be translated as "breath" or "wind" or "spirit." The Bible also wants us to know that God was nostril to nostril with the very first man. And then, after Adam received God's breath, or spirit, he became a living creature. That means that the very first thing that the very first man saw was the face of God. That moment has been imprinted on us all. We long for that moment, and sin separates us from seeing God. But at the cross and empty tomb, Jesus made it possible for you and me to be face-to-face with the Father again. Jesus makes us pure in heart. You know why? Because it isn't your heart anymore. Ezekiel 36:26 says, "And I will give you a new heart, and a new spirit I will put within you. And I will remove the heart of stone from your flesh and give you a heart of flesh." God rips your wretched heart out, sends it to hell all by itself, and gives you a new heart. His heart.

But I can hear your response. You say, "But why do I still struggle?"

Because He didn't give you a new mind. This is why you still have the same jacked-up thoughts that you've had for a long time. This is why Paul says in Romans 12:2, "Do not be conformed to this world, but be transformed by the renewal of your mind." You've got to get your mind to line up with the pure heart that Jesus has given you. When that happens, you will see God.

Paul's second letter to the Corinthians 5:17 says it this way: "Therefore, if anyone is in Christ, he is a new creation. The old has passed away; behold, the new has come." Do you know what that means in our day-to-day living? You're not the person you used to be. He or she is dead. Crucified with Christ. And the new creation has the heart of Christ—which is pure.

For every single one of us who has been given a new heart, who has surrendered our lives to the lordship of Christ, there will be a day when we breathe our last on earth and breathe our next in heaven—face-to-face with our heavenly Father. And unlike Moses, who had to cover his face and hide behind a rock, we will not burn up. We will glorify God forever and ever and ever. John said it this way: "We shall be like him, because we shall see him as he is" (1 John 3:2).

Pure in heart.

Step Seven: Peacemakers

"Blessed are the peacemakers, for they shall be called sons of God."

Notice He doesn't say peacekeepers. A peacemaker and a peacekeeper are not the same thing. A peacekeeper prevents war. A peacemaker ushers in the shalom, the completeness, the wholeness of God into a given situation. And when you do this, you are a son of God. By the way, the Greek language used adverbs differently than we do. When referring to James and John, Jesus called them "sons of thunder." Not "thunderly." So this phrase is the Greek way of saying that you will be godly.

Prior to Jesus, every single one of us was an enemy of God. And when Jesus came, He made peace between a treasonous race like ours and the great and mighty King. What He's saying here is blessed are you when you, like Jesus, do whatever it takes to introduce people who are far from God to the God who loved them so much that He sent Jesus on their behalf. This is ushering in peace, and blessed are you when you do this.

There's nothing you can do to be more like Jesus than when, at great expense to yourself, you help reconcile men and women to God. Paul says it this way: "All this is from God, who through Christ reconciled us to himself and gave us the ministry of reconciliation" (2 Cor. 5:18). In other words, made peace.

"In Christ God was reconciling the world to himself, not counting their trespasses against them, and entrusting to us the message of reconciliation. Therefore, we are ambassadors for Christ, God making his appeal through us. We implore you on behalf of Christ, be reconciled to God. For our sake he made him to be sin who knew no sin, so that in him we might become the righteousness of God." (2 Cor. 5:19–21)

In other words, blessed are you when the moment you are rescued you begin to understand that you are a part of the rescue team and that God's desire is to use you to make peace between enemies of God and God Himself. Through the reconciling work of Jesus Christ, He made peace between us and God. And so when we become like Him, we make peace between other rebels and the Father, showing once again how our vertical relationship with Jesus bleeds into our horizontal relationships with one another. Which leads to the last Beatitude.

Step Eight: Persecuted

"Blessed are those who are persecuted for righteousness' sake, for theirs is the kingdom of heaven."

Remember where we started: "Blessed are the poor in spirit, for theirs is the kingdom of heaven." These two, the first and the last, are bookends. Jesus is bringing us back full circle. How should you respond when you're persecuted? You should respond the way Jesus responded.

Jesus hung on a cross over the men who literally nailed Him up there, and when He was reviled, He did not revile in return, but He uttered these words: "Father, forgive them, for they know not what they do." You want to call yourself a Christian? Then forgive those who nail you to the tree. Being persecuted and being a Christian have gone hand in hand since Jesus was here. And by the way, who most often persecuted Jesus? Was it the world or the religious? It was always the religious.

The gospel will blow up religion because the gospel says it's not about your religious activity; it's about Christ's activity on the cross. The gospel is about trust, and religion is about good behavior. Most evangelical Americans like me assume that this world ought to accept us, especially in America. This cultural phenomenon is new because, for a long time, men and women were persecuted for the sake of Jesus' name. And today in places all around the world, the persecuted church faces threats of violence and even death. Not in spite of their faith, but because of their faith.

I think this is why Jesus adds a little bit of commentary. He says, "Blessed are you when others revile you and persecute you and utter all kinds of evil against you falsely on my account. Rejoice and be glad."

It's a weird response, isn't it? Rejoice and be glad. Why? "For your reward is great in heaven, for so they persecuted the prophets who were before you." In other words, don't get too comfortable here, because this world is not your permanent address. Jesus is lifting our eyes off our circumstances and onto our reward. We are residents of another kingdom, and if you're not being persecuted, why? If you've never felt any kind of persecution because you're a Jesus follower, then check which team you're on. And do those around you know which team you're on? Or are you a secret member? If you don't feel a significant push of our current culture against you and your way of life, it could be because you are just going with the flow. People who live out the gospel as laid out here in the Beatitudes, who have surrendered their life to the lordship of Jesus Christ and begin to live by a brand-new ethic, don't fit into this world very well.

The rest of the Sermon on the Mount is about what it looks like when the gospel as laid out in the Beatitudes takes hold of your life. It changes your marriage, changes the way you forgive, changes your generosity. When you become salt and light, everything about you is different. It seems to me that most evangelicals have just replaced the law of the Ten Commandments with the law of the Sermon on the Mount. Which means you missed the whole point. The Sermon on the Mount is not a suggestion on the Mount. It's not an op-ed by Jesus on the Mount. It's a sermon. And in it Jesus describes what it looks like to live rightly before the Lord. And if you're honest, your only conclusion is, "There's no way. There's no way I can nail this thing. I'm toast." Which is why I believe He started with the invitation of the gospel. Blessed are you when you read the Sermon on the Mount and you think, *I can't pull this off.*

Perfect. You're poor in spirit.

You know that you need Jesus to do for you what you could never do for yourself, which means you're perfectly positioned to hand over the reins to your Master and Maker and watch Him guide your life. When you're wrecked by the gospel train, everything about you changes.

Look how Jesus ends the sermon. And if you take your Bible seriously, these verses will freak you out. He says, "Not everyone who says to me, 'Lord, Lord,' will enter the kingdom of heaven, but the one who does the will of my Father who is in heaven." When Jesus speaks this, there are a lot of people on the mountain, and He's issuing a warning: "Listen, man, wake up. There's going to be a bunch of surprised church people who don't get into heaven." Then He says to them, "On that day many will say to me, 'Lord, Lord, did we not prophesy in your name, and cast out demons in your name, and do many mighty works in your name?'"

In essence, they are showing Jesus their religious resume. "Look at the many good things I have done!" And I don't know about you, but at a first glance at their resume, I would think they are a sure thing. Prophets and exorcists? I mean, have you ever cast out a demon? I have not. I sent a seventh grader home from camp once. That's the closest thing to an exorcism that I've been involved in. I would think they would be in. Jesus is like, "No, man. It's not about the good work that you have done. By trusting in your own good works, a works-based righteousness, you have declared yourself righteous. By definition, you are self-righteous, making you your own king, not Me."

For us today, we would say, "I sang the songs with one hand up. I tithed. I went on a mission trip. I sponsored kids. I led a disciple group. I was on staff." But look at what Jesus says: "And then will I declare to them, 'I never knew you; depart from me.'"

In the Sermon on the Mount, Jesus is describing what happens in you when you walk with Him and deepen your relationship. When you know Him, do your activities change? For sure. But your activities do not determine your destiny. Your identity in Jesus does. Finally, Jesus gives this illustration: "Everyone then who hears these words of mine and does them will be like a wise man who built his house on the rock. And the rain fell, and the floods came, and the winds blew and beat on that house, but it did not fall, because it had been founded on the rock."

The rock here is the person and work of Jesus Christ. The gospel of grace through Jesus Christ. Contrast that with the alternative: "And everyone who hears these words of mine and does not do them will be like a foolish man who built his house on the sand. And the rain fell, and the floods came, and the winds blew and beat against that house, and it fell, and great was the fall of it."

Let me just ask you this: On what have you built your life? Solid rock or shifting sand? Maybe some of you have been going to church for a long time, but for what? Works or relationship? I'm not knocking serving the body—we all should—but what identifies you? Why do you serve? I have met a lot of churchgoers who are proud of what they do in church and for the church but have little relationship with the One who died for His bride.

Jesus says, *Come to me, all you who are weary and heavy burdened.* He didn't say come to a disciple group or come to church or come to better behavior. He didn't say come to right doctrine or right theology. Yes, those things are good, but they're the fruit of having come to Him. They're not the goal. He says, *Come to Me. Come to the person who died on the cross for you, and I will give you rest for your soul.*

In the old covenant, the covenant on Sinai, God declares, "I am God. You are My people." Then He gives us the commandments that we must follow to be in right relationship with Him. Following the commandments, we get instructions on how to build altars and how to make sacrifices. Why? Because God knows we can't live the commandments.

In the Sermon on the Mount, Jesus does the exact opposite. He says, *I have made the sacrifice. Therefore, blessed are you if you'll accept that sacrifice. You don't do all these things to earn My favor. You already have it.*

Jesus is the greater Moses. And while the Sermon on the Mount is a reflection of Moses at Sinai, the order is reversed. Turned on its head. If you get infected with the gospel, the symptoms of the gospel-infected life are love-driven obedience to the life of Jesus. Not works-based adherence to a set of rules in order to earn something from Him. What most evangelicals have done is take out the Levitical law and add an evangelical law that includes things about lust and money and forgiveness. Which is totally missing the point. Being a Christian is not about sin management. Sin management is like holding a beach ball under the ocean. You think that if you can just get a hold of your sin by your might and willpower, you can force it under the water. Take hold of your sin and you control it. How long can you do that? Depends on how strong you are. And on the waves. But eventually, your hand will slip. No one can do that very long. Especially in a storm. And when we lose our grip, the beach ball never gently floats back to the top. It explodes in your face. That is what works-based sin management looks like. In the Sermon on the Mount, Jesus walks by with a pocketknife, punctures the beach ball, and takes the power out of it. By defeating sin, Jesus has not given us a license to sin, but rather freedom from it. These are two very different things.

We started with the 11:22 service at Beach UMC, but we soon went to multiple services because we didn't have enough room for all the people who showed up. Then a really significant thing happened. This fifteen-year-old girl started coming to the service. She was a tenth-grade cheerleader and softball player at The Bolles School. She was an influencer. About this time, we did a series called Inked. We studied tattoos in the Scripture. Like Jesus returning with *King of kings and Lord of lords* written on His thigh. I don't think He's gonna use a Sharpie. I got a tattoo and kept it hidden for four weeks, and then on the last week of the series, I revealed the tattoo. Normally I'm a verse-by-verse expository preacher, but that weekend, I just shared my testimony about what my tattoo meant.

Long story short, I was a troubled teen. With emphasis on *troubled*. A local football coach from Dillon got me out of some trouble by giving me a job mowing grass at a summer camp. Next thing I know, I'm attending camp. I got saved at camp. I already told you that story. Then I started working at camp. Then, one night, about five minutes before he was to step up there and preach, Coach Lee said to me, "Joby Martin." He always called me by my first and last name. "When the singing is done, you are gonna preach."

A college kid was onstage leading a heart-stirring rendition of "I Am a C." I said, "Coach…preach? I'm not comfortable speaking in front of people."

He said, "Comfortable? Did you say comfortable?" Then, with his voice escalating like a halftime speech, he said, "Boy, do you think Paul and Silas were comfortable in prison? Boy, do you think Daniel was comfortable in the lions' den? Do you think Jesus Christ was comfortable on the cross?!"

"Uh, no, sir." And then I said, "But, Coach, what do I talk about?"

Without hesitation he said, "Boy, that's easy. You talk about Jesus and you talk for about thirty minutes. Go!"

And I did. I talked about Jesus to a bunch of high school kids for about thirty minutes. God saved a few. When I walked off the tiny little platform, Coach met me halfway.

He said, "Joby Martin, when you preach the Bible, I see two things happen. I see you come alive, and I see them come alive." From that moment, I've pretty much been doing that thing. Every week.

Looking back across my life, that moment is as big as any.

At the end of camp, the counselors dressed up in sheets and reenacted the death and resurrection of Jesus again, just like they had when I got saved. Part of that story is a crown of thorns, hanging on a cross. That image stuck with me. Years later, I was on a mission trip in Jamaica, and Coach Lee died. I thought it was pretty appropriate that I couldn't go to the funeral because I was leading a mission trip. He'd love that. Probably did it on purpose. The guy who did Coach Lee's eulogy read Acts 11:24: "He was a good man, full of the Holy Spirit and of faith. And a great number of people were brought to the Lord" (NIV).

Back to Inked and McKenzie. I finished telling this story and revealed my tattoo—a cross, a crown of thorns, and Acts 11:24 on my arm. Ultimately that's what I live for and I pray is the fruit of my life. When I finished, I shared how Coach Lee led me to Christ. I shared that he said, "I believe there is one more out there that is ready to ask Jesus in their heart." And I closed the service asking if there was one more that was ready to respond to the gospel. And this fifteen-year-old girl named McKenzie Wilson let go of her mom's and dad's hands and then raised her hands and surrendered her life to Christ. I didn't know it at the time, but after that she wrote these words in her Bible: *I want to make my faith public.*

Four weeks later, she was lying in the hospital in a coma. Rare brain disease. I didn't know her or her family, but I'd heard that a high school girl who had been attending Eleven22 was in the hospital, so I decided to go visit. When I was let into the hallway, her dad came walking straight to me. Some family friends had briefed me on the severity of her condition on the elevator ride up. Her dad, Blake, walked with deliberate steps straight up to me. He had a Bible, one of the ones we give out at Eleven22, in his hand. He said something like, "I have been listening to you for the last several weeks with my family. Now I need you to listen to me." He proceeded to tell me McKenzie's story. So I walked into the room to find the mom lying in bed, cradling her nonresponsive daughter.

I lost it. I can still see it. McKenzie was a beautiful, athletic blonde young woman. All I could think of was the one-year-old beautiful blonde baby girl at my house. I couldn't stop crying. I met her parents and led them to Christ right there in the room with McKenzie. I spent several hours just being present with her family. I didn't try to find the right words. I was just there. We cried. We prayed. We cried some more. Gretchen and I came back every day and sat with the family and prayed some more. God wove our families together during that time.

Four days later she died.

Her time of death was 11:22 a.m.

You can't make this stuff up.

Her parents wanted to do the funeral at the church and her mom said, "Gretchen was her favorite singer. I just want it to be like a service at Eleven22. I want to sing the songs that we sing." Then she said, "Joby, can you be funny?"

And I was like, "I don't think I can, but I'll try." And then she said, "You know how at the end, you ask people to raise their hand if they want to surrender to Jesus? I want you to do that."

Mind you, McKenzie's dad was at that time president of a large bank. All of his friends from Wall Street pulled into the parking lot for the service. In all, 1,750 people showed up for the funeral. Our overflow area overflowed.

I am an unashamed gospel guy. But I wanted to make sure I honored the family while also being aware of who was in the room. So I just took McKenzie's Bible, trying to be sensitive to a really diverse crowd, and preached her own notes that she'd written in her Bible. Basically, I said, "McKenzie's dying prayer was she wanted to make her faith public. So I want to talk to you about her faith."

During that service, 175 people surrendered their lives to Jesus. Many of whom are now deacons and things like that at our church. Shortly after that, our 11:22 service blew up. Overflow and more overflow. And Pastor Jerry, literally the best Christian I have ever met, came to me and said, "I think it's time that we plant you and launch you as lead pastor of your own church." To my knowledge, it is the first time that the United Methodist Church has ever launched a nondenominational church. I will be forever grateful.

So with a lot of help from a lot of people and much wise counsel, we found an abandoned Walmart we could convert into a church building. But we needed $4 million, so we started raising money. Pastor Jerry allowed Eleven22 to meet at BUMC while we cast vision and raised support. We raised $5 million. We leased the Walmart with an option to buy (from Toney Sleiman, without whom there would be no Eleven22), renovated it, and gave $1 million back to Beach United to pay off their debt.

September 23, 2012, was our very first service at our own facility, and 3,364 people attended. In the first service, when the countdown clock hit 11:22 a.m., I said, "Let us pray." Those were the first words ever spoken in our church. I preached out of Luke 4, where Jesus unrolls the scroll, quotes from the prophet Isaiah, and says,

> "'The Spirit of the Lord is upon me,
>   because he has anointed me
>   to proclaim good news to the poor.
> He has sent me to proclaim liberty to the captives
>   and recovering of sight to the blind,
>   to set at liberty those who are oppressed,
>   to proclaim the year of the Lord's favor.'
> And he rolled up the scroll and gave it back to the attendant and sat down. And the eyes of all in the synagogue were fixed on him. And he began to say to them, 'Today this Scripture has been fulfilled in your hearing.'" (vv. 18–21)

This blows their minds. They have no box for this. Jesus is claiming to be the anointed Son of God. He's saying, "This is what I'm about." So, looking at our church, I said, "If that's what He's about, then that's what we should be about." And it's ultimately the gospel and the implications of the gospel.

Every Sunday for eight years I preached from what used to be Ladies Accessories. I had to check with Gretchen to find out what that was. Turns out it was not underwear and stuff. It was cheap jewelry.

In December 2020, we opened a new worship center in the other half of the renovated Walmart. So now I preach from Layaway. Millennials and Gen Zers, you'll need to google it. It's crazy—when

I was growing up, you actually needed money before they would let you buy something. Before we opened our new worship center in the other half of the Walmart, we read the entire Bible out loud nonstop. It took us about seventy-two hours. Before a sermon was ever preached in there, every word of God was proclaimed.

And one of the implications of this is that we can look out from where we sit and ask, "Who can I serve? Who can I lift up? Whose stuff can I make more important than my stuff?"

In our church we have a pretty tight relationship with Compassion International. We believe in their ministry. And by believe in it, I mean we invest in it. I mean, like, a lot of us. On one weekend, our church sponsored 1,795 children. I'm not saying that to brag. It's a fact. And it's not a competition, but if it were, we'd be winning. And I admit, that weekend, because I wanted to drive the point home, I brought my daughter up onstage with me. Talked about her life. The fact that she didn't choose where she was born or to whom she was born. How she does not have parasites and has all her teeth. And how God gave her to us. I know it was very manipulative, but I don't care. It worked, and almost 1,800 kids were rescued from poverty in Jesus' name. We have sponsored a total of over 13,000. It's not expensive. To save one child only costs thirty-eight dollars a month. Just over a dollar a day. Our church believes in it so much that our kids, our youth, even sponsor kids. With their chore money. Or they get jobs. They email their kids. Send pictures. Visit them. It's crazy.

Interestingly enough, during that weekend, a girl named Prossy that our church sponsored emailed me. She was a part of Compassion's Leadership Development Program, which means that we sent her through college. Before she got sponsored through Compassion, she grew up in a mud house with no shoes. She got her first pair of shoes when she was eight years old. She graduated from high school at the top of her class, but she had no family and no possibilities. Her life was changed with sponsorship, and she was able to attend college.

A few years ago, a few of us from the church were in Africa training some of the pastors of the churches we planted there. Before my arrival, I emailed Prossy to let her know we'd be near her and would love to see her. "Can I send you some money to get you some bus fare or taxi fare over to the city?" I asked.

She responded, "I don't need money. I have a job."

We as a church sent her through college, and for whatever reason, she just happened to email me on that Compassion weekend. Her email read, "Hello, Daddy."

She calls me Daddy because she doesn't have a daddy, and she doesn't have a mama, so she calls Gretchen Mom. In fact, she's changed her name to "Prossy Joby" because she doesn't have a family. She says we're her family, and apparently she doesn't understand how last names work. But whatever—that's a different thing, "Hello, daddy. Well done." Where she's from, that means "Hey." That was followed by "How is everyone? How is the ministry? I really miss my father. Regards to the entire family of CoE22 and my siblings." That would be JP and Reagan. "All's well."

I wrote back, "Praise the Lord, Prossy—this weekend is our Compassion Weekend and our church sponsored 1,795 kids."

This was her response: "Wow, this is so amazing, daddy. I am humbled. Glory to God. Send my gratitude to everyone who has stood with us."

The *us* there means every child in poverty.

She said, "Send my gratitude to everyone who has stood with us and Compassion at large. For sure, if it wasn't for God and Compassion, I don't know how life would be by now. I can now testify for God's faithfulness and goodness that through Compassion, my life was turned around for good and through God's grace. I am even speechless. I am a living testimony. My heart is full of joy unspeakable, which causes me tears. Not that I am hurt, but because I am happy and grateful. You"—she's talking to our church here—"are great people to us, sent from heaven, not just mere men, but extraordinary. I love you all. Hope to see you again soon. God bless you, Prossy."

Today, Prossy has eight people working for her, and she can pay her own bills. It's just an incredible story. True and undefiled religion is to take care of widows and orphans, and in my opinion, nobody does it better than Compassion International.

As I write this, our church is almost ten years old, has nine campuses, and will soon be at eleven in a year and a half—two of which are in prisons. And we have an online platform now reaching hundreds of thousands of people a week with the gospel. We've planted over 350 churches—over 200 in Africa—and sponsored over thirteen thousand Compassion kids. Again, it's not a competition, but if it were, we'd be winning. And we welcome all comers to try and best us.

Since we started, there have been over ten thousand salvations— or at least people have let us know that they've made a first-time decision for Christ. Sometimes some church people say, "How do you know all those people are saved?" To which I say, "Well, if you make it to heaven, I'll introduce you to them."

I've seen a lot of people use their church as a platform for themselves. For self-promotion. But there are no rock star shepherds; that doesn't even make sense. And Lord forbid that I ever attempt to become one. I just know I love our church, I love to preach, and I'm thankful my church lets me preach. I am so thankful to our staff that does such a great job at being the part of the body God has called them to be so that I can be the part He has called me to be. I hope when I'm dead and done, somebody can say that "he was a good man, full of the Holy Spirit and of faith. And a great number of people were brought to the Lord." To be a good man, I mean I want to be a good husband and a good dad. If I'm an average preacher at best, no problem. I want to be good to my wife, good to my kids, and full of the Holy Spirit. I want to be led by the Spirit. You know if you ever ride a really well-trained horse, you just barely have to touch that rein and he'll go exactly where you want him to go? That's how I want to be with the Lord. Just so full of the Holy Spirit that at just the slightest little nudge, I will change directions and do whatever the Spirit wants me to do.

And let me be found full of faith, not fear. I refuse to be ruled by the tyranny of fear. Faith roots out fear. Love casts it out. Fear is a spirit, not a feeling. And we have not been given a spirit of fear. But we have been given a spirit of power and a spirit of love and a spirit of self-control. I want my life to be spent in such a way that a great number of people will be brought to the Lord. So far He's used me to reach thousands, but in God's economy, a great number is just one more person.

For the record, I did eventually get another tattoo. A cross and crown of thorns on one side. And the initials of my family—Gretchen, JP, and Reagan Capri—on the other: *JP, G, RC*. Instead of my name, it's my family. On one side, I have my God. On the other, my people. That's who I live for.

Which brings me back to you. Who do you live for? I tell you the story of our church because in it I saw then and continue to see now the undeserved and unmerited blessings of God. Eleven22 is so far beyond anything I could have comprehended and it's so disproportionate to my gifts and abilities that it has a humbling effect, and not the other way around. People look at our explosive growth, our campuses, and they say all kinds of cool stuff that, if I let it, would really blow my head up, but the truth is this: when a mosquito grabs on to a freight train, that mosquito does not feel bigger. He's just hanging on for dear life. That's what it's like. I do not feel bigger, because I simply can't get over the gospel—the fact that God would save me, use me, not disqualify me because of all my sin, AND anoint me to do something just blows my mind.

At the end of the day, I just want to be faithful, not famous. A shepherd, not a celebrity. I couldn't care less about being famous. But I do want to be effective and I want to share the gospel. I've said it before, and I'll say it again:

I'm just a nobody trying to tell anybody about the Somebody who wants to save everybody.

Given that this is the third time I've written that, maybe you should highlight that too. Print a T-shirt. It's catchy because it's true. And in truth, it should describe all of us.

If we are run over by the grace train of God, the way we live changes forever, not because we focus on doing "right" things but because we are in right relationship with Jesus. Because we love Him, we obey Him. And the fruit of that obedience is these blessings. Our problem is that most of us chase the blessings rather than the One who blesses.

Pray with Me

Our good and gracious heavenly Father, I thank You for the gospel. I thank You that by the power of Your Holy Spirit, You make us aware of our spiritual poverty apart from You. I thank You for the good news that because of Your great love and unending mercy, the verdict comes before the performance. Lord, I lift up to You the exhausted soul that has bought into the lie of religion that one's works can earn a right standing before You. Lord, I ask that Your Spirit would convict us, that we would mourn our sin and our sinful condition. God, I thank You that You are pleased to take the reins in our lives. I thank You that the gentle nudges of the Spirit lead us to abundant life, because life to the full is only found in You. God, I pray that Your peace transcends understanding in our own lives, that it would spill over into the lives of those around us. God, I pray for the persecuted. I lift up the men and women around the world who faithfully serve You in the face of the threat of violence. And Lord, if we call ourselves followers of Jesus and don't ever get a bloody nose from bumping up against the broken world, would You show us where we are indistinguishable from this world? God, I pray for my brothers and sisters at Eleven22. I thank You for the way they live out the gospel in front of me. God, thank You for allowing me to be a part of that faith family. Lord, may we all be conduits of Your good news in this broken world. We pray this in the matchless name of Jesus Christ our Lord. Amen.

CHAPTER 5

Mount of Temptation—With What Weapon Will You Fight the Enemy?

> "Then Jesus was led up by the Spirit into the wilderness to be tempted by the devil."
>
> Matthew 4:1
>
> "Again, the devil took him to a very high mountain."
>
> Matthew 4:8

We don't know the exact spot where satan tempted Jesus, but tradition holds that it was actually a thirteen-hundred-foot mountain in the wilderness that rises up out of the rock on the road between Jericho and Jerusalem. Today, the mountain is well-known because of a monastery that seems to cling to the rock face. You can climb to the top by a winding and steep path or ride a cable car.

I think I like the cable car better. Better view. I bet Peter would have taken the cable car.

Let me start with a question: Have you ever tried to make someone you love, love what you love? In my experience, it doesn't work out too well. I tried to make Gretchen love sweet tea because, I thought, *How could you not love sweet tea? What is wrong with a human being who doesn't love sweet tea?* But Gretchen's not having it.

Then we moved to Jacksonville in 2003 and I discovered Angie's sweet tea. Angie's is a sandwich shop about two miles from our church. I'm a frequent visitor. When we first moved there, I took Gretchen, and I was like, "Now listen, baby. If you don't like this, you ain't never going to like sweet tea at all." Angie's sweet tea is straight from heaven.

She sipped it. But she still didn't like it. And I thought to myself, *Something is wrong with this woman.*

I learned this lesson a second time with my kids. I'd been invited to Europe to preach, so, while on the train to London, we detoured through Oxford because I'm a huge C. S. Lewis fan. I was in heaven. Totally geeking out. Somewhere on our tour, we went to The Eagle and Child. This is where C. S. Lewis would sit with J. R. R. Tolkien and a group of men they called The Inklings. And they would just nerd out about imagination and fairies and story and how to communicate the gospel through story. I mean, the level of nerddom happening in that place...I wish I could have just been there.

The hostess took us to our table, which just so happened to be their table. The one next to the fireplace. I couldn't believe it. I was just eating it up. I turned to my kids and said, "Do you guys understand? We're sitting with C. S. Lewis and J. R. R. Tolkien. We're sitting right here. They wrote parts of *The Hobbit* and *The Lion, the Witch and the Wardrobe* right here. In that chair." I turned to my daughter. "What do you think about it, Reagan?"

She nodded. "Dad, do they have fries?"

This was my first clue that maybe they weren't digging it.

After lunch, we set out on a two-hour walking tour of Oxford, including the classrooms where Lewis taught and the halls where he debated. We stood around the pulpit where he preached.

No lie…I was freaking out.

My kids were too, but not in the same way at all. Until we walked into one part of Oxford, and the guy said, "This is where they filmed *Harry Potter*."

My kids came alive. I scratched my head. "Are you serious right now?"

We ended our tour on a path called Addison's Walk—a really famous stretch of dirt.

According to C. S. Lewis, after years of conversation with J. R. R. Tolkien, and after a particular discussion about how the human mind could create this idea of myths and fairies—along with a few pints—Tolkien told Lewis, "You see, the reality of the gospel is that the myth is true."

Lewis was a teacher of medieval mythology at Oxford and this idea freaked him out. He left The Eagle and Child and entered Addison's Walk—a trail next to his college. Lewis says when he got on that trail, he was not a believer, but when he stepped off, he was. Somewhere between the beginning of the trail and the end, Lewis believed that Jesus Christ died on the cross and it counted for him. That what he'd long thought was only myth was true. It was on this trail that he pondered a thought that he later captured in *Mere Christianity*: "If we find ourselves with a desire that nothing in this world can satisfy, the most probable explanation is that we were made for another world."[8]

I already told you that I have a tattoo on my arm. It reads Acts 11:24: "For he was a good man, full of the Holy Spirit and of faith. And a great number of people were brought to the Lord." I talk about this a lot, but "a great number" is really just one more. My kids know this and can quote it, so as I'm walking down

---

8   C. S. Lewis, *Mere Christianity* (London: Macmillan Publishing, 1952), 68.

that path, I'm explaining how Lewis was Tolkien's one more. I was totally freaking out. This was absolutely the best come-to-life classroom they've ever had and I wanted them to remember it, so I said, "Let's take a picture."

Looking at that photo, you have never seen two more bored and unenthused kids in your life. They're totally over it. Somewhere in there I realized my family is not exactly crazy about sweet tea and Lewis, and I can't make someone I love, love what I love.

I tell you all of this because I love—with all that I am—the Word of God. And I want you to love God's Word. And I know that, no matter how hard I try, I can't make you love it. I've seen this time and time again. But in this chapter, I am going to do my best to shove it down your throat like a parent shoves Brussels sprouts down their kid's throat, because it's not just good for you; it's better than life. It's the sword against the enemy. It's life-giving. It's food for our soul. It's always true. Always trustworthy. It's not even really an it. It's living. It's breathing. It's active. It gets into places in your soul that I can't.

Truth is, I don't know anybody who loves Jesus like crazy who doesn't also love the Word of God. His spoken Word. If you love the Lord your God with all of your mind, then you love His Word. I want to teach you a principle. Normally when I teach, I take one passage, and we just sort of soak in it. That's how most of the chapters in this book have been set up so far. But in this chapter, I'm going to take you through seven different passages, because if you can grab on to this, it could revolutionize your walk with Jesus.

In Romans 12:1, Paul says this: "I appeal to you therefore, brothers." Now, the reason that *therefore* is there in Romans 12 is because this is the transitional verse in the book of Romans. Chapters 1 to 8 are all about how the gospel says that we are saved not by our good works. We are not made righteous because we obey the law, but an alien righteousness has been manifested. His name is Jesus. And when we put our faith in Jesus, His righteousness is counted unto us. *Therefore, now there is no condemnation for those who are in Christ Jesus.* Romans 1–8 is all about the gospel. Chapters 9, 10, and 11 are about Israel's role in God's redemptive story for all peoples. And then you get to chapter 12 and there's the *therefore*. And the rest of the book of Romans is all about how the gospel changes and impacts our life and our role in God's redemptive story.

"I appeal to you therefore, brothers"—because of the gospel and because of your role as the church in the spreading of the gospel until the coming of Jesus—"by the mercies of God, to present your bodies as a living sacrifice." This is Paul's way of saying what Jesus says in the book of Mark. I appeal to you, therefore, brothers, to love God with all. That's what he's saying. "To present your bodies as a living sacrifice, holy and acceptable to God, which is your spiritual worship." Literally in Greek, it means, "This is your logical response."

Remember the Shema? Shema, Israel: The Lord our God, the Lord is one. And when you see God for who He really is, the one true God, then your logical response, the only natural response to that, is to love God with your all. All of your heart, all of your soul, all of your mind, and all of your strength. And so you say, "Okay, Paul. So how do we do that?" How are we to present our bodies as a living sacrifice, holy and acceptable to God, which is our spiritual worship? Paul answers, *Okay, there are two steps. Number one, do not be conformed to this world. And number two, be transformed.*

That's how you do it.

The word *conform* is a construction term. When you pour concrete, you first build a form because the concrete takes the form of what you built. If you want to make a heart, you build a wooden heart frame, pour concrete in it, and when it hardens, you've got a concrete heart. Right?

Paul is telling us not to be like the concrete—don't be conformed to the pattern of this world. From the day you were born until this very day, you have lived in a world that has a certain form to it, and it's trying very, very hard to mold you into that form. Paul comes along and says, "Don't do that." This means when you're talking about the way we do money, the way we do sex, the way we do generosity, the way we do family, the way we do forgiveness, the way we do friendships—for everything, there's the world's way and there is Jesus' way. Don't conform to the pattern of this world. That's step one.

Step two: *but be transformed.* That word is *metamorphoō.* This is total and radical and complete change from the inside out. You were a caterpillar; now you can be a butterfly. It's a change to the point that you're not even recognizable anymore.

It's not easy, so you might ask, "Well, Paul, how am I to not conform and be transformed?"

Paul's answer is simple: *by the renewal of your mind.* Now back to my question: How do you love the Lord your God with all your mind? Paul's answer is, *Do not be conformed to this world, but be transformed by the renewal of your mind* (v. 2).

I don't know if you've noticed, but when you surrender your life to Jesus, chances are about 100 percent that you'll still have struggles and temptations and sin. Why is that? When you surrender your life to Jesus, you get a brand-new heart. God reaches in, grabs that cold, dead, rock stone heart, rips it out, and gives you a new heart. One that is His with Jesus on the throne of it. The problem with each of us is that we still have the same mind. The same family influences. The same birth order. All the scars and insecurities. Your Enneagram number doesn't change. It's not like once you meet Jesus, everybody's a ten and you're perfect. That's not how it works. You still have the same worldview.

So what do we have to do? While our heart is changed when we surrender to the lordship of Christ, we spend the rest of our lives renewing our mind. The way you renew something is you take off the old and put on the new. Right? When my wife and daughter paint their toenails, they don't just keep stacking the polish on, layer upon layer. If they did, they'd have crazy-looking toes. They have to strip off the old before they put on the new. If you paint your car, you've first got to strip off the old, take it down to the metal, and then put on the new coat.

What Paul means here is that you have to strip off the old way of thinking that was conformed to the pattern of this world and you've got to renew your mind by putting on the new way of thinking. Which is standing on the truth of the Word of God. "That by testing you may discern what is the will of God, what is good and acceptable and perfect."

You want to know how to renew your mind with His Word? Go to Ephesians 6. Pentecostals love Ephesians 6. And I love it too. Paul says, "Finally, be strong in the Lord and in the strength of his might. Put on the whole armor of God, that you may be able to stand against the schemes of the devil." *Stand against* doesn't mean "stand up." It means "take a stand because the enemy is coming against you." It means "do not give ground." We call this "spiritual warfare." When the enemy comes against you, you stand your ground against the enemy so that you may be able to stand against the schemes of the devil.

This word *schemes* here is *methodeia*. Like the methods or methodologies of the enemy. *For we do not wrestle against flesh and blood.* You thought your problem was your boss, or your pride, or your ex, or your addiction. And the Bible would say, "That's not your problem." Your problem is not out there. Your problem is a spiritual problem.

But here's the thing. When we hear the word *battle*, or we think about warfare, most of us immediately go to a World War II mentality, thinking there are two kinds of equal and opposing forces, and it's the good guys versus the bad guys. And they meet on the battlefield, and the good guys eventually win. But the kinds of international fights against cells and sects that we have today are a lot more closely aligned with the spiritual warfare of Ephesians 6 than they are with the warfare of World War II, and here's why. Because spiritual warfare between the enemy and God is not like two equal, opposing forces that meet out on the battlefield. All throughout the New Testament, we find out that the determinative deathblow has already been dealt to the enemy, and he is but a shadow of his former self. Colossians says Jesus Christ took all of satan's accusations against us and nailed them to the cross and rendered him—satan—powerless in the spiritual realm. This means the battle is over. The serpent has been defanged. We won. Victory formation.

This is not to say the enemy doesn't have power. He does. And demons are real and they scheme and manifest, but while that power is real, all of it was given to the enemy by Jesus. Remember this. It is a lesser power. A defeated power.

Today, if somebody wants to attack America—al-Qaeda, ISIS, Russia, whatever, whoever—they can't just say, "I'll meet you on the battlefield," because we would just squash them. So the way we get attacked today is what is called dirty war. Guerilla war. Snipe and run. Did you know that there are bots in Russia that monitor your online activity and can measure what you're most afraid of? They know when to drop that tweet in your inbox to raise up fears or to fuel some misinformation. It's a misinformation campaign. Misinformation is the primary scheme or method and tactic of the enemy, too, because he can't meet us on the battlefield anymore.

Another word for misinformation is *lie*.

This is why Paul says, "Finally, be strong in the Lord and in the strength of his might. Put on the whole armor of God, that you may be able to stand against the schemes of the devil. For we do not wrestle against flesh and blood…"

The primary battle in the Christian walk is in the mind. Satan's scheme is primarily a misinformation campaign. Lies that exalt themselves against the knowledge of the truth.

If the primary battlefield is the mind, how do we fight back? How do we as children of God fight back against *the rulers, the authorities, the cosmic powers over this present darkness, and against the spiritual forces of evil in the heavenly places?*

The spiritual forces of evil are in a battle for everyone's mind right now. I call these whispers. Unexplainable whispers lodged in the back of your mind that try relentlessly to get you to believe your doubts and doubt your beliefs.

Remember that the enemy wants you to believe your doubts and doubt God's Word.

In contrast, God wants us to believe our beliefs and doubt our doubts. To help us out, Paul says, *Therefore take up the whole armor of God, that you may be able to withstand in the evil day, and having done all, to stand firm.* That's four times he's said to take a stand against this.

Look at the first piece of armor Paul mentions: "having fastened on the belt of truth." His Word. "And having put on the breastplate of righteousness." That's about identity, which we derive from His Word. "And, as shoes for your feet, having put on the readiness given by the gospel of peace." That's the life, death, and resurrection of Jesus—which we know by His Word. And "in all circumstances take up the shield of faith, with which you can extinguish all the flaming darts of the evil one." We get this faith through hearing His Word. "And take the helmet of salvation, and the sword of the Spirit, which is the word of God."

So what do you do when the enemy launches that dirty war campaign against your mind? Or they're trying to get you to conform to the pattern of this world? You stand firm. In the power of the Lord—which only comes through His Word. And you put on your identity in Christ—which we learn only in His Word. Everything Paul mentions in the armor of God is defensive except one weapon. The sword of the Spirit, which is the Word of God, is offensive.

In John 8:31–32, Jesus said to the Jews who believed in Him, "If you abide in my word, you are truly my disciples, and you will know the truth, and the truth will set you free." The reason I want you to love this Word is because there's freedom here. And only here. Where you and I have areas of our life that are in bondage, it is because we are not in line with and obedient to the truth of the Word of God.

His Word is the tool He has given us to set us free. This is the key to unlock the chains of the lies that have kept us bound up by the enemy. "You will know the truth, and the truth will set you free."

Where is His truth? In His Word. The psalmist says, *The entirety of Your word is truth.* That means every word.

If you drop down to John 8:44, you'll see that Jesus gets into an argument with a bunch of religious people. Religious people love to argue with the Lord. You ever notice that? Jesus doesn't flinch. He says, "You are of your father the devil, and your will is to do your father's desires. He was a murderer from the beginning, and does not stand in the truth, because there is no truth in him. When he lies, he speaks out of his own character, for he is a liar and the father of lies."

If you lay John 8 over Ephesians 6, you'll understand that the spiritual battles that we face are not on typical battlefields. The battle is a battle of the mind. The enemy wants to speak lies in our mind to conform us to the patterns of this world. The paths of this world lead to death and destruction and bondage.

But the paths of Jesus lead to truth and freedom. Let me ask you this: What would you do with freedom?

Think about that.

As Christians, we are commanded to love and accept the people of this world and reject the values and patterns of this world. Yet most of us reject the people of this world because they are not like us, and we accept the values and the patterns of this world. Totally backward.

In 1 John 2:15–16, John says, "Do not love the world or the things in the world. If anyone loves the world, the love of the Father is not in him. For all that is in the world—the desires of the flesh and the desires of the eyes and pride of life—is not from the Father but is from the world." I like to use the old King James here because it says, "The lust of the flesh, and the lust of the eyes, and the pride of life."

These are the three primary weapons—or lures or lies—that are used against us by our enemy: the lust of the flesh, the lust of the eyes, and the pride of life. These are THE only three temptations that exist on planet earth. There they are. The Bible says it. That's it.

The enemy is like a bass fisherman with three lures in his tackle box. He's got the lust of the flesh, the lust of the eyes, and the pride of life. So if you know that, if you know that's all he can throw at you, then when you are tempted, you can begin to know what category you're being tempted in. How you're being tempted and what is tempting you. Knowing and identifying your enemy helps you—by the power of God—overcome these things.

And when you do this, you are renewing your mind.

A good bass fisherman puts on a top water plug, throws that thing out there, and begins making what is fake look like it's real. He does this to lure the fish. This is why we call it a "lure." It's alluring. The thing about temptation is it's tempting. So he works that plug across the top, and it splashes and flashes right across the face of Big Billy Bass where Billy immediately spots it as a fake and he thinks, *I don't want that. I mean, that's loud, and it's noisy, and I can tell from here it's a big plastic thing with hooks hanging from it.*

But there it is. Every lure has a hook. Every lure has something you want. With every temptation there is a "gotcha."

The fisherman is not deterred, so he clips off that one, tucks it away for a later day, puts on a spinner bait, and drops it on Big Billy's nose. Big Billy laughs and thinks to himself, *Man, that stupid thing looks like a helicopter with a skirt on. I'm not even hungry for that.*

But a good fisherman knows sometimes you've got to change baits more than once. So, he clips that off, tucks it away, and ties on the bass bait of all bass baits. A purple plastic worm. He casts, reels, and that plastic worm jiggles and wiggles and Billy can't help himself. "Yes, got it." Chomp! And about the time the worm hits Billy's throat, the fisherman snatches the line. This is the lure of the enemy.

The lust of the flesh is a desire to feel. When we hear "lust of the flesh," we think sex, and that's part of it—an important part of it, because ultimately the problem in sex outside of marriage in any kind of fashion is the desire to feel a certain way. The lure and lie of the enemy is, "No, no. You deserve to feel this way." Because you don't like the way you currently feel with one person, you try feeling with another. Maybe that will satisfy your need to feel. The enemy lies to you and tells you that you deserve to feel a certain way, and then he lures you with what would feel good. Which is always outside the design and will of God.

The lust of the eyes is the deep desire to have something you don't currently have. Something you didn't know you needed until you saw it. The lust of the eyes says, "That possession will satisfy me." What's it look like? If you're bored at home, think, *I wonder what's on Amazon right now,* and you start clicking buttons, and you think, *Oh, I've got to have that,* you've just been duped by the lust of the eyes. It happens to all of us. I'm as bad as anyone. Is stuff bad? No. Unless you put your hope in it, and then it'll kill you.

The pride of life is a deep desire to be something. It's about power, position. About comparison, ego, and insecurity. About the applause of man over the applause of God. The pride of life is that deep desire to prove all the haters wrong and make something impressive out of yourself regardless of who you have to walk over to get there. The pride of life is about retweets and thumbs-ups and likes. It's about craving a blue check mark next to your name.

Lust of the flesh: sex, passion, feeling.

Lust of the eyes: stuff, possession, having.

Pride of life: status, position, being.

These three are all the enemy has to offer, *all that is in the world.* Our problem is he really doesn't need more because he's wearing us out with just these three. Why change what's working?

Here's why this is important. The Bible says that *the devil prowls around like a roaring lion, seeking someone to devour.* Now, you might read that verse and go, "Yeah, whatever. Okay," but it's more true than your front teeth. If a real lion were prowling around trying to get you, and I told you, "Hey listen, man, the zoo called. A lion got loose. He's after you. He's in the garage," would you walk to your car a little different?

You'd open the garage door and holler for help. "Yo, anybody seen a lion? Anybody heard a lion?" What if you knew that a lion was coming after you, but you knew he could only come after you three ways: he's either going to jump off the top of the building, spring from the back seat, or be waiting in the trunk? When you walked up to your car, you'd know where to look.

Knowing where to look helps you stand against the methods or the schemes of your enemy. And if you know how the enemy is going to attack you, then don't you clearly have the advantage?

Now, go all the way back to Genesis 3. I want to show you how this principle is all throughout the Bible. This has been the enemy's tactic from the beginning. In chapter 2, God is creating everything. He breathes the *ruach* of life into Adam, and Adam becomes a living being. When he opens his eyes, he's face-to-face with God. God looks at him and says, This is very good. And then God says the first thing that is not good in the world— it's not good for man to be alone. So He puts Adam to sleep and gives him a wife and He tells him, *Don't eat from that tree, but you can eat from every other tree, so enjoy, be fruitful, and multiply.* Praise God. Adam and Eve are just hanging out, naked and unashamed.

And in that context, here comes the enemy, in Genesis 3:1. "Now the serpent," who is the enemy, "was more crafty"—this means conniving; it means he's a twister—"than any other beast of the field that the LORD God had made. He said to the woman"—don't miss this—" 'Did God actually say…?' "

This is how every temptation begins. "Did God actually say…?" And whenever you hear this, the lie is not far behind. Jesus said when he, the enemy, is lying, he is speaking his native tongue. And notice what the serpent did. He showed his hand. The enemy always wants you to doubt at least three things. The enemy wants you to doubt (1) the Word of God, (2) the work of God, and (3) the worthiness of God.

Think about it. When the whispers start coming, he always says, "Can you really trust the Word of God? I know the Bible says that, but that's not what it meant. I mean, come on. What did Paul really know about dating and marriage? He wasn't even married. And what did he know about suing people? I mean, come on, give me a break. Did God really say He wants us to…?" Fill in the blank.

The enemy is hell-bent on us questioning the Word of God, and he wants us to question the work of God. He whispers, "When Jesus died on the cross, do you think that really counted for you?" Or this is one of his favorites: "If you really loved Him, you'd quit sinning all the time. You're not even a Christian." The enemy wants you to doubt that when Jesus said, *"It is finished,"* that His finishing work counted for everybody else—just not you.

Lastly, the enemy wants you to doubt the worthiness of God. It sounds something like this: "If God really loved you, don't you think He'd take better care of you? He is not worth your worship because He's not treating you very well right now."

This is what the enemy does.

"Did God actually say, 'You shall not eat of any tree in the garden'?" And the woman said to the serpent, "We may eat of the fruit of the trees in the garden, but God said, 'You shall not eat of the fruit of the tree that is in the midst of the garden, neither shall you touch it, lest you die.'"

Note that God never actually said the *touch it* part. This is classic legalism. Adding your own extra clause to God's command.

At this point in human history, the Word of God is very limited. There are only a few commandments. There's not even, like, a whole book. It could all have been written on a three-by-five card: be fruitful, multiply, cultivate, stay away from that tree. Got it? That's it. All of the Word of God.

"But the serpent said to the woman, 'You will not surely die.'" *And here comes the lie:* "For God knows that when you eat of it your eyes will be opened, and you will be like God, knowing good and evil." If you unpack this, here's the lie—you can't trust God. You've got this. You know better.

What's this sound like in our lives? Well, the Bible teaches that sex is for married people. One man and one woman. It is not for "going to be married," or "married in your heart." Both are counterfeits. They're lies. But we do it anyway because we think, *Nah, I got this. You see, God? I know how to do life better than You know how to do life.*

Take finances. The Bible is pretty clear about what we are to do with our finances. There are only three things we can do with our money. We can spend it, give it, and leave it if you've saved it, because you can't take it with you.

That's all you can do with it.

God knows you need it, so He commands you to give a portion back to Him. We are to bring our first and best back to God because God is first, God loves first, and God went first. What we do with our money reflects what's most important in our hearts. Therefore we, by faith, gladly bring to God our first and best because God first loved us by giving us His best in Jesus Christ. Then enjoy the rest like crazy and be a multigenerational blessing to your kids, and their kids, and their kids, etc. But we think we know better, so we look at it like, *God, forget that. No, no, no, no, no. I'm getting credit card points, and that's way better. I'm going to buy stuff that I can't afford and go into debt. Why? Because I want it.* But when we're leveraged and in credit card debt up to our eyeballs, we can't respond when God calls us to be generous, because we're still paying for stuff we finished using two years ago.

What Eve saw was that the tree was good for food. That's lust of the flesh. She looked at that, and she thought, *Oh, this will satisfy me. This is about my appetite. I deserve this.* Then the Word says, *It was a delight to the eyes.* This is the lust of the eyes. Eve thought, *I didn't even know I wanted this until I saw it.* Then it reads, *And that the tree was to be desired to make one wise.* This is the last one, the pride of life.

Do you see this?

From the Garden of Eden, the enemy has never changed his tactics. Because all he's got in the world are these three things, these three lies: the lust of the flesh, the lust of the eyes, and the pride of life. They were there in the beginning. They're here now. So Eve took of the fruit and ate it and she gave some to her husband who was with her.

Huh? He was standing there the whole time?

I want to ask him, "Adam, you were silent! Why? What happened to defending the garden?" How different the world would be if Eve had told the serpent, "I never speak to strange snakes without my husband," and, more important, if Adam had defended the garden.

Notice we're not even to the temptation on the mountain yet. Everything I've written to this point is setup. I know I started by describing a steep path and a cable car and you keep waiting for me to get back to it, but I'm laying the groundwork—and trust me, the payoff is worth it. For now, focus on this: We have an enemy. He can't meet us on the battlefield. Can't go toe-to-toe. Because the deathblow has been struck against him. *Tetelestai*—"It is finished." And he has no defense against the truth. So, he attacks us with a dirty war campaign, a misinformation campaign. He sells us lies, wanting us to buy into the lies of this world and be conformed to the pattern of this world.

The lust of the flesh, the lust of the eyes, and the pride of life.

And he's been at it over and over and over in our lives since the beginning of human history. So what do you do when temptation comes your way? What do you do when the whispers start coming your way?

This is the question.

Paul says, step one: don't be conformed to the lies. Step two: be transformed by God's truth.

How did Jesus answer temptation?

Matthew 4:1: "Then Jesus was led up by the Spirit into the wilderness to be tempted by the devil." Let that rattle around for a minute. Maybe this is why in the Lord's Prayer, Jesus says, *Lead us not into temptation,* because He did once, and it wasn't awesome. And don't forget, this came right on the heels of His baptism. So pay close attention in your life. Often the enemy comes on strongest in the valley at the base of the last mountain.

Verse 2: "And after fasting forty days and forty nights, he was hungry." You think? Verse 3: "And the tempter came and said to him, 'If you are the Son of God...'" Stop there. Look where he starts. Identity. The enemy wants Him to question God. Same tactic he used in the garden. "If you are the Son of God."

The enemy always comes at you with condemnation because of your past, because of your desires, because of something you struggle with. All of which is rooted in your identity. The implication is "You really think you're a Christian? A son of God? No, no, no. You're condemned. Unfit for use." He always starts there. He starts there with me and he starts there with you.

"If you are the Son of God, command these stones to become loaves of bread." You think Jesus is hungry? He hasn't eaten in forty days. You think satan knows this? Of course. Satan is like the original social media analytics bot. He is watching your every move. You think he's going to start there? Absolutely. The unspoken implication is this: "You have the ability to meet your own needs with the resources that God has given you, and you should use that for yourself. Because you deserve it."

You know what that's called? Lust of the flesh.

Don't miss this—the Bible says that Jesus was tempted. This means that Jesus must have, in some way and to some extent, wanted to do this. Even just a little. Here's the thing about temptation—it's tempting. If it ain't tempting, it ain't temptation. Case in point: A friend gave me a hundred-dollar gift card to KUIU. KUIU makes hunting clothes. Some of the best on the planet. I think I'm going to start preaching in it. So I get online with my hundred dollars in hand. By the time I checked out, I'd spent over five hundred. Why? Because I was tempted and gave in to temptation. Can I get a witness? And KUIU...maybe a sponsorship?

Jesus is hungry. The humanity of the Son of God is fully present in this moment. He has the ability and the God-given resources at His disposal. To use at will. But is that use outside the will of God? Here's what I mean. You get home from work, and you're like, "I need a drink." Is a drink a sin? No. Of course not. Unless it's fruit in beer, which is definitely a sin. But that's another sermon. Jesus can fix His own problem, and in the same way, you could numb yours. The question is this: Is our response in or out of the will of God?

Here's the problem. When you begin to go, "I deserve to feel this way." Or, "I'm entitled." So, we go well beyond what is okay. Look, I'm into freedom and grace, but is grace still grace if we use it as a license to sin? It's lust of the flesh. Maybe you don't drink but you go to food for comfort, and you just can't stop. Is food bad? No way. It is supposed to be a tool in our life not only for our health but also to stir in us worship for the Giver of all good things. But when you look to food for your comfort and you won't stop, you're being tempted by, and giving in to, the lust of the flesh.

Or you begin to tell yourself that pornography is actually a good idea for your marriage because your wife won't give you what you want. And then you ramp it up, telling yourself that at least you aren't with somebody else. You tell yourself, "No, no, I deserve this. I'm faithful. I'm not touching anybody."

You do realize that is actually another human you're looking at? Not to mention that the Bible says as a man thinks in his heart, so is he.

This is lust of the flesh.

Take note, because Jesus is about to answer satan. He says, "It is written." This is it. Jesus answers with what Paul will call in Ephesians 6 "the sword of the Spirit." He goes on the offensive against the devil, and He says, "It is written." Look at what He says: "Man shall not live by bread alone, but by every word that comes from the mouth of God."

See that *every word*? It matters.

In John 4, Jesus sends the disciples to get something to eat. When they come back, they find Him talking to the Samaritan woman, and when they ask Him if He's hungry, He says, "I have food to eat that you do not know about." They're confused, so they ask each other, "Has anyone brought him something to eat?" Jesus answers them, "My food is to do the will of him who sent me and to accomplish his work" (vv. 31–34).

Jesus is saying to His disciples, "I've got spiritual food you don't even know about. My Father in heaven fills me up in a way I can't even explain to you." Don't miss the "It is written."

Verse 5: "Then the devil took him to the holy city"—that'd be Jerusalem—"and set him on the pinnacle of the temple and said to him, 'If you are the Son of God…'" See where he went? Straight back to identity. Which means the attack is relentless. Then he says this: "Throw yourself down, for it is written…" Check this out. The devil quoted Scripture.

Don't forget that the devil's been around a minute and he can read. He knows the book too. This is why you have to not just know about Scripture but actually know the Word. This is why Jesus would look at the Pharisees, who had memorized what we call the Old Testament, and He'd say to them, *You don't even know the Word. If you did, you'd live it, and if you did, then surely you would know Me.* Their problem was that while they'd memorized, they weren't living it. Point being, there's a difference between knowing about it and knowing it.

The devil says, "If you are the Son of God, throw yourself down, for it is written, 'He will command his angels concerning you,' and 'On their hands they will bear you up, lest you strike your foot against a stone.'" This is the pride of life. He's tempting Jesus to show the entire world what a big deal He is. Problem is, Jesus is not, and never has been, into self-promotion. *He did not think equality with God something to be grasped.*

Essentially, the devil is saying, *Jesus, let's just skip to the end, because we both know that God sent You into the world so that everyone would worship You.* Fact is, he's half-right. Yes, God sent Him, but He did not send Jesus to gain our worship by showing off, but by humbling Himself and going to the cross.

Sometimes we think—through perverted logic—that the end justifies the means. That if the end goal is good, then we can do whatever it takes to achieve that end. Our problem is that the life and words of Jesus would disagree with this. God will not bless perverse or sinful means. No matter the end. This temptation is the pride of life: to make much of yourself. Jesus said He came to serve and not to be served, but to give His life as a ransom for many. To this temptation, Jesus says, "Again it is written." Notice how Jesus responds. A second time, He responds with the truth of the Word of God. "You shall not put the Lord your God to the test." Jesus is saying, "I don't have to make much of Myself. I obey My Father and trust Him with the results." Jesus rejects satan's offer and does not conform to the pattern of this world but chooses rather to stand on the truth of the Word of God.

Temptation number three. You want to guess what part of us this will tempt? "Again, the devil took him to a very high mountain and showed him all the kingdoms of the world and their glory." Look closely and there's a clue. The devil tips his hand: "All these I will give you, if you will fall down and worship me." This is textbook lust of the eyes. What's crazy is that all that satan is offering will one day be Jesus'. He will return to rule and reign over it all. Satan is offering a shortcut absent the cross. He's tempting Jesus with this unspoken message—*What if I give you that without suffering and dying?* But there's a catch. *If you'll just fall down and worship me.* And Jesus said to him, "Be gone, Satan! For it is written…"

Three temptations. Three responses. And in all three, Jesus responds to the lie of the enemy with the truths of the Word of God.

"'You shall worship the Lord your God and him only shall you serve.' Then the devil left him, and behold, angels came and were ministering to him."

Do you see a pattern? If it worked for Jesus, do you believe it will work for us?

Let me come closer to home: Do you have *it-is-written*s in your life? This is why I started with the question "Have you ever tried to make someone you love, love what you love?" I love the Word and I want you to love it. I know it's a big book, and I know it can be hard to understand sometimes, but the Bible promises—Jesus promises—that the Spirit of God, the Holy Spirit Himself, will teach you all the things that you need to know when you need to know them. And you can trust Him with that.

God has given us His Word, the Bible, not to defeat the devil but to remind us that the devil has already been defeated, and we are standing on that victory. That we are not fighting for victory, but from it, and because we are fighting from victory, we can stand on the truth of that victory.

If you want to stand in victory against the enemy—the victory that Jesus has already secured for us—then stand on the truth and don't waffle on the lies. You decide. Either you will be conformed to these lies, to the patterns of the world, or you will be transformed by the renewing of your mind. Which means you have to identify the lies that we buy into and say, "I am not condemned.

I am not unfit for use. I am a child of God even when I don't feel like it." Stand on the truth that *there is therefore now no condemnation for those who are in Christ Jesus.* And if you don't believe it yet, just quote it and claim it again. *There is therefore now no condemnation for those who are in Christ Jesus.* Do it over, and over, and over. Eventually your feelings will fall in line with God's truth.

Here's another lie: You wake up every day in a world that lies to you, in billboard after billboard, commercial after commercial, and magazine cover after magazine cover. The world says if you're not beautiful, then you're not lovable. And the description of beauty they show is not even a reality. It's more like a cartoon character. Instead, stare back and stand on the truth of Psalm 139:14: *I am fearfully and wonderfully made. Fearfully* means "reverently." It means God made you on purpose. Each freckle. Each wrinkle. To the Creator of the universe, you're His masterpiece.

Every night when I put Reagan Capri, my eleven-year-old daughter, to bed, I pray this over her. You know why? Because she lives in a world that will always lie to her, and when it does, I want to anchor the truth of God so deep in her soul that when this world lies to her, she sniffs it out and realizes, "Nah, that ain't true. That ain't true."

God knit you together in your mother's womb. Slowly and purposefully. He took His time. So, memorize Ephesians 2:10: *you are God's workmanship.* The Greek word for *workmanship* is *poiēma.* From this we get *poem.* The word means a "woven fabric." You ever seen someone weave? It takes time. And nothing about it is haphazard. Meaning, you're not a mistake.

In my case, I can get caught up in what everybody else thinks about me. Why is that? Why does the approval of man and the applause of men play such a big role in my life? In response, I ask myself Galatians 1:10: Am I seeking to please God or man? That question alone identifies the lie and reshapes everything.

Here's another: my past somehow defines my future. That's a lie from the pit of hell. Actually, all lies are from the pit of hell. So, I tell the enemy, "There is therefore now no condemnation for those who are in Christ Jesus."

Which begs the question—are you IN Christ Jesus?

The lie of pride tells you, *I should be treated this way.* But Paul told the Galatians, *I have been crucified with Christ. It is no longer I who live* (Gal. 2:20). Do crucified people have rights? When I chose to follow Jesus, I laid down those rights. Do you understand? How about when we begin to think a little too highly of ourselves? We might need to reflect on Galatians 6:14: "Far be it from me to boast except in the cross of our Lord Jesus Christ, by which the world has been crucified to me, and I to the world."

This is a decision to take off the old and put on the new.

Maybe your problem isn't pride but self-deprecation. Thinking too little of yourself. That you're worthless. You need 1 Corinthians 6:19–20: "Do you not know that your body is a temple of the Holy Spirit within you, whom you have from God? You are not your own, for you were bought with a price. So glorify God in your body."

You want the Joby version? *Because of what Christ did for me, I'm a pretty big deal. I'm a child of God.* Notice my identity is in what He did. Not in what I did.

Maybe nothing lies to us more than our money. Our money says, "I'll take care of you. I'll make you happy. I'll keep you safe. I'll make you important." All lies. Money can do none of those things. Only God can. Money is a good tool and a terrible god. Paul told Timothy, "As for the rich in this present age, charge them not to be haughty" (1 Tim. 6:17). God alone has the power to care for us, give us joy, keep us safe, and cause us to know our own importance—because of Him.

If you're only digging into the Word of God for an hour once a week, it won't stick. You'll be a baby forever. A big, fat, diaper-wearing, umbilical cord–swinging, crying, sloppy, milk-drinking, half-worthless baby. At some point, you've got to eat solid food. The writer of Hebrews says this: "For everyone who lives on milk is unskilled in the word of righteousness, since he is a child. But solid food is for the mature, for those who have their powers of discernment trained by constant practice to distinguish good from evil" (5:13–14).

I dare you to do this. Write it down. Identify the lie, then write down God's truth that counters it. Write it on a three-by-five card and tape it to your bathroom mirror or dashboard where you can constantly stand firm against the schemes of the lying enemy and not be conformed to the pattern of this world but be transformed by the renewing of your mind. And if you don't know where to look in the Bible, then use this amazing miracle tool God has provided for His children: Google.

All the enemy can tempt us with is lust of the flesh, lust of the eyes, and pride of life. Everything we need is found in Him and Him alone. You want to feel something? *Come to me all those who are weary and heavy burdened, and I will give you rest for your soul.*

You want to feel better? Jesus offers rest for the soul. He offers peace that transcends understanding and circumstance. He offers the secret of contentment no matter what. Jesus is the fulfillment of the lust of the flesh.

You want some stuff? How about an everlasting inheritance that no rust can ruin and no thief can steal and no moth can eat?

Jesus is the fulfillment of the lust of the eyes.

You want to be a big deal? Put your trust in Jesus, and not only will you be more than a conqueror, but you become a child of God, a coheir with Christ. Your Dad is the King of the universe.

Jesus is the fulfillment of the pride of life.

God has given us His Word not to defeat the enemy, but to remind us that he is already defeated. And we can stand on His promises. God's Word is not only true, it is trustworthy. You can stake your life on its claims. Paul told the Ephesians, "Finally, be strong in the Lord and in the strength of his might" (6:10). Where do you get that might? His Word.

Let me end with this—Paul told the Corinthians, "For the weapons of our warfare are not of the flesh but have divine power to destroy strongholds. We destroy arguments and every lofty opinion raised against the knowledge of God, and take every thought captive to obey Christ" (2 Cor. 10:4–5). Another translation says, *Every argument that exalts itself against the knowledge of God.* These strongholds and lofty opinions exist in the mind and they are fed by lies of the enemy. How do we tear them down? The grappling hooks of the truth of God.

On the Mount of Temptation, satan tempted Jesus by twisting Scripture. He used the same "Did God actually say…?" lie he used in the garden. In response, Jesus countered every temptation with the written Word of God. If God's Word is good enough for Jesus when He fought the devil, is it good enough for you? With what weapon will you fight the enemy?

Pray with Me

Our good and gracious heavenly Father, I thank You for Your Word. What a gift. Thank You that You would reveal Yourself and Your heart for humanity through the Bible. Thank You that not only did You carry men along by Your Spirit to write it, but You also assembled it and protected it through the ages, that we might hold in our hands the very Word of God. Thank You that we live in a time and place that we have such unfettered access to Your Word. God, we often take it for granted. Forgive us when we neglect time in Your Word. God, I pray that as we abide in You, we would abide in Your Word. I pray against the enemy and his evil schemes. I pray that You would protect every believer from the lies of the enemy. I pray that we would be so rooted in the truth of the Word of God that we would immediately be able to discern the lies and lures of this world. I pray that whenever Your children hear the whispers of condemnation and fear, they would recognize that it is not You. That is not the language of the Father. Lord, I pray that we would be people that hide Your Word in our hearts that we might not sin against You. I pray that You would stir in us an affection for Your Word and that we would love it and meditate upon it day and night. I pray that we would not only believe in You but that we would also believe You. Your promises are trustworthy and true. Lord, I pray that as we renew our mind with Your truth that at just the right times and in just the right circumstances, Holy Spirit, You would bring to our hearts and minds Your perfect Word. We pray this in the good, strong name of Jesus Christ our Lord and Savior. Amen.

CHAPTER 6

Mount of Transfiguration—Will You Cast Out the Demons That Torment You?

"After six days Jesus took with him Peter and James, and John his brother, and led them up a high mountain by themselves. And he was transfigured before them, and his face shone like the sun, and his clothes became white as light. And behold, there appeared to them Moses and Elijah, talking with him. And Peter said to Jesus, 'Lord, it is good that we are here. If you wish, I will make three tents here, one for you and one for Moses and one for Elijah.' He was still speaking when, behold, a bright cloud overshadowed them, and a voice from the cloud said, 'This is my beloved Son, with whom I am well pleased; listen to him.' When the disciples heard this, they fell on their faces and were terrified. But Jesus came and touched them, saying, 'Rise, and have no fear.' And when they lifted up their eyes, they saw no one but Jesus only."

Matthew 17:1–8

Matthew 17 and Mark 9 describe Jesus' transfiguration from two different perspectives. Both start on the mountain and end in the valley. Matthew's account says, "After six days Jesus took with him Peter and James, and John." As we discussed earlier, Matthew is a Jewish man writing to a Jewish audience, and from the beginning, he wants his audience to understand that Jesus is the greater Moses—doing what Moses did, only greater.

Let me circle back around to Moses on Sinai:

> *"The LORD said to Moses, 'Come up to me on the mountain and wait there, that I may give you the tablets of stone, with the law and the commandment, which I have written for their instruction.' So Moses rose with his assistant Joshua, and Moses went up into the mountain of God. And he said to the elders, 'Wait here for us until we return to you. And behold, Aaron and Hur are with you. Whoever has a dispute, let him go to them.'*
>
> *Then Moses went up on the mountain, and the cloud covered the mountain. The glory of the LORD dwelt on Mount Sinai, and the cloud covered it six days. And on the seventh day he called to Moses out of the midst of the cloud. Now the appearance of the glory of the LORD was like a devouring fire on the top of the mountain in the sight of the people of Israel."* (Exodus 24:12–17)

When God told Moses, *I'm going to meet with you on a mountain,* how long did God make Moses wait on Him?

Six days.

Matthew is doing this on purpose. He's equating Jesus with God in Exodus 24. Jesus is God.

Jesus takes with him Peter, James, and John. Some of you look at this and you say, "Well, that's not fair. Jesus always picks Peter, James, and John to do the cool stuff." Those three witness Jesus raising Jairus' daughter back to life after He healed the woman with the issue of blood. And in the Garden of Gethsemane, Jesus tells the other disciples, *Hey, y'all stay right here and pray, except for you three. Peter, James, and John…you come with Me.* I know that some of you are like, "Well, that's not fair. What about the rest of them?" I mean, there are twelve of them, right? You could break them into groups of four and run a three-team rotation. Maybe even a March Madness bracket. Well, you should write this down, especially if you're a millennial or younger: fairness is not a biblical value. God does what He wants, with whom He wants, when He wants. Why? Because He's the sovereign King of the universe. That reality should comfort you more than it ruffles you, because He is good.

Theologians talk about why He continues to use this little inner circle of three. Even here, He led them up on a high mountain by themselves. The other nine were at the base of the mountain. Why only three? Why'd they get to go? Many people will say, "Well, those were His favorites. Those were the ones that He loved the most. They were the earliest disciples; they displayed the most faith."

I disagree.

I know some of you will say, "No, no, no, no. The Bible says that John is the one that Jesus loves." Yes. That's true. As written by John in the book of John. I firmly believe that the Word of God is inerrant and infallible, but you don't get to give yourself your own nickname. Man code prevents it. I'm sure when they all got to heaven, Doubting Thomas was like, "I got the short end of the stick on this one."

I pastored for fifteen years in student ministry, and here's what I believe is happening. Jesus is like, *All right. You boys stay here by the campfire and write worship songs or whatever you're going to do. I've got some work to do with the Father. I'm going up on the mountain in My glory. It's going to be kind of awesome. You guys stay here.* And I think Peter, James, and John were like, *Sweet.* They had some M-80s from Tijuana or something. But the smirk on their faces convinces Jesus He'd better not leave them alone. *Hold on. I don't trust you three alone. Peter, James, and John, get in the truck.*

Here's why I say this: Peter is going to screw up in this chapter. Not to mention that in the previous chapter, Jesus called Peter "satan." And in Matthew 20, after Jesus casts out a demon, declares the gospel, and transfigures Himself, James and John are going to convince their mom to go to Jesus to try to make them senior VP over Israel. They ignore the gospel and make a power play. And use their mom, of all people.

These are the biggest screwups of the bunch. Jesus knew He couldn't leave them alone.

Which is good news for all of us. God can and does use cracker-jacks and messed-up disciples—like this redneck from Dillon, South Carolina—to change the world. There is hope for us all.

Jesus and the three walk up the mountain and in verse 2, "he was transfigured before them." I don't even know exactly what all this means. *Transfigured* is a metaphysical term meaning that although He was still recognizable, something happened that made Him almost unrecognizable. My friend Chris Brown—not the recording artist—is a pastor in San Diego at North Coast Church. He says this about the transfiguration: "His divinity is bursting forth through his humanity...the miracle is not that Jesus was transfigured on the mountain, and the miracle is not that Peter, James, and John could see His glory. The real miracle is that His divinity was shrouded in humanity for 33 years." The real miracle here is that Jesus walked among us and the Word became flesh and people could hang out with Him. Here on the Mount of Transfiguration, God is pressing Pause on the miracles and allowing His divinity to burst forth.

"And he was transfigured before them, and his face shone like the sun, and his clothes became white as light." Strange, isn't it? Matthew is searching for language to try to describe what is happening on the mountain. Luke describes it this way: "And as he was praying, the appearance of his face was altered, and his clothing became dazzling white" (9:29). Mark is always the most direct and to the point. Mark says it this way: "His clothes became radiant, intensely white, as no one on earth could bleach them" (9:3).

Kind of understated, don't you think?

I wish I could have heard the conversation in heaven when Matthew and Mark and Luke compared notes. One of them asks, "Hey, dude. You remember the transfiguration?"

Matthew says, "I was trying to think of the brightest, most amazing thing I could in all of the solar system. So I just imagined the sun inside Jesus and sunbeams are bursting forth through His face. What about you, Luke?"

"To me, it was like walking along at night and your eyes are adjusted to the darkness and then out of nowhere, boom, a big clap of thunder and bright lightning so you can hardly see. Mark?"

"Um...Clorox."

Look at all three accounts—something amazing is going on. And of the three, Matthew is on to something. Back up one chapter into Matthew 16. Jesus has just affirmed Peter's declaration that Jesus is the Christ, the Son of the living God. Then Jesus lays out the gospel: *I'm going to be handed over to the scribes, to the chief priests, and to the Pharisees. I'm going to be crucified, dead, and buried. And on the third day, I will be resurrected.* The white clothes matter because on the day of the resurrection, when the disciples show up, they see angels dressed in white robes. And those robes are brighter than lightning.

John and Jesus were fishing buddies. They camped together for three years and John reclined against Jesus' bosom on the night of the Last Supper. But when John sees Jesus in His glory, as recorded in Revelation, he does not walk up and give Him a man hug and say, "What's up, bro? You're my homeboy."

Hardly.

He falls down on his face as though dead. Jesus declared the gospel in Matthew 16 and is now demonstrating the gospel in Matthew 17. In a sense, He is saying, *My story does not end at the cross. It goes all the way to My resurrection, to glory, to the Father, and to My return.*

From bleached and lightning-tinted clothes, Scripture records, *There appeared to them Moses and Elijah, talking with him.* As twenty-first-century evangelicals, when we read that Moses and Elijah appear on the mountain, we just stare off into the distance. We think, *That's neat. I've heard of those guys.* These are details that don't really strike us as all that important. But if you were a first-century Jewish boy or girl, the moment you read or heard that Moses and Elijah showed up on the mountain, you'd start listening. Intently. You would be overwhelmed with anticipation. Moses and Elijah are the two primary superheroes in the old covenant. By the time of Jesus, Moses has been dead for fourteen hundred years, and Elijah—who didn't die but was taken up into heaven—has been gone from planet earth for nine hundred. But now, they've shown up and they're talking to Jesus.

A few steps away, these three Jewish boys, Peter, James, and John, are staring at this and they are blown away.

Here's why.

Moses represents the law and Elijah represents the prophets. In fact, standing there on the mountain are the law and the prophets bearing witness to the Messiah, to the gospel. This thing that's happening, this "transfiguration," is the personification of the very Scriptures happening on the Mount of Transfiguration. This should blow your hair back. Paul will later talk about it in Romans 3. After he says, *No one will declare themselves righteous by works of the law,* he goes on to say, *But the Law and the Prophets bear witness to a righteousness manifested apart from the Law.* This manifestation is what is happening on the Mount of Transfiguration. The law and the prophets are bearing witness to Jesus, who would fulfill every law in the Scriptures and fulfill every prophecy in the Scriptures.

Amazingly, the three have a conversation. They're talking and Luke tells us what they're talking about. It's Jesus' return. Look at this through the eyes of Peter: There's Jesus. Transfigured. Sunbeam-faced. He's talking to a guy with a staff and a beard and two stone tablets. Peter looks closely and says, pointing, "I think that's Moses." And then another guy shows up with a staff and a beard and his name tag reads ELIJAH. Peter, James, and John are dumbfounded. *Are you serious?* They are watching the law and the prophets bearing witness to the righteousness manifested apart from the law and the prophets.

This is a really big deal.

Peter, who's never one to miss a chance to speak, leans into the huddle and says to Jesus, "It is good that we are here." My thought is this—if you ever find yourself in a place where you see the glorified Christ and Moses and Elijah discussing the gospel among themselves, maybe it's not about you. Maybe that is not the time for you to just speak up and say something. Maybe you should just be still.

I think in that moment that Jesus and Moses and Elijah look at Peter and think, *Are you even being serious right now?* To which Peter—again, never one to miss an opportunity to open his mouth—says, *If you wish, I can make three tents here. One for you, one for Eli, and one for Mo.* In fact, Mark records it this way: "And Peter said to Jesus, 'Rabbi, it is good that we are here. Let us make three tents, one for you and one for Moses and one for Elijah.' For he did not know what to say, for they were terrified."

Note to self—when you do not know what to say, don't. It's

better to sit quietly and let everyone assume you don't know what you are talking about instead of opening your mouth and removing all doubt. Listen, Christians are notorious for saying the dumbest stuff at the worst times. When you don't know what to say, just don't. And if you ever find yourself qualifying what you have said with the phrase, "I'm just saying," then you probably shouldn't. That's how it goes.

There are a couple of reasons I think Peter's out of line. One, it's not about him. What could he possibly add to this moment? Why in the world is he bringing up anything? Maybe he's trying to put Jesus on the same level as Moses and Elijah, but they're not. These three are not roommates. Not equals. Jesus is God. The Second Person of the Trinity. The Son of God. He was in the beginning, all things were created by Him, for Him, through Him, and to Him. Moses (the law) and Elijah (the prophets) are attesting to Jesus' divinity.

I don't mean to suggest that Peter isn't well-intentioned. He is. He's just missing the point. Entirely. But his heart is good. He's thinking to himself, *We have arrived. It doesn't get any better than this. I mean, the very presence of the glorified Jesus? Why don't we just stay here forever and ever and ever? Forget the rest of those guys down there at the bottom of the mountain. I don't know what they're doing. But maybe, when they're dead, they can come join us.*

Have you ever had that kind of worship experience where you felt the manifest presence of God in an emotive way that's almost hard to put into words? Maybe on a mission trip? Maybe alone in the Scriptures? For me, it often happens at our Sunday-morning gatherings. And, if I'm honest, I am addicted to that feeling. Like many churches, God has blessed us with amazing worship pastors and leaders. Their songs lift us up to the very feet of Jesus. That's what they do. Sometimes when I'm just singing or praying with my eyes closed, I have this strange impression that if I were to open my eyes at that second, I'd be staring into the very face of God.

You ever been there?

Sometimes I just wish I had a cot and I could park it right there. Like Samuel in the temple. Sleeping in His presence. Reacting like Peter: "It is good that we are here." And Jesus loves it, too, but our problem is we want to just stay there. Forever. And while that is the eternal cry of our hearts, and one day we will stay in His presence forever, that moment is not yet. Even after He was transfigured, Jesus walked down the mountain.

Why?

Because we were at the bottom of the mountain. And there was work yet to be done. *For the joy set before Him* He didn't stay up there in the tent.

One of my good friends is a worship pastor. One of the most incredible and anointed voices I've ever heard. His name is Michael Olson. He used to travel with Michael W. Smith. Early in our friendship, he asked me, "What's more important—the mission of God or the glory of God?" He asked because he's worked in other churches and he often experienced this tension where he felt they put the glory of God on the back burner for the sake of the mission of God. He was wanting to make sure we don't do that. Why? My response was simple. "Brother, the mission of God...is the glory of God."

These are not to be divided.

In Peter's mind, he's wanting to mark the moment. But look at what he's doing. Verse 5 reads, "He was still speaking when, behold, a bright cloud overshadowed them." What's he saying that's so important? I imagined it sounded something like, *Well, Sir, no, seriously, I can make tents. Cool ones. With a canopy. Multiple colors...* He just won't stop. But then the cloud appears and a voice from the cloud says, "This is my beloved Son, with whom I am well pleased."

Look back to Jesus' baptism. Who showed up? The Father. What'd He say? "This is my beloved Son. Listen to Him." That's Hebrew for "Shut up and quit talking." Which, by the way, it's really hard to listen, especially to God, when you're doing all the talking. It's almost impossible to simultaneously talk and listen. Peter's just running off at the mouth. Maybe it's time to shut up and listen. I can't tell you how many times I've been with people in groups and we say, "Hey, man. We need direction. We need a word from the Lord. We need to pray." And then we pray and we do all the talking and zero listening. Maybe a significant part of our prayer life should be listening to what God has to say to you instead of informing Him about the circumstances that you find yourself in. How dumb are we when we pray? "Dear God, I just want to pray about the situation; not sure if You know about it, but here's what's happening in the stock market right now."

I'm pretty sure Jesus knows. Maybe if we quit talking the whole time, He would tell us what we should do and how we should respond.

Maybe we should listen more than we speak when we pray.

When Peter, James, and John heard this, they fell on their faces. Afraid. You know why? Because they grew up studying the Torah—the first five books of the Bible. They had memorized them—word for word. So they knew the Scriptures inside and out. One of the most significant events in all of the Old Testament was the day Moses went up Mount Sinai—hence, chapter 2 of this book—and God came down in the form of a cloud on the mountain. And Moses takes up three named people.

When Peter, James, and John are staring at this event, in their minds the picture of Moses on Sinai returns, and they're like, "Uh-oh. There's our leader. We're up on a mountain. Here's the cloud, and there's three of us. I think we're dead." Because at Mount Sinai, in the old covenant, God says, "Unless I invite you to come up here, you better not come up here. You better not even get close enough to the mountain. If you bump into the mountain, you or your kid or your goat or your dog or your anybody, I will burn you up because you can't handle My glory."

Then comes the beauty of verse 7. "But Jesus came and touched them, saying, 'Rise, and have no fear.'" The Bible says, *Perfect love drives out fear.* How? Jesus perfectly loved us in this, that *while we were still sinners, Christ died for us.* In Christ, the new covenant understanding of the fear of God is radically different than the old covenant fear of God. Yes, there is reverence. Yes, there is understanding that He is the cosmic King of the universe. But in Christ, we understand Him as our Dad.

Think of it this way—my kids have access to me in a way that others don't. If I'm sitting on the couch, my daughter, Reagan Capri, will jump up next to me, put one leg over mine, then rub my bald head. If you do that to me, you'll be in trouble. Other people don't touch me like that. But my little girl? Anytime. No problem.

As they lie on their faces, afraid Elijah is about to call down fire, Jesus puts His hand on them—"Rise, and have no fear." Why? Because He knows what's coming—God is going to demonstrate that He loves you through the life, death, and resurrection of Jesus. *This is love. Not that we love God, but he loved us and sent his son as a propitiation for our sin.* Jesus knows that the Father is sending Him to the cross where He will become sin and the payment that satisfies the wrath and judgment and law of God. Jesus knows the Father is going to make Him, who was without sin, to be sin for us, that we would be made the righteousness of God.

Because if we knew that, what would we fear?

You need to hear this—for anyone who is in Christ, God is not disappointed in you. He is not dissatisfied with you. Because if Christ is in you, He was (and still is) the full payment that satisfied.

God delights over His children. Yes, even you. This means that your sin doesn't define you. Your past doesn't define you. Your mistakes don't define you. Your habits don't define you.

If you are "in" Jesus, then Jesus defines you. He alone tells you who you are. And according to Jesus, you are a child of God. Your understanding of the character and nature of God not only defines who you are but also determines how you deal with your sin, shame, and guilt. A. W. Tozer says, "The most important thing about you is what you think when you think about God." So, when you think about God, I need you to think that this is love. Not that we love Him, but He loved us and sent His Son as a payment that satisfies. Therefore, if I am in Him, then He is not dissatisfied in me. Zephaniah 3:17 says,

> *"The LORD your God is in your midst,*
> *a mighty one who will save;*
> *he will rejoice over you with gladness;*
> *he will quiet you by his love;*
> *he will exult over you with loud singing."*

Some versions translate *he will rejoice* as he will dance over you with gladness. I love that.

Verse 8: "And when they lifted up their eyes, they saw no one but Jesus only." Listen. When you're afraid, look only to Jesus. He's the only one that can cast out our fear. "And as they were coming down the mountain, Jesus commanded them, 'Tell no one the vision, until the Son of Man is raised from the dead.'" In other words, *Boys, you might want to keep this to yourself until I pull off Easter. Because they won't believe you.*

Flip over with me to Mark 9. Here, Mark tells us about this same event, but he includes some different details. If you're new to Bible study, it's basically like if you're watching ESPN and then you flip over to FOX Sports. It's the same game, the same event, but different channels decide to highlight different things. So Mark is going to highlight what happens next.

In Mark 9, Jesus and the disciples are walking down the mountain into the valley. Notice they're walking down the mountain. The hair on the back of your neck should be standing up. Because sometimes, right on the heels of your most intense spiritual encounters with the Lord, those high holy moments, those mountaintop experiences, where you've never felt so close to God, the very next event that happens is down in the valley. What makes me say that? Remember His baptism in the Jordan. The heavens split open. God the Father said, "This is my beloved Son, with whom I am well pleased." And immediately after that, He's walking through the desert, being tempted by the enemy.

Sound familiar?

Walking down the mountain, Mark 9:14–16: "And when they came to the disciples, they saw a great crowd around them, and scribes arguing with them. And immediately all the crowd, when they saw him, were greatly amazed and ran up to him and greeted him. And he asked them, "What are you arguing about with them?" Notice what does not happen—the scribes don't answer and the disciples don't answer. Have you ever heard your kids fighting, walked into their bedroom, and asked, "What are you all fighting about?"

And they say, "Oh, we were sharing prayer requests."

Right.

Someone from the crowd answers. A dad. "Teacher, I brought my son to you, for he has a spirit that makes him mute. And whenever it seizes him, it throws him down, and he foams and grinds his teeth and becomes rigid. So I asked your disciples to cast it out, and they were not able" (vv. 17–18). Matthew records that this dad comes forward, falls down on his face before Jesus, and says, *Rabbi, teacher, I've brought my son here to be healed, and the disciples could not do it.*

If you've been around Bible study for a really long time, you already know how this story is going to end. In fact, I don't even like to use the word *story* when I describe the events of the Old and New Testament. Because when you hear the word *story*, you're likely to think *Bible stories*—some of you think flannelgraphs or VeggieTales or "A long time ago in a galaxy far, far away..." This is not a story. This is an event and this man is as real as you and me. He has a name. We don't know his name, but his friends call him by his name. And he has an address. He has a job. He gets up every day and finds himself in this place of utter desperation because his son is sick.

If you're a parent, you don't need me to tell you that there's no pain like kid pain. This dad knows kid pain. It's why he's on his face before Jesus. And like all of us, I'm sure he's tried to do everything he can think of.

What would you do if your kid was sick? You would do whatever it takes. You'd sell the house; you'd sell the cars. Whatever. Now he hears that the Miracle Worker has shown up in town. He's heard that He raised a dead girl to life. That He can walk on water. He can feed thousands of people with almost nothing. He can make the wind and the waves stop. Hearing this, the man thinks, *Maybe He can do something for my boy.* So, don't think *Bible story.* Think *dad and his son.*

The happiest day of my whole life was the day I found out that we were having a boy. We were in that little room and they waved that little wand over Gretchen's tummy and they said, "It's a boy." And I was like, "You're dang right it is." I hugged that lady and called my daddy. I said, "Daddy, I made a boy." And he said, "I knew you had it in you, son." Then that little guy was born and they wrapped him up like a little burrito and they handed him over to me with all his little hairs sticking out. "Oh, it's a skullet." Bald on the top and mullet in the back. He looked like Hulk Hogan. My chest puffed up. "You can take the boy out of Dillon, but you can't take Dillon out of the boy. Just look at him."

I love my wife. More every day. Didn't think I could love anyone else that much. But when JP was born, love multiplied. Became something more. Something greater. I named him after me. I'm the third. He's the fourth. Truth is, I was almost Junior Junior. That happens where I'm from. We're into us at my house. All the love I had to give, I gave to that little human. Years pass, and Gretchen gives birth a second time. Reagan Capri. My daughter. I know this sounds terrible, but during the pregnancy, I began to wonder, *Can I love the second one like I loved the first one?* And then I'm holding Reagan and I realize that love is an inexhaustible resource, because love is from God. You don't cut it in half or thirds; it doubles and triples. So I gave all the love that I have to my son, and then, when I'm holding Reagan Capri, this precious little daughter, I gave it all to her too. I looked at her and I simultaneously thought, *I would die for you, and if some boy ever gets out of line with you, I'll make someone die for you. I'll start my prison ministry from the inside.*

At the foot of the Mount of Transfiguration, this heartbroken dad, spilling tears on Jesus' feet, is desperate for God to do something. He's at this low place: *Jesus, if you don't come through, I don't know what I'm going to do.* The Bible says, *Hope deferred makes the heart sick.* I think I'd rather have a sick body than a sick heart. This man has tried everything everywhere, and now finally he has found the disciples of Jesus, but when he gets his boy to them, they get into a denominational argument about the ministry of Jesus. While they're arguing, this boy is still foaming at the mouth.

So, Jesus, along with Peter, James, and John, walks down the mountain, where they meet this frantic father who says, "Teacher, I brought my son to you, for he has a spirit that makes him mute.

And whenever it seizes him, it throws him down...So I asked your disciples to cast it out, and they were not able."

Verse 19: "He answered them." He's not talking to the dad; He's talking to the disciples. "O faithless generation, how long am I to be with you? How long am I to bear with you? Bring him to me." The disciples' problem is they are trying to operate apart from the power of Jesus. Trying to maybe mimic what they've seen Him do rather than lean into the power of Jesus Himself.

Verse 20: *They brought the boy to him. And when the spirit saw him, immediately it (the demon) convulsed the boy, and he (the boy) fell on the ground.* By the way, in the Bible, the demonic are always the first to recognize Jesus and the religious are the last. Let that rattle around for a second. The reason that the demons recognize Jesus is because they see Him for who He is and they quake. The reason that the religious can't see Him is because He doesn't fit their mental construct. The number-one question religious people ask Jesus is, "Why are You hanging out with those people?"

And Jesus says in response, *Because I came to seek and to save that which was lost.* I like to tell the folks in our church that we're not a country club. We're a hospital. Sometimes a triage. If it's a little bit grimy, it's because we want to be like Jesus. We want to display Him to the people who are furthest from God, who need Him the most, while the religious people are mouthing off and the demons are quaking. And if you think you have to get your life straightened out before you plug into a local church, that would be like thinking you can't go to the ER until the bleeding stops.

Jesus asks the father, "How long has this been happening to him?" And notice Jesus knows the answer. He's asking for the benefit of those standing around.

The dad says, "From childhood."

This is important. He could have said, "From birth." He didn't say, "From birth." He said, "From childhood." In other words, the boy and his mama come home from the hospital, and everything seems to be going fine. For years, everything is going okay. And then one day something's wrong. He starts to get sick. This is not how they planned their life. They start praying and they start begging God and it gets worse and it doesn't get better. The dad goes on to say, "It has often cast him into fire and into water, to destroy him."

Why?

Because that's what demons do. Steal, kill, and destroy everything good that God has for you, and the good that God has for you is Himself. Think about it. First century. Everywhere this family went, they encountered fire and water. Every meal was cooked around a campfire. And they live on the edge of the Sea of Galilee. This means every step of this boy's life, the enemy is trying to take him away from his dad.

Look at what he says next: "But if you can do anything, have compassion on us and help us." Not just "Help my son"—"Help us." Because what's affecting his son is impacting and affecting the entire family. And notice the *if* there. That's a big *if*. "If you can do anything…" It's interesting when you stand it up next to what he doesn't say. He doesn't say, "You owe me something," but instead, he pleads, Jesus, would You look at us and have compassion? Not because we deserve it. Not because we've done anything right. And he isn't trying to broker a deal by saying, "If I give money to the poor and attend Sunday services for a month, then would You heal?" Just, "Would you be so moved that You would do something that I have not been able to do?"

And Jesus says to him, "'If you can'! All things are possible for one who believes."

Verse 24: Immediately the father of the child cried out—and notice, he does not whisper. He screams this from his belly: "I believe; help my unbelief!"

You ever been there?

You ever been in that spot of utter desperation?

I've stood in hospital rooms with desperate parents and cried for help with everything I'm made of—"God, I need You to come through. Come on, God. Do this thing. Just step in. I believe. I believe. You brought life. You give breath. You heal. You bring sight to the blind. The lame walk. You can do it. I know if the tomb is empty, anything is possible. God, come on. I believe." And then there are times I walk in there and my unbelief is a lot more than my belief. I got this little itty-bitty tiny belief.

If you're looking for a church where the pastor's got it all together, you should skip mine. I'm the most jacked-up one in the room, which is why I need Jesus today as much as I've ever needed Him in my entire life, because I believe, but I need Him to help me with my own unbelief.

Maybe you've been praying for twenty years that God will save your dad and it hasn't happened. Maybe you went back to the doctor and you thought the cancer was gone but it's back. Maybe you've got a prodigal son, or a prodigal daughter. You raised them in the church. You raised them in Sunday school. They've been to VBS a hundred times. They prayed the prayer when they were eleven. You baptized them. And now they're running from God. They're destroying not just themselves. They're destroying your entire family. Maybe your marriage is broken. You see a hundred testimony videos about how God has put a marriage back together, and you're just begging God to do a thing in your husband's life, and He just hasn't done it. You want to believe. With all that you are. But deep down in your soul, unbelief still rattles around.

You know what Jesus does not do to this man? When the desperate dad says, *I believe; help my unbelief!* the Bible does not say, "And Jesus took His pinky finger and flicked him into the center of the sun so that he would burn forever." No. Jesus does not say, "Away from Me, you wretch, until you can get your faith meter up to miracle level, and then come back and see Me and I'll do something for you." Jesus meets this man right where he is.

A while back, my sister-in-law, Maggie, was thirty-six weeks pregnant. She's the sweetest girl ever. One night, she didn't feel the baby, little Nash, moving. She went to the doctor the next day and there was no heartbeat. He was gone. But he was still in her and so she had to give birth. Go through the whole thing.

While this was happening, I was with my buddies, hunting in Kentucky, and Gretchen called me. Every deer in Kentucky could hear me wailing because I was like, "Why, God, why? I mean, I can't... Tell me You understand her. She and her husband, Justin— they love You. They go to church. They serve. All they want to do is be parents. The most ill-deserving mamas on the planet seem to just crank out babies all the time, and these people that are chasing after You...I believe, but help me overcome my unbelief."

And then that next Sunday, I'm sitting in church and some lyrics to the first song that we sing, "Great Are You Lord," are "You give life. You give breath in our lungs." And I believe that, but in that moment, I'm like, "Well, God, why didn't You do it this time? Why not with little Nash?" When Maggie delivered him, they celebrated his life. Hugged him. Kissed him. Took pictures. To me, he looked like he just needed to wake up. "Just open your eyes, buddy."

Have you ever been there?

When we look at the circumstances of our lives, maybe we should pray what this dad prays, which is maybe the most honest prayer in the entire Bible. "I believe; help my unbelief!" Unpack his words and here's what you find: "God, I trust You. Except for this area where I don't. I need Your help. I believe in You, but there's a whole bunch of stuff I don't understand. I have faith in You that You're a good, good Father, except for all this part over here, where

I'm struggling, God." Honest, right? In this moment, this dad does not come to Jesus on his own terms. He just brings his true self to Jesus and surrenders. Everything. He surrenders both his belief and his unbelief. And Jesus receives him and his offering.

Now, look at what Jesus does. Verses 25–27:

"And when Jesus saw that a crowd came running together, he rebuked the unclean spirit, saying to it, 'You mute and deaf spirit, I command you, come out of him and never enter him again.' And after crying out and convulsing him terribly, it came out, and the boy was like a corpse, so that most of them said, 'He is dead.' But Jesus took him by the hand and lifted him up, and he arose."

Don't miss the signal Jesus is sending. This is a precursor to Easter. To the resurrection.

Verses 28–29: "And when he had entered the house, his disciples asked him privately, 'Why could we not cast it out?' And he said to them, 'This kind cannot be driven out by anything but prayer.'"

Let me ask you a tough question. Be honest. Is prayer your first response or your last resort?

The disciples are trying to do ministry apart from Jesus. They're just trying to mimic His actions instead of plugging into His power. Jesus is telling His followers, "Whether I'm up on the mountain or right here beside you, you can connect to My power at any point through prayer."

In my house, we have a dozen charging blocks or Apple cubes plugged into the walls. They are everywhere. But for the life of me, we can't keep up the cord that connects my dying iPhone to the block. My two precious children, who I love with all my heart, are the primary culprits of this conspiracy against my happiness. And truth be told, I don't think their mom is helping. What is so frustrating is that I know I am so close to an infinite source of power that can recharge my iPhone; I just can't connect. Think of prayer as that cord. You and I are a prayer away from connecting to the source of infinite power that can change everything.

Let me ask a second tough question. Maybe tougher. If the Holy Spirit left your house, how long would it take you to realize it?

Do you operate your house on tradition and good conservative moral values, or are you plugged into the power offered to you by the presence of the Spirit of God? I think the point of this whole thing is that God does not reveal Himself to us so that we can sit and soak it up on the mountaintop, but so that we can be sent to serve on mission. You should read that again: God does not reveal Himself to us so that we can sit and soak it up on the mountaintop, but so that we can be sent to serve on mission.

Jesus comes off that mountain and He runs into this dad who's in a place of utter desperation, and He lays His hands on this boy and He prays for this boy and He casts a demon out of this boy. Are any of you like this dad? The Bible says, *We cast all our cares upon him because he cares for us.* The book of James says, *Is anyone among you sick?* That could be financially sick, it could be relationally sick, it could be mentally sick. *Let him gather the elders together and pray and anoint with oil.*

I grew up Southern Baptist. This whole "anoint with oil" thing is outside of my comfort zone. We didn't do this stuff. But James 5 tells me to, so you and I are just going to do what the book says. We're going to pray for deliverance. We're going to pray for healing. We're going to pray to cast out demons. I am not claiming to be a faith healer, but I am trying to be a Bible obeyer.

People have asked me, "Do you believe in demons?" Let me respond with some questions: Anybody struggle with an addiction? Anybody addicted to porn? Pills? The bottle? Is there something that seems to have control over you and over which you have no control? You've been to meetings—and I'm pro meetings—and you try and you try and you try, but something on the inside of you seems to take over and lead you down a path that you swore you'd never walk again. What do you call that? You think that's just chemical? Or do you think there's some darkness that has some grip on you that only the power of the resurrected Jesus can break?

You think your marriage problem is poor communication? Some of you reading this right now are in a difficult marriage and you need Jesus to step in the middle of that thing and reconcile what you have been unable to reconcile. Some of you have a prodigal son or daughter and you think that their life is just a series of unwise choices and that's why they're in the pit. Maybe, but what if there's a demon that is currently working to take your son or your daughter away from you?

Some of you are dealing with depression. It doesn't make sense. You wake up and your circumstances tell you, "I should be happy about my life," and you just can't make the happy turn on inside of you. You don't think the enemy is trying to oppress you?

Some of you are so riddled with fear your every decision is filtered through its lens. You say you have faith, but you live in fear. If that's you, that's not Jesus. Paul told Timothy, *He has not given us a spirit of fear.* Stop right there. Fear is an emotion that God gave us—like, "That lion wants to eat me—I should run." That's good and we should listen to it. But fear can also be a spirit—one that's not good and one that we should not listen to. And I don't quite understand it, but these demons seem to latch onto or attach to wounds. Sometimes very deep wounds. And it's like we need the very Spirit of God to come heal that wound and pluck off anything attached to it. Like maggots.

Some of you hear about the forgiveness of sin, when Jesus on the cross says, "It is finished," and you don't think it counts for you. You think He forgave some of that stuff, but that abortion? You don't think He can forgive you. But why do you think that? Because the enemy keeps whispering, "You are condemned." Where does that whisper come from? Because according to Jesus, you're not.

The fruit of the Spirit of God is love, joy, peace, patience, kindness, goodness, faithfulness, gentleness, and self-control. This is what the Spirit of God produces in us. If there is something in you, some feeling or desire or compulsion, that is not one of these things, then it might have a demonic influence. And notice I said "might," because until you dig around a bit, you just don't know. It might also just be your carnal nature that needs to be crucified. Jesus commands us to crucify the flesh and cast out the demonic. Which means, logically, you can't crucify the demonic (that's His job) and you can't cast out the flesh (it's got to be put to death).

Do you wrestle too much with things like anger, rage, depression, suicidal thoughts, murderous thoughts, adulterous thoughts, self-hatred, unforgiveness, or lack of self-control? How about some form of addiction or inexplicable compulsion? Are any of you "cutters," and you can't stop cutting yourself? How about porn? Can't stop looking? How about lying? Are you a compulsive liar even when you want to tell the truth?

Deliverance in the ministry of Jesus was the norm. Why isn't that true with us? And who told you it shouldn't be? I'm looking at the Word, and according to the Word, we should be doing what Jesus did. He regularly cast out the demonic. It happened everywhere He went. In the ministry of Jesus, casting out was commonplace. The norm. In fact, casting out demons by the Spirit of God was the proof that the kingdom of God had come upon them (Lk. 11:20).

I believe Jesus has given us His authority and power and commanded us to do what He did. And even though it makes me uncomfortable and even though it's been abused, and even though I didn't grow up in a church like this, I don't want to be disobedient. Further, He told us to "proclaim as you go, saying,

'The kingdom of heaven is at hand.' Heal the sick, raise the dead, cleanse lepers, cast out demons. You received without paying; give without pay" (Matt. 10:8).

Let me give you one more:

"And he said to them, 'Go into all the world and proclaim the gospel to the whole creation. Whoever believes and is baptized will be saved, but whoever does not believe will be condemned. And these signs will accompany those who believe: in my name they will cast out demons; they will speak in new tongues; they will pick up serpents with their hands; and if they drink any deadly poison, it will not hurt them; they will lay their hands on the sick, and they will recover.'"
(Mark 16:15–18)

"These signs will accompany those who believe..."

So...what do you believe?

I'm not naïve, I realize this has been abused. But that abuse does not excuse us from walking in obedience to His Word, and when I read His Word, He tells me to preach, cleanse, raise, cast out, and heal.

Paul, in 2 Corinthians 10:4–5, says, "For the weapons of our warfare are not of the flesh but have divine power to destroy strongholds. We destroy arguments and every lofty opinion raised against the knowledge of God, and take every thought captive to obey Christ."

Paul knew that you're in a war whether you like it or not. And we are destroying strongholds and arguments and everything that lifts itself up and tries to compare itself or equal itself to the knowledge of God. That phrase *destroying strongholds* paints a picture in Greek of throwing grappling hooks over walls and pulling them down. Forcibly. That's what we're doing. If you look at the ministry of Jesus, in over 60 percent of His healings, He first cast out the demonic, then healed the patient. And in many cases, casting out the demonic brought the healing. It was the ministry of Jesus, and He said, "Truly, truly, I say to you, whoever believes in me will also do the works that I do; and greater works than these will he do, because I am going to the Father. Whatever you ask in my name, this I will do, that the Father may be glorified in the Son. If you ask me anything in my name, I will do it" (John 14:12–14).

This is either true or it isn't. I'm believing that it is as true today as it was the moment He spoke it two thousand years ago.

My litmus test is this: Are you free? It's a gut-check question. And only you truly know the answer. *It's for freedom that He came to set us free* and *where the Spirit of the Lord is, there is freedom.* So, where are you not free? Where are you in prison to some sin? Where are you enslaved by something that is not the Spirit of God? And you'll know the answer by the fruit it produces. Now, look at that thing and let me ask you this: Is there a chance its source is demonic?

Let me take you back to the desperate father at the foot of the mountain. "I believe; help my unbelief!"

There's something about when spiritual authority puts that oil on your head and puts that hand on your head, and it's not because of any of that stuff. It's just because of Jesus' blood. It breaks the power of sin in your life. "There is therefore now no condemnation for those who are in Christ Jesus."

Our battle is not just unwise choices—it's not against flesh and blood. It's against the demonic. It's against darkness. Against principalities and powers. And these are not just words on a page that pertained to people two thousand years ago. I don't see an expiration date in the Scriptures on the power of God working through His children. These words are life to us and they pertain to us. Today. Right now. The book says it, so it's true. You and I have an enemy that wants to take us out. He prowls around and he wants to kill you and enslave you and the ones most precious to us. Demons entice, they dominate, they control, they manipulate, and they're as real as the book you're currently holding. Can I see them? No, but that doesn't make them any less real. And the fact that you can't see them doesn't make the words of Scripture any less true. Let me ask you this: If you were your enemy, what would you want you to believe (falsely) about you? Now let's flip that: If you were Jesus, sitting next to you right this moment, what would you want you to believe about you? And what would He want you to believe about Him...and His Word? And why?

Remember that whole discussion we had about *pisteuō* and "believing in" versus "believing that"? This is where that rubber meets this road. Let me ask you again: What do you believe? I believe that if we believe Jesus and what He has told us and we are obedient to Him, then we will do what He did and cast out the demons that imprison us and walk in the freedom that His blood purchased on Calvary.

You want freedom? You want the power of God to step into that prison and fling wide the door? You want Jesus, right now, by the very hand of God, to pluck that thing out of your chest and heal your wound forever?

Matthew finishes up this whole event this way: The disciples say, "Why can't we cast it out?" And Jesus says, "Because of your little faith. For truly, I say to you, if you have faith like a grain of mustard seed, you will say to this mountain, 'Move from here to there,' and it will move, and nothing will be impossible for you." It's not the size of your faith; it's the object of your faith. You take that little, itty-bitty, tiny sort of almost-belief faith, and you put it in the infinitely powerful resurrected Jesus, and it is infinitely more powerful than putting all of your trust in the little temporary idols of this world.

So that's what we're going to do. If you're by yourself, then find some olive oil and you can put it on your own head and I'll invite the Spirit of God as we pray together. The centurion told Jesus, *You don't need to come to my house; just speak the word.* So, we're going to believe like the centurion and just believe that Jesus will show up. If you've got friends around, maybe a disciple group, or a pastor, or someone with some spiritual authority who actually believes the Word of God is true and walks in obedience, then great. Ask them. Either way...

My friend, co-laborer on this project, and deacon at our church is Charles Martin. He has lots more experience than I do in prayers of deliverance. He wrote a book called *They Turned the World Upside Down*. In it, there is a chapter or two on spiritual warfare. When you finish this book, you should immediately read that one. With his permission, I have borrowed this prayer in its entirety.

Pray with Me

Lord Jesus Christ, I believe You are the Son of God and the only way to God—that You died on the cross for my sins and rose again so that I might be forgiven and receive eternal life. Here and now I receive that forgiveness and that life.

Father, I renounce all my pride and religious self-righteousness and any false dignity that does not come from You. I have no claim on Your mercy except that You died in my place, and I know there is more mercy in You than sin in me. Please forgive me of my pride. Of my rebellion. Lord, I'm so sorry. I don't want it to keep me from You any longer. Today, I choose to crucify my pride, laying it down at the foot of Your cross.

Lord, I confess all my sins before You and hold nothing back. Especially I confess...(Let the Holy Spirit bring to mind any unconfessed sin. And don't hurry through this. There's no pressure here. He'll wait on you.)

Father, I repent of all my sins. Known and unknown. Things said and left unsaid. And all my actions and thoughts not inspired by You. In this moment, I turn from every decision or action or thought based in me, my selfishness, and my wicked, black heart. I turn away from them and I turn toward You, Lord, for mercy and forgiveness.

By a decision of my will, I freely forgive all who have ever wronged or harmed me. I lay down all bitterness, all resentment, and all hatred. Specifically, I forgive... (speak their name[s] out loud).

I sever all contact I have ever had with the occult or with any and all false religions, particularly... (horoscopes, mind readers, mediums, fortune tellers, Ouija boards, and any and all forms of witchcraft and/or secret societies). Lord, I repent for any place where I've sought power or solace or comfort in any power other than You. Forgive me, please. In this moment, I make a full break from that false power and I raise my hand in covenant with You and You alone. I know that it is Your blood which cleanses me from all unrighteousness, and so I plead the blood of Jesus now over my mind, soul, spirit, and body.

Lord, I commit myself to get rid of all objects associated with the occult or false religion(s). I will purge my house now or when I get home and, regardless of earthly value, I will throw all of it in the trash.

Lord Jesus, I thank You that on the cross You were made a curse, that I might be redeemed from every curse and inherit God's blessing. On that basis, I ask You to release me and set me free to receive the deliverance I need, which You promise me in Joel 2:32 and Acts 2:21.

Lord, I take my stand with You against all satan's demons.

I submit to You, Lord—You and You alone—and I resist the devil. Greater are You who are in me than he who is in the world. And I overcome him, satan, by the blood of the Lamb and the word of my testimony; and my testimony is this: the blood of Jesus has set me free, once and forever, from any and all attacks, schemes, plans, or activity of the enemy, and I willingly come under the full and complete tetelestai authority of the precious blood of Jesus.

Having done all this, in faith and belief, I now speak to any demons that have control over me. I am a blood-bought, blood-washed, and blood-redeemed child of the Most High God, Possessor of heaven and earth, the God of angel armies, and I (speak directly to them) command you—go from me now in the name of Jesus! Leave! Get out! I expel you! The blood of Jesus cleanses me. The name of Jesus frees me!

If you just prayed this, now just breathe, and let me (Joby) pray over you. And you don't need to do anything. Just let the Holy Spirit have His way. He's working, even now in this moment. So relax. Just breathe in and out, let me pray, and let Him do what only He can do:

Our good and gracious heavenly Father, You know I start my prayers that way because I just want to be daily reminded of those two unchanging attributes of Yours. I declare that You are good. Even when the circumstances around me are not good, You are good. Even when I don't understand why this is happening, You are good. Even when my faith is small, You are good. And Father, You are so gracious. You proved it once and for all at the cross. Father, if anyone knows that there is no pain like kid pain, it is You. I praise You for sending Your Son to suffer and die in our place. God, I praise You that You often use our pain as a platform for Your praise. God, I praise You in advance for the miracles that will happen, for the chains of addiction that will be broken, for the sins that will be forgiven, for the spirit of fear that will be cast out, for the marriages that will be reconciled, for the prodigal sons that will come home, for the cancer that will disappear, and for the depression that will be replaced by joy. For if the tomb is empty, anything is possible. In Jesus' name. Amen.

Now just praise Him.

Note: If you've just prayed this, you might want some further prayer. Folks at my church will pray with you if you email or call…Sometimes this stuff isn't "one and done," so hang in there and contact us.

CHAPTER 7

Mount Calvary—What Is Finished?

We started this walk on Mount Moriah—eighteen hundred years prior to Christ—where Abraham built an altar, bound Isaac, and raised the knife. And on that mountain, rather than take Isaac, God provided a substitute. A ram in place of Abraham's son. Now, two thousand years after the resurrection of Christ, you and I have returned to that same mountain. But we know it by another name.

Mount Calvary.

It just blows me away that the very place where Abraham, the father, was willing to sacrifice the son of his love, Isaac, is the very same mountain where our Father in heaven, God Most High, did offer and sacrifice His own Son. A substitute. To take our place. Abraham was called a friend of God. And through the blood of Jesus, you and I can be called friends of God.

Jesus was and is the Lamb that was slain for you and me.

Whether you are a weekly churchgoer, or a CEO (Christmas and Easter Only), or rarely if ever attend, chances are good we all agree on this—something has gone wrong with the human condition. Even if we can't agree on the solution, we agree there is a problem. We are broken. CNN believes it. Fox News believes it. Buddhists,

Muslims, Christians, atheists—we all believe something has gone wrong. This is why "self-help" is the largest section in the bookstore. Every other world religion, every other worldview—whether a major world religion that's been around for thousands of years or a secular, atheistic worldview—has something in common, and it is this: "I must do something to make this thing right." With emphasis on *I*. What we're going to discover is that the gospel of Jesus Christ is unique in its response to the human problem.

And the response is not me, but Him.

The gospel of Jesus Christ is not about what you can do to please God, but what He has done to rescue you. Or, as He said to Moses, "To bring you to Myself" (Exod. 19:4). To really understand the glory of the rescue, we need to dive into what was required. The price that was paid. Hence, the Crucifixion.

The rescue started in the Garden of Eden and finished at the cross and empty tomb. Just like Abraham climbed Moriah, Jesus climbed Calvary, and His last few steps started at the base of the Mount of Olives. In another garden. The Garden of Gethsemane. *Gethsemane* is the English corruption of the Hebrew words *gat* and *shemanim*. It means "the place where the olive is pressed." Or "the place of the crushing." Jesus knows His hour has come, so He brings His disciples to the base of the Mount of Olives and says, "All right, boys, you hang out here and you pray. Peter, James, John, you come with me a little farther. Will you stay awake and will you pray for me?" From there, the Bible says that Jesus falls onto His face, and His soul is so sorrowful that He thinks He is going to die, because He knows that the cross looms. As His blood vessels burst, and His sweat literally turns to blood, He prays this prayer: "My Father, if it be possible, let this cup pass from me."

Do you realize what Jesus is saying? He's saying, "Okay, Father, if there is some plan B that I'm not aware of, if there is some other way for You to rescue and redeem all of humanity and make all things new, if Oprah's right and all roads lead to heaven, if you can align your chakras, if you can obey the Ten Commandments, if you can meditate and find peace and nirvana, if you can obey the five pillars and visit Mecca—if any of these ways are going to work, if there be any other way, it seems like an awful waste of My blood tomorrow on Mount Calvary. Father, if there be any other way, let this cup pass from Me. Not My will, but Your will be done."

After Jesus prays the third time, He looks over the Kidron Valley, up into the gates of Jerusalem, and watches as men with torches and soldiers with swords exit the city and wind a serpentine path toward Him. When they show up, they arrest Jesus and lead Him to a mock trial, but nobody wants to be the person to convict Jesus. So, they pass Him back and forth. Herod doesn't want to do it. Pilate doesn't want to do it. Caiaphas doesn't want to do it. Nobody wants to be the person who slams the gavel down and says, "This man deserves death." Why? Because everyone in town knows He's innocent. And the town is packed. Why? Passover. There are people everywhere, which is part of the reason the chief priests and the Pharisees want Jesus to die that weekend. So the largest number of people in that region would see Him and spread the word about what happens to people who claim to be the Son of God, so that nobody else would have the gall to claim the kinds of things Jesus claimed. They think they're solidifying their power. God Most High had another thing in mind.

In a public trial, Pilate puts it up to a vote. "What shall I do with Jesus who is called Christ?" By the way, that is the most important question that you will ever deal with in your entire life. What will you do with this man called Jesus? And the crowd screams out, "Crucify him, crucify him!"

These are the same people who, just days prior, on what we call Palm Sunday, were waving palm branches, celebrating His entrance into Jerusalem, wanting to make Him king, screaming, "Hosannah...blessed is he who comes in the name of the Lord!" This is the same crowd that is now screaming, "Crucify him!" Pilate knows Jesus is innocent, but he doesn't want to look weak, so he offers to free one prisoner—either Barabbas, a convicted murderer and insurrectionist, or Jesus. He's trying to find an out and release Jesus. He's also a pansy, trying to wash his hands of this whole affair so he doesn't have to make a decision.

None of us have that luxury. Every single one of us must answer this question: What will YOU do with this man called Jesus?

The crowd chooses Barabbas. The crowd says, "May the blood of Jesus be on our heads and the heads of our children." To anyone who believes, that blood will be a great blessing of salvation. But for anyone who does not believe, this is an everlasting curse. Having sentenced Jesus to die, they begin to beat and mock Him, starting with putting a sack over His head and punching Him in the face, saying, "You call Yourself a prophet? Who hit You?" Pulling it off, in an effort to shame Him, they pluck out His beard. Then they parade Him to the praetorium, Pontius Pilate's house, tie him to a post, and beat Him with a Roman scourge. Also known as a cat-o'-nine-tails.

You can't rightly understand the glory of the resurrection if you don't understand the brutality of the Crucifixion.

For decades, I think we mostly breezed by words like *flogged* in the Scriptures until Mel Gibson's *The Passion of the Christ* showed us a version of what actually happened. Because of that image, we now think differently about that word. Each of the nine tails is tipped with metal and glass so that when swung, it sinks, or embeds, into the flesh. When pulled off, it strips off chunks of flesh. Exposing ribs. Very few human beings could survive this beating. This mutilated Jesus. Isaiah, prophetically describing this event seven hundred years before it occurred, said Jesus would become unrecognizable as a man. To continue to mock Him, they laid a purple robe across His back. Having shredded Him, they fashioned a crown of thorns made from an acacia tree. Interestingly, the ark of the covenant was also made out of acacia wood. The very thing that held the Word of God and the law of God is now the very thing that crowns the Son of God. Once they pressed it into His brow, they beat it into place with rods and then forced Him to carry His own cross to Golgotha, the place of the skull.

In the beginning of the first century, because the Romans did not have helicopters and tanks and guns, what they did was brutally oppress anyone who would rise up. To not only strike down a rebellion, but make a statement with the bodies of those who attempted it. When Spartacus was defeated, Rome crucified six thousand men down a road 120 miles long. In one day. Crucifixion was the most brutal form of punishment and death in the history of humanity. It's where we get our English word *excruciating* from. It literally means "from the cross."

Nails would be put into the hands and feet, a couple of the most sensitive nerve centers in the human body. By the way, in the first century, your hand was considered anything from your elbow to your fingertips. Once nailed to the tree, the soldiers weren't finished. They stripped those they crucified. Naked. To shame them. And they didn't crucify them ten feet in the air; they did so just a foot or two off the ground. Where passersby could see them. Hear them. Smell them. And they did it on the busiest of roads. Again, as a deterrent. So low to the road people would mock them and spit on them and curse them.

When Jesus was a little boy, there was a Jewish rebellion in Jerusalem, and Rome crucified hundreds of Jewish men in the city. Maybe Jesus saw it as a little boy, and maybe—this is total speculation—that's what He knew He was headed toward. The

Bible says one sentence, *And they crucified him.* Let the reader infer. It's always struck me as strange that the death of the only innocent man to ever live is given so little ink.

To drag things out, make the fun last longer, the soldiers would give you wine vinegar to numb you a little bit. Maybe keep you alive and awake longer. Some people died from the pain, some people bled out, but most died from asphyxiation. Drowning in their own lung fluids. This meant every single time you wanted to take a breath or say something, you would have to push up on your nail-pierced feet, take as deep a breath as the pain would allow, and find the strength to speak. The Romans had perfected the brutal, excruciating killing of others.

Because last words, like first words, matter, let's look at Jesus' last words. On the cross, Jesus says seven things. Seven different times, He pushes up on His feet and speaks. I think maybe we should pay attention.

In most of the paintings we see of Jesus, He's wearing a loin-cloth. Nice, but it's not true. To complete the shame started with plucking out His beard, Jesus was stripped naked. Very shameful for a Jewish man. This is why the Bible is careful to point out that the women that were following Him followed from a long way off. Because they didn't want to see that.

In Luke 23:34, Jesus says, **"Father, forgive them, for they know not what they do."** Listen, the first thing I think Jesus wants us to know on the cross is that this is why He came. He did not come to be a good moral teacher. Good moral teachers don't say the kinds of things that Jesus said. Jesus says, "I am the way, and the truth, and the life. No one comes to the Father except through me." Jesus says, *I am the resurrection and the life. Apart from me, you don't have life.* Jesus says, "I and the Father are one." Either He's a crazy man, or He's lying, or He's telling the truth—in which case, He is, in fact, Lord of the universe. Hanging there on the cross, He wants us to know first and foremost that He's not just a rabbi, not just a teacher. He is the Savior. This is why He came. And in these words, He's reminding the people.

Remember what the angel said to the shepherds in the field? *Behold, I bring good news of great joy, for unto us is born this day in the city of David, a savior for all the people.* And remember what his cousin, John the Baptist, said about Him? *Behold, the lamb of God who comes to take away the sin of the entire world.* Jesus was sent to save and deliver. And in order to do that, to return us to His Father, to present us holy and blameless before Him, He must first forgive our sin. To make the payment we couldn't make in ten thousand lifetimes. That payment is the cross.

Despite preaching to the contrary, Jesus did not come to make bad people better. Jesus did not primarily come to instruct you how to live a better life. Make no bones about it. Jesus died on the cross for the glory of God and the forgiveness of your sin. To suggest He was simply a good moral teacher and not understand Him as Savior is to reject who He is and what He came for.

After Jesus says, "Father, forgive them, for they know not what they do," Luke 23 says, they cast lots to divide his garments. And the people stood by, watching, but the rulers scoffed at him, saying, "He saved others, let him save himself, if he is the Christ of God, his Chosen One!" The soldiers also mocked him, coming up and offering him sour wine and saying, "If you are the King of the Jews, save yourself!" (vv. 34–37).

Verses 38–43 read,

> *"There was also an inscription over him, 'This is the King of Jews.'*
>
> *One of the criminals who were hanged railed at him, saying, 'Are you not the Christ? Save yourself and us!' But the other rebuked him, saying, 'Do you not fear God, since*

you are under the same sentence of condemnation? And we indeed justly, for we are receiving the due reward of our deeds; but this man has done nothing wrong.' And he said, 'Jesus, remember me when you come into your kingdom.' And Jesus said to him, 'Truly, I say to you, today you will be with me in paradise.'"

This is nothing but pure, unadulterated grace poured out on all mankind. By grace we have been saved, through faith, and in this moment, the dying hour of this thief, he understands, by faith, the grace of Jesus Christ. Jesus is crucified between two thieves who deserve to be there. One of them surrenders to Jesus as King; the other comes to Jesus on his own terms. "If You are who You say You are, then why don't You do Your thing and do it for me too?"

I preach a lot, so I look out across a lot of faces. All of us fall into one of two categories: We come to God on our terms, saying, "God, if You are who You say You are, then why don't You get me out of this mess? Prove Yourself." The rest of us hear this and think, *Bro, are you even serious right now? Do you know who you're talking to? We deserve to be here. This man has done nothing wrong.*

Somehow, hanging in a lot of pain in what are his last minutes on planet earth, this second thief understands that Jesus is who He says He is, and that somehow—even though he may not totally understand it—what Jesus is doing in that minute on the cross counts for him. Jesus is making his payment, and he knows it. He's watching it happen in real time. So convinced is he that he asks Him for a favor. If you've ever prayed a prayer of salvation, you've done the same thing. You asked God for a favor. The good news is that He answers that prayer 100 percent of the time—*everyone who calls on the name on the LORD shall be saved* (Joel 2:32).

Some of you have trouble with this. Can't believe it. You ask, "Even me?" Yes, even you.

Some of the rest of you are thinking you're so good you don't need Him. I've got good news—you too can be saved.

Some of you think you're too bad, too far gone. Let me ask you this: Who do you think you are? You think your sin compares to the grace of Jesus Christ poured out on the cross? Look at what Jesus does not say. He does not say, "Okay, well, you've got some stuff to work on while you're hanging there, so why don't you get to work and then before I check out, I'll come back and see if you deserve to make the trip." There's no "you've got work to do..."

Of all the people we read about in the New Testament, we are the most certain that this brother makes it into heaven. Why? Jesus tells us. *"Today you will be with me in paradise."* This man is saved by lavish, unmerited grace. By grace. Now, I know sometimes you might look at this and be like, "Well, that's not fair."

Look, man. You don't want fair. Fair is not a biblical value. And fair is you pressing up on your nail-pierced feet.

Gretchen and I have two kids. Sometimes I'll give one something and not the other. The second will be like, "That's not fair." Look here, Scooter, fair ended at the Garden of Eden. You want fair? All right, let's do fair. Let's divide up the mortgage among the four of us. Hey, look! Now we have homeless kids. Or how about this one? Whoever paid for the Xbox plays the Xbox. Looks like Daddy's got an Xbox.

The Bible says the wages of sin is death, but the gift of God is eternal life. This man on the cross does not say, "Jesus, from now on I promise I will..." You will what, bro? There ain't no "from now on." There ain't no tomorrow. Your now and your tomorrow are over. All he has to offer Jesus is his broken and contrite self.

The Bible says even our righteous deeds are like filthy rags before the Lord. You know what this thief on the cross brings Jesus? Himself. That's all he brings. He surrenders all of himself to the Lord, and the Bible assures us that by grace this man is saved. "Truly, I say to you, today you will be with me in paradise." Listen, good people don't go to heaven. Forgiven people go to heaven because there are no good among us. I know what some of you are thinking. *Well, look. I'm a good guy.* Compared to who? The nightly news and your college roommate? Sure. You're doing okay. But how good do you have to be? God says, "Be holy, for I am holy." Anyone want to raise their hand on that one and offer, "Nailing it"? If you do, the only thing you're nailing is your pride. The granddaddy of all the sins. Making you the worst among us.

This is the truth of us—none of us are good. Not one. Let me ask you this. Put aside for a moment the righteous law of God. Can you keep your own laws? Can you even keep your own commandments? How many times have you told yourself that you would never do that again and then you did it again? Anybody ever been there? Has anybody ever kept a New Year's resolution till Easter? No. Have any of us ever looked in the mirror and asked, "What is wrong with me?" No one has lied to you more than you. No one has broken more promises to you than you. The heart of the problem is that you and I have a heart problem.

Not going to lie. You are wrong with you. But I've got really good news. Your rescue is not about you being a better version of you to make yourself right before God. That's self-righteousness. Which is a sin. Scripture says no one will be declared righteous by fulfilling the law but God manifested righteousness apart from the law through faith in Jesus Christ. Don't miss those two words in the middle. They matter. A lot. *But God.* Exhibit A is this brother on the cross who receives salvation not by any good work, but as a free gift of Jesus. "Truly, I say to you, today you will be with me in paradise."

The Bible doesn't tell us when, but at some point after the conversation with the thief, Jesus looks out in the crowd and sees his mother standing next to the disciple John. Despite the pain,

He musters the strength to say, **"Woman, behold, your son. Son, behold, your mother."** Seems strange, doesn't it? Why does He do this? Think about this through Mary's perspective. See it through her eyes. Do any of you mamas have a son? What's the first thing you did when he was born? If you're anything like Gretchen, you grabbed those feet and started counting: "One, two, three, four, five...one, two, three, four, five." Then you started bragging. "Look at these little feet." Crazy. I know—I was there. They look like little hospital gloves somebody blew up. Just fat little toes. Next thing you do is look at the hands. "One, two, three, four, five...one, two, three, four, five. Look at these hands. Look at these little fingernails. How're they so small?" Crazy. Right? Then every mama I've ever met gets all up in their faces and smells them and nuzzles their noses. We all do.

Now Mary is looking at her boy's hands and feet. Those tiny hands where she once counted fingers and toes are now nailed to a cross. And she can smell him. Essentially, Jesus—who was Mary and Joseph's firstborn child—is saying, "I need somebody to take care of My mama. John, that's you." Maybe this is the reason why John outlived all the other disciples. Maybe this is the reason that when they tried to martyr John, it wouldn't work. Church history tells us that all the other apostles were martyred—not for what they believed but for what they said they saw: Jesus Christ risen from the dead. And the people who saw this were rather vocal about what they saw.

What does this mean for you and me? Look closely. Jesus is a little busy in this moment. He's got some stuff going on. This is THE most pivotal moment in all of history. He's redeeming the world and making all things new and yet He still cares about the needs of those who He loves and who love Him.

You know why this matters? This matters because God is still running the universe. Still in control. Still got the whole world in His hands. He tells us to cast all our cares upon Him because He cares for us, and yet some of us think, *I probably shouldn't bring this to God because it's not that big a deal*. You're right—it's not that big a deal. But *you* are. To Him, you're a big deal, and that makes your deals a big deal to Him. Like a good dad, He looks to His kids and says, "Come on. Bring it to Me."

You ever go to pick up your kid after Sunday school—in our church, we call it "New Gen"—and they walk out carrying these little art projects? Just being honest—some of them are pretty terrible. That said, I have a few of Reagan's. And I treasure them. I compare them to what your kid makes and I'm like, *Your kid's art project is not good. It's junk. My kid's making art*. Why? Because I don't know your kid. But my kid's stuff, man—we frame it. Put it on the wall. Treasure it. Why? Because it's Reagan. My kid. For anyone who is in Christ Jesus, God says, "Come on. Bring it to Me. Cast all your cares upon Me. Any of you weary, tired, and heavy-burdened, bring that to Me." Jesus is taking care of our temporary physical needs while He is dying on the cross. Why? Because God loves you, not some future version of you once you get your act together. God's not only interested in getting you out of this world and getting you to heaven, but God has a purpose and a plan for you. Here and now. He is a good shepherd and He came that you may have life and have it abundantly. *Woman, behold, your son. Son, behold, your mother.*

Following these two conversations, the earth goes dark for three hours, and then in Matthew 27:46, in what can be a very confusing verse, Jesus pushes up on His nail-pierced feet and says these words: **"My God, my God, why have you forsaken me?"** In Aramaic, *"Eli, Eli, lema sabachthani."* Those around him are confused. They ask, "Is He calling for Elijah?" Most of my life, the way I have been taught what's happening here, the reason that everything goes dark and Jesus says, "My God, my God, why have you forsaken me?" is because God is turning His back on Jesus.

Is He? For sure, Jesus is receiving the full wrath and punishment from God the Father because He is bearing our sin and actually becoming our sin. Yes and amen, and without a doubt.

But it's kind of a troubling thing in Matthew 28 to hear the promise of Jesus, *And lo, I will be with you to the very ends of the age,* or to hear the promise of Romans 8, *Nothing can separate us from the love of God, neither height nor depth nor things to come nor things in the past. Neither angels nor demons nor anything in this world could separate us from the love of God.* And then we hear Him speak these words. It makes you wonder, *"Okay, what's exactly happening?"*

There's a lot more to it than just the words that Jesus said. Jesus says, "My God, my God, why have you forsaken me?" Jesus was a rabbi, and rabbis had four levels of exegesis, or four levels of interpretation of the Scripture. And the second level of interpretation of the Scripture was called a *remez*. *Remez* is a Hebrew word that just means "hint." It's a small part of something bigger. So, as soon as He says the words "My God, my God, why have you forsaken me?" every Jewish boy and girl there, every Jewish man and woman immediately knows that Jesus is quoting Psalm 22. The psalms were songs, and every little boy and girl, when they were in the equivalent of first grade, would go to Hebrew school and study the Torah—the first five books of the Bible. Not only would they study them, they'd memorize all of the Torah and all of the psalms. All of them. In fact, most of the time when they would show up on their first day of school, they would get a tablet. If you're in your twenties, note that this tablet was not electronic. It was a chalkboard kind of thing.

During class, they would write the words of God and do their schoolwork—on that tablet. But on the first day, the main rabbi— the main teacher—would have soaked their tablet in honey. Honey was very expensive, very precious, and obviously very sweet. These children had heard of honey but had probably never tasted it. When given their honey-soaked tablet, these little first-grade Jewish boys and girls would just lick the honey. Had honey everywhere. In their hair, on their elbows, on their neighbors. It was everywhere, causing each of them to think, *I love school. This is the greatest day of my life.* And about that time, the rabbi would say something like, "Just as you crave the sweet taste of honey, may your soul crave the life-giving taste of the Word of God." And they would memorize the Scripture, the whole thing.

This love of the Word created a process whereby, when they taught, Jewish rabbis could teach an entire passage by just giving you a hint of the passage. Maybe just the first few words.

Back to Jesus. "My God, my God, why have you forsaken me?" For all of you in your midforties, this is the equivalent of me saying to you, "Stop, collaborate, and listen." How many of you just sang the next line? It's in there and I never taught you that.

The New Testament does not describe the Crucifixion of Jesus. All it says is, *And they crucified him.* Have you ever wondered why there is no description of the most important death in the history of history? Because it's already in here. Psalms, chapter 22.

Psalm 22 was written by King David (like David and Goliath—that David) a thousand years before Jesus was born. And when Jesus says, "My God, my God, why have you forsaken me?" He is describing His own death. Imagine if you were there that day, watching what was happening, and as Jesus said this, you began to roll the verses of Psalm 22 through your head. As you did, you realized that Psalm 22 was a play-by-play, blow-by-blow account of everything Jesus experienced and that you were witnessing that day.

"My God, my God, why have you forsaken me?
Why are you so far from saving me, from the words of my groaning?

O my God, I cry by day, but you do not answer,
and by night, but I find no rest.
Yet you are holy,
enthroned on the praises of Israel.
In you our fathers trusted;
they trusted, and you delivered them.
To you they cried and were rescued;
in you they trusted and were not put to shame." (Psalm 22:1–5)

Jesus wants us to know that He is descended from the line of David. From the root of Jesse. The one that Abraham was talking about. The one Moses was talking about. The one Elijah prophesied about and Isaiah foretold. In these few words, Jesus confirms for those watching that the God of Abraham and Isaac and Jacob is the one hanging on a cross. In Psalm 22, David goes on to say, "But I am a worm and not a man, scorned by mankind and despised by the people. All who see me mock me; they make mouths at me; they wag their heads." Then the next part is in quotes: "He trusts in the LORD; let him deliver him; let him rescue him, for he delights in him!" In Luke 23:35, the Roman soldier says these words almost verbatim. Imagine the impossibility of this. David wrote these words a thousand years before Jesus and they are coming true. Verbatim. In verse 8, one of the soldiers says, "If you could save yourself, go ahead. You say you're the king of the Jews, save yourself and save us with you." The psalmist keeps going. "Yet you are he who took me from the womb. You made me trust you at my mother's breasts. On you was I cast from my birth, and from my mother's womb you have been my God."

Who could this be true of? David? No. David said he was born in iniquity. Has it been true of you? No. The only human being this could be true of is Jesus Christ, because every single one of us was born in sin, and Jesus alone was born perfect. Sometimes people tell me, "I've been a Christian my whole life." I know what you mean, but you haven't. You can't be born into it. There are no grandchildren in the faith. There are only firsthand faith recipients. Your name is written in the Lamb's book of life upon confession and belief. Not before. A thousand years before Jesus is born, David is prophesying—or, rather, the Holy Spirit is speaking prophetically through David—about the one who would be born sinless, in right standing with God.

In verse 11, it goes on to say, "Be not far from me, for trouble is near, and there is none to help. Many bulls encompass me; strong bulls of Bashan surround me; they open wide their mouths at me, like a ravening and roaring lion." A bull was one of the signs of the Roman army, and the Roman sign for the emperor was a lion, but we have a problem—the Roman empire does not appear in history for another three hundred years.

David continues: "I am poured out like water, and all my bones are out of joint; my heart is like wax; it is melted within my breast." The Gospel of John, chapter 19, verse 31, lets us know that it was at the end of the day, because it was the Sabbath, and to appease the Jewish leaders, they wanted to make sure that everybody on the crosses was dead so that they could take them down before the Sabbath set in. To do this, they broke the legs of the two thieves at the sides of Jesus, but when they came to Jesus, they said, *He's already dead.* And so the Bible tells us that they took a spear and they shoved it up under His ribs and into His heart.

John 19:34 tells us, "But one of the soldiers pierced his side with a spear, and at once there came out blood and water." Imagine you're standing there and you know that Psalm 22 says, "I am poured out like water, and all my bones are out of joint; my heart is like wax; it is melted within my breast." Then the soldier shoves a spear in Jesus' chest and blood and water gush out. Right before your very eyes.

Psalm 22:15: "My strength is dried up like a potsherd, and my tongue sticks to my jaws." Maybe it's in this moment that Jesus pushes up on His nail-pierced feet and says, **"I thirst."** Because John 19:29 tells us that the Roman soldiers take a sponge and mix it in wine vinegar or sour wine, depending on your translation, and they shove it into His mouth.

Archeologists tell us that there would only be two reasons a sponge would be there. Roman soldiers carried certain things in their backpacks or travel kits. One of those things would have been a sponge to clean themselves up after they went to the bathroom. Also, right outside the city, there would have been public bathrooms, and slaves would put a sponge on the end of a stick to clean up the marble bathrooms. People shared these sponges as first-century toilet paper.

But bacteria would also be shared, so they would drop the sponge in what was called wine vinegar to keep the sponges from transmitting germs. These Roman soldiers were not being kind to Jesus. They were mocking Him. Essentially, they shoved first-century toilet paper into the mouth of our King and God. Jesus then says, *I thirst.*

"You lay me in the dust of death." "For dogs encompass me; a company of evildoers encircles me."

This is unbelievable. Word for word.

"They have pierced my hands and feet." This psalm was written a thousand years before the event it describes. In fact, crucifixion as a form of punishment had not yet been invented and wouldn't be until 300 BC. Persia invented it in 300 BC and Rome perfected it when Alexander the Great came through. This means that seven hundred years before anybody in all recorded history had been pierced in their hands and feet as punishment for a crime, the Holy Spirit was writing about it through His servant David.

A lot of us wear a cross around our neck, and yet very few of us have any understanding of what it means. It was the symbol of shame. The symbol of oppression. The cross was the way Rome crushed anybody that rose up against them. And somehow, today, it is the symbol of freedom. Of God's grace. Of how much God loves us. *For God demonstrated his love for us in this, that while we were still sinners Christ died for us.* Can you imagine walking into the Roman Colosseum, where they fed Christians to the lions and where they crucified people all over the place, and saying, "Hey, look here, emperor. One day that symbol of shame, it will stand in this Colosseum as a symbol of the forgiveness of sins." Unbelievable.

David again: "A company of evildoers encircles me; they have pierced my hands and feet—I can count all my bones." Notice they did not break His legs. "They stare and gloat over me; they divide my garments among them, and for my clothing they cast lots." This happens in Luke 23:34. "But you, O LORD, do not be far off! O you my help, come quickly to my aid! Deliver my soul from the sword, my precious life from the power of the dog!" By the way, *dog* was a slang term for a Gentile. "Save me from the mouth of the lion! You have rescued me from the horns of the wild oxen!" But watch what happens next. The psalmist begins to shift from the cross to the resurrection. He says, "I will tell of your name to my brothers." How's He going to do that if He's dead? Three days later, the stone will be rolled away and Jesus will be resurrected, and He will appear to His brothers, to the Jewish people in Jerusalem, in the place where He was crucified.

The psalmist says, *"In the midst of the congregation I will praise you."* Not only did Jesus teach in the temple before He was crucified, but He appeared to over five hundred people in the city where He was crucified. Verses 23–24 say, "You who fear the LORD, praise him! All you offspring of Jacob, glorify him, and stand in awe of him, all you offspring of Israel! For he has not despised or abhorred the affliction of the afflicted, and he has not hidden his face from him." At the cross, God's not turning His back on Jesus. He is pouring out His wrath on Him. No doubt about it. But this is not like God and the devil are playing chess, and the enemy's like, "Ha ha, I see Your move." This is not how this works at all. This has been the plan to redeem the entire world from the very beginning. God utters this out loud in Genesis 3: *I will put enmity between your offspring, Eve, and this enemy, this serpent, this satan. And one day a single Jewish man from your line will come, and this enemy will bruise His heel at the cross, but He will crush his head.*

Even though He doesn't quote Psalm 22 in its entirety, remember the *remez*. Every listener, young and old, as soon as they heard those words, would "hear" the entire Psalm in their mind. In short, Jesus is preaching the gospel from the cross. He says, "For he has not despised or abhorred the affliction of the afflicted, and he has not hidden his face from him, but has heard, when he cried to him. From you comes my praise in the great congregation; my vows I will perform before those who fear him. The afflicted shall eat and be satisfied; those who seek him shall praise the LORD! May your hearts live forever!" Jesus is talking about eternity here. About forever. About how heaven is coming and how, in this moment, Jesus is making it possible for your hearts to live forever because of what He is doing on the cross. When Jesus says He is the way, the truth, and the life, and no one comes to the Father but by Him, this is that moment, and this is that way.

Psalm 22 ends this way: "All the ends of the earth shall remember and turn to the LORD, and all the families of the nations shall worship before you." Jesus wants them to know, through Psalm 22, that this event, this happening before their eyes on a hill outside of the city of Jerusalem, will affect every tribe, tongue, and nation— it's the beginning of what we know as the Great Commission—and that God is using this brutal method of execution to accomplish His will. *It pleased the Father to crush him.*

A few years ago at our church, we were doing twenty-four hours of preaching. Nonstop. All our pastors were rotating. At my house, we were listening to the livestream, so my family was watching it either directly or indirectly because it was blanketing our home. Following one of my segments, I walked in the door and found JP (age twelve at the time) sitting at the table with several Bibles spread out in front of him. I said, "What you working on there, buddy?"

"Writing a sermon."

When I sat down, JP explained to me that it had been God's plan, from the beginning, for His Son to die on the cross for the sins of all mankind, and he was tracing it through—from Genesis to the gospels. Later that year, a hurricane shut down Jacksonville, so Gretchen and I had church at home. Our pastor? JP. His sermon was about eight minutes long and his point was simple: "The execution of God's Son was the execution of His plan."

I can't say it any better myself.

Jesus is putting the world on notice. He will be resurrected and will send His disciples to the very edge of the earth, and all nations will be saved—through this singular event right here. "For kingship belongs to the LORD, and he rules over the nations. All the prosperous of the earth eat and worship; before him shall bow all who go down to the dust, even the one who could not keep himself alive."

And then there's this. Try to get your mind around this. David is talking about us. "Posterity shall serve him; it shall be told of the Lord to the coming generation; they shall come and proclaim his righteousness to a people yet unborn." On the cross, Jesus is laying down His life for the glory of God, and yet in the middle of that, He wants the people standing there, who are starting to put the pieces of Psalm 22 together in their mind, to understand that literally, Jesus had you and me in mind. A people yet unborn.

"Posterity shall serve him; it shall be told of the Lord to the coming generation; they shall come and proclaim his righteousness to a people yet unborn"—*Ready for this part?*—"that he has done it." In Hebrew, literally, "it has been done."

On the cross, Jesus says, "My God, my God, why have you forsaken me?" He says, "I thirst." He says, **"Father, into your hands I commit my spirit!"** Then don't miss this. Jesus is hanging in what are the last few minutes of His life on this earth. He pushes up on His nail-pierced feet and the last thing that He says with a scream is **"It is finished."**

Tetelestai.

Archeologists have found bank records in the first century where loans that have been paid off have the word *tetelestai* printed on them. Paid in full.

Stand for a minute at His feet. At the foot of the cross. Listening to His last words, you begin to see the very words of the psalmist that are a thousand years old play out before your eyes. You see the people rail against Him and wag their fingers and their mouths at Him—"You saved others; save Yourself." You see Him cry out, "I thirst," and they take the sour wine and shove it in His face. You see His pierced hands, pierced feet. You watch as they pierce His side and blood and water flow from His heart. And in your mind, you hear the echo of His words, "It is finished," and you begin to think, *Oh my goodness. He is who He said He is. This is the Messiah. The Anointed One. The Lamb of God who's come to take away the sin of the entire world.*

A few hundred yards from where Jesus hung stood the temple. And in the temple, in the Holy of Holies, hung a curtain. Meant to separate the people of God, like us, from the presence of God. It was made of fine wool, several inches thick. And when Jesus says, "*Tetelestai,*" that curtain tears—from the top to the bottom. Not bottom to top. We also know from Scripture that when the earthquake rumbles, and the sky turns dark, the centurion, standing at the feet of Jesus, says, "Truly this was the Son of God!"

Even to the unbelieving Gentile, there was no doubt.

The question is this: *What* is finished?

Some people think Jesus is saying He's finished, but that's not what He's saying. Jesus does not say, "I am finished." Because He isn't. Far from it. Three days later He is going to walk out of a borrowed tomb. Borrowed because He only needs it for the weekend and then He's gonna give it back. Jesus is saying that the wrath of God has been satisfied and the requirement for the payment of sin under the sacrificial system is finished. No more is the blood of bulls and goats needed to cover the sins of the people for one year, because the Lamb of God has—once and for all—taken away the sin of the world.

Let's bring it home. What does *tetelestai* mean for you? Because God is just, your and my sin must be paid for, but because He knew we could not live up to that requirement since none of us is sinless, He gave His only Son in our place. Why? Because He loves us with a love we can't fathom. The death of Jesus on that cross means you are no longer required to pay the penalty for your own sin. He took your place. Your debt has been paid for. *Tetelestai* means the enemy doesn't get to tell you who you are anymore. It means your habits and your addictions don't define you. Why? Because their legal hold on your life is finished. Guilt is finished. You don't need to carry it around on your shoulders anymore. Why? Because you're no longer guilty. Condemnation is finished. Why? Because "there is therefore now no condemnation for those who are in Christ Jesus." Being good enough through religion is finished. Trying to come up with some kind of religious checklist that leads to nothing but exhaustion and pride is finished.

Finally, Jesus says, **"Father, into your hands I commit my Spirit!"** And there on the cross, to the shock of those who loved Him,

Jesus died. His friends took His body down, put Him in the grave, and the soldiers rolled a stone in front, sealed it, and stationed a garrison to stand guard.

But on the third day, His heart began to beat. The *ruach* of God reentered His lungs, the stone was rolled away, and the Roman guards scattered. From there, Jesus appeared to over five hundred people for six weeks. Why? Because He wasn't finished. And let me tell you why this matters right now, because not only is "it" finished, but He's not finished with you. The empty tomb and your alarm clock are empirical evidence. The fact that you woke up this morning and are currently sitting somewhere reading this book is proof that God is not done with you.

And the same power of the Holy Spirit of God that brought Jesus out of the grave is the very same thing that's swirling around in you right now, helping you understand that Jesus took your place. My place. The same Spirit of God that resurrected Jesus from the grave is the same Spirit saying something in your soul that only He can say. That's what's happening. Which means this: He's not done with you.

If the tomb is empty, anything is possible.

When we surrender to His lordship, then the event that happened at the cross—the shed blood of Jesus, the payment that satisfied the wrath of God—makes us right with God, despite your and my complete and total depravity. On the cross, Jesus put us back into right relationship with the Father. He forgave us, and not only that, He gave us the right to become children of God. Heirs and coheirs with Christ. Because the tomb is empty, your prodigal isn't too far gone and your marriage isn't beyond rescue.

Surrendering isn't simply a head thing. It's a heart thing. Bend the heart and the body follows. The centurion wasn't raised in church. Didn't know the Bible. Didn't know a single verse. He was as lost as it gets, and yet he found himself watching this man die and something on the inside of him changed. In the blink of an eye, he went from thinking *This guy is just one more inept leader of a failed insurrection* to *This is the Son of God.* Big difference. Somehow, he went from not understanding who Jesus is to knowing. And when he knew, he bent his knee as a symbol of bending his life before not just the good moral teacher, but the Savior of the universe.

Out in ministry, I got in trouble for doing something because the leaders of my church didn't understand what Jesus meant when He said, "It is finished." I was in seminary in Virginia but spent a summer in the Myrtle Beach area working three jobs. I worked at the gym, I waited tables, and on Wednesdays and Sundays, I worked at a very small legalistic denominational church—with emphasis on *legalistic.* But I needed the job and I thought it'd be a great opportunity for me to get some youth ministry experience.

Directly across the street from the gym where I worked sat a strip club. Seeing the possibilities, the owner of the gym, in a rather brilliant marketing move, gave all the dancers free memberships. And because those girls were always working out, our gym was packed with guys. I worked both the check-in counter and the smoothie counter, so over time, I got to know the girls, and given that I was pretty unfamiliar with the exotic dancing world, I found out they each had two names—their real name and their stage name. What's more, almost all of them had kids and none of their kids knew what they did for a living. Each one started out thinking they were going to dance for a few months, make a little money, and then exit. Dancing was never their plan A. Nor their plan B. Their problem was they started making money because they were all gorgeous and Myrtle Beach was littered with men away from their families on multiday golf trips. Making money was followed closely by needing to make expensive car payments and the need to support some sort of substance habit, because all of them needed something to help them climb up on stage night after night. Every Wednesday and Sunday, I had to write a talk for that night's youth service, so when I wasn't making smoothies, I'd spread my Bible and notebook out across the counter and work on my sermon. Sermon prep for teenagers. After these girls worked out, they'd sit at my countertop bar and order their smoothie, and since I wasn't asking them for their phone number and they thought me relatively harmless, they'd ask, "What're you doing?" Knowing I needed practice, I would ask them if I could go through my little sermon with them, and they'd all say yes, so I'd just go through my talk with them and then ask what was confusing. I'd ask, "Did this make sense?" I figured if it was clear to my stripper friends, then it would be clear to my students. (I know this sounds disparaging, but I'm not sure which group should be offended.) Inevitably, somewhere across that counter, I'd share the gospel and invite them to church. About a month in, this super sweet girl whose stage name was Sunshine said, "Well, I'll go to church with you." And about there, I thought, *Oh no. I didn't think this through very well.* But how do you uninvite somebody to church? So I said, "All right."

Sunshine said she'd drive, which was awesome because her car was a lot nicer than mine. So Sunday morning, she showed up at my little apartment in a brand-new white Corvette convertible. Just her, her daughter, and me. It was a two-seater, so her daughter just sat on her lap. The church was twenty-four miles away from my house, inland, and she let me drive. The license plate read TPLSS FUN. A little play on words. So we drove to church. I got there in sixteen minutes.

I don't know how to say this delicately, but she wore a short little sundress and some really high-heeled shoes. Add to that the fact that she was heavily invested in her career from a surgery standpoint, and she didn't look like your typical front-pew Baptist.

We dropped her daughter off at the children's church and then the two of us walked into church—together—at which point the stares and the looks started. Boring a hole into both of us. She was uncomfortable and I was uncomfortable. The judgment was tangible. I think we sang a few hymns. I seem to remember "Amazing Grace" was one of them. I did the announcements, and the pastor preached, and I have no idea what he preached on because I was feeling so bad for her. Afterward she and I were walking out of the sanctuary to pick up her daughter when one of the deacons said, "Hey, we need to talk to you for just a minute in the office." I had a feeling this was not going to go well. I was like, "All right."

She picked up her daughter and waited by the car while I walked into an ambush in the senior pastor's office. In the Bible, the title *deacon* means servant. In this church, it meant power broker. They looked down their noses at me. "Why are you bringing somebody like that here?"

I said, "What do you mean?"

One of the other deacons started hammering me. "The reason this church exists is to protect our children and good, clean people like us from people like that at the beach. And for you to bring her in here, what kind of example is that setting for the kids and for the students that you're supposed to be in charge of?"

To this day, I'm still ashamed of my answer. I just caved and said, "I'm sorry."

I knew that their response to her was wrong and my response to their response was wrong. To this day, I still know it's wrong. At the time, I was twenty-two years old and didn't want to get fired from my little job. To be honest, I don't really know what I was thinking. I'm not really proud of my answer. So I got done taking my twenty-minute thrashing and then walked out to the parking lot.

Hers was the only car there, and her kid was sitting in the car, finishing coloring a picture of Jesus she got in Sunday school. When I walked up to Sunshine, she was wearing aviators and tears were cascading down her face. She said, "That was about me, wasn't it?"

I couldn't bring myself to tell her the truth, so I lied. "Nah, man, nah." I made some stuff up. And then we got into her car and I didn't know what to do. She was upset. I was upset. But it was my fault. We drove back a lot slower and the silence was just so awkward. I was trying to make conversation and I didn't know what to say, so I said, "What did you think about church?"

Without hesitation, she said, "I've never felt more degraded in my whole life."

She said this while her daughter was coloring a picture of Jesus.

The night before, Sunshine had danced naked on a pole for money in front of strange, gropey men while high on something, and somehow the men and women in my church made her feel worse than how she'd felt the night before. And just for the record, she said she recognized a couple of men's faces.

For the rest of the summer, my friendship with Sunshine was significantly strained. She didn't sit at the counter, didn't order smoothies, and wasn't a part of Bible talk. And then, quietly, she left town.

When I realized she was gone for good, I promised myself that if I ever had the chance, I was going to make sure that any church that I was a part of would be welcoming to the people that Jesus welcomed, which was everybody. That's one of the reasons the vision of The Church of Eleven22 is that we are "a movement for ALL PEOPLE to discover and deepen a relationship with Jesus Christ." That *ALL PEOPLE* includes Sunshine. It includes you.

I've been a pastor for more than twenty years, and this memory hurts as much today as the day it happened. If you've ever been rejected by a church, if you've ever taken a chance on us only to be judged and looked down upon, would you please allow me to tell you that I'm so sorry? Please forgive us. We are all just broken and sometimes we get it wrong more often than we get it right. That response, that shame, that judgment are not what Jesus bled and died for.

Today, in our church, we have a strip club ministry. Once a month my wife, along with several other ladies, goes in and sits with the girls in the dressing room. They take them dinner, ask about their kids and their plans, and just share the love of God and an invitation to our church. We just get to know them and we don't judge them. And I thank God that we've had multiple girls come to our church, feel loved and welcomed, and walk away from that lifestyle.

When Jesus said, "It is finished," He also put to rest your and my right to judge others—of which we are all guilty. As a twenty-two-year-old naïve youth pastor, I caved and let the judgment of older men keep me from just loving on a lady who needed Jesus. A lot. Who knows how many times she'd been betrayed and rejected and here we were, doing it all over again.

The word *tetelestai* allows every one of us, regardless of our sin, to walk into His presence without shame and without judgment. Each of us, because of the shed blood of Jesus, has not only the right, but also the invitation to stand before the throne of God and receive the love He alone offers. "It is finished" drove a stake in the ground for all of us who would cling to it, and it means exactly what Paul told the Romans. Nothing can separate us from His love. All barriers have been torn down and our behavior and our unrighteousness can no longer exclude us from Him. That doesn't mean He won't look at our behavior and say what he said to the woman caught in adultery, *Go and sin no more.* Some of us are just flat-out walking in sin and it's time we give that to Jesus. *"It is finished"* is not a license to sin; it's an invitation to walk through the doors and bring it to Jesus without condemnation or finger-pointing shame.

According to Paul in his letter to the Colossians, the written record of my wrongs—everything I've ever done wrong, every sin I've ever committed—has been nailed to the cross, where Jesus made a spectacle of the author. Satan. *"It is finished"* means my identity is no longer found in my guilty verdict or my prison sentence or my divorce or my addiction or name-your-sin, but *"It is finished"* means that now, only Jesus gets to tell you who you are and who I am. And there on the cross, He invites us to be His children. Without the cross of Jesus, you and I are guilty. Destined to hell. For all eternity. Through the cross, Jesus triumphed, and continues to triumph, over the devil. Once and for all. Permanently. For all eternity. And because of the cross, no matter my history, no matter my past, no matter my sin, when I believe and confess Him as Lord, I am redeemed, forgiven, cleansed, made righteous, sanctified, and brought by the hand of Jesus up to the Father, who lifts me into His lap and calls me, "Child."

In Jewish tradition, when you were eating at the table, if you were done, you would just kind of toss your napkin. But if you got up with the intention of returning, like to go to the bathroom or whatever, you would fold it. A folded napkin signified *I'll be back.* When Peter and John walked into the empty tomb, they found the face covering, the shroud, folded at the head. Jesus was putting the world on notice that He was returning. Which He did. And He will again.

And because He did, you and I can have this conversation. Some of you are surrendered, kneeling at the feet of Jesus. Some of you are hardheaded, making excuses, clinging to anything but Jesus. You're thinking to yourself, *I'll get around to that someday.* But what if these are the last few minutes of your life? What if you close this book and get hit by a truck? Or your widow-maker breaks loose? Or a vessel bursts in your head? What if?

I'm not Jesus, but through me, He is asking you—that's right,

YOU—are you fully surrendered to the lordship of Jesus Christ? Have you believed in your heart that He is Lord and have you confessed Him as your Savior? And if you have, are there places in your heart where He is not Lord? Places you are holding back?

Why?

Last chance. Do you want to?

Pray with Me

Our good and gracious heavenly Father—God, we love You more than anything. We love You because You first loved us. We thank You, Jesus, that in the Garden of Gethsemane, You said, "Not my will, but yours, be done," and that You went through the excruciating, humiliating, shame-filled cross for our sake. God, I thank You that we are saved by grace—pure, unadulterated grace through faith. God, we thank You for the gift of faith that You have given to Your people on this day. God, I thank You that it's not by works but by grace that we are saved. And Lord, I thank You for that empty tomb. God, I thank You that Jesus is alive. God, I thank You that as Christians, we are not just mimickers of a teaching, but we are followers of a living Savior. And Lord, I pray that we would be forever changed because Jesus is alive. Because Father, You love us, and the Spirit lives in us. Lord, I thank You for my salvation and I pray that You would ransom the hearts that read the words of Your sacrifice and triumph over death. And God, I pray for Sunshine. I pray that maybe, just maybe, she picks up this book and she reads how wrong I was. And that the grace of God breaks through the pain we caused and that she comes to know Your perfect love. If the tomb is empty, anything is possible. I pray this in the name of the one who died for her and the rest of us. In Jesus' name. Amen.

Epilogue

I was on a mission trip when my phone rang. It was a guy from our church, a really gifted doctor with the Mayo Clinic. He said, "I want you to pray about something."

"Yeah, man."

"How would you feel about eating dinner with Dr. Billy Graham at my house?"

I looked at my phone. "I don't even have to pray about that," I said.

I don't know what I was expecting, but when Gretchen and I arrived, we were met by the doctor and his wife, their daughter, Dr. Graham, and the man who traveled with him. That was it. Just us. For four or five hours on a Friday evening.

Of all the humans I could have ever hoped to meet, this was the guy. So, just to polish up on my Billy Graham history, I read a biography of his life. And when we walked into the doctor's house, there was Billy Graham. The man. He was way up in age and he was leaning on a walker, but it was Billy Graham. I was a little fuzzy on etiquette, so I was unsure how to introduce myself. I mean, what do you say? So, I just said, "Dr. Graham, I read in your biography that you were most excited to meet Joe DiMaggio. That was one of the highlights of your life. Well, this is that moment for me."

He smiled. "No, pastor, I'm just happy to meet you."

I nudged Gretchen and whispered, "Did you hear that? He called me pastor."

Gretchen shook her head. "He probably doesn't know your name."

And I was thinking, *Woman, why you got to do me that way?*

So we got to talking and he said, "Tell me a little bit about your church."

The previous weekend, we'd baptized maybe two hundred people at a beach baptism. So, I said, "Things are going pretty well. We've grown to a few thousand people. And we just baptized a couple hundred…"

When I said this, he physically jolted and shook his head. "Well, I've never heard of such a thing."

I didn't say this but I thought, *Um, sir, I'm pretty sure you have—1973, Seoul, Korea. Between May 30 and June 3, you preached to 3.2 million, 1.1 million on June 3 alone. And in that time, some seventy-five thousand people got saved. I think you've heard of such things.*

Here's what's crazy. That moment reminded me of the parable of the talents. If anybody's a five-talent person, it's Dr. Graham. But despite that, he never compared what he did with what we were doing. He was just excited for what we were doing. Genuinely.

So, we ate dinner, and at one point he looked over to Gretchen. He said, "Well, ma'am, I hear you're a worship leader."

And you need to understand that while Gretchen was and is a worship leader with an incredible voice, she was really struggling with this at the time. With calling, gifting, every-thing. What I'm getting at is that when Dr. Graham asked her this, she was not overly confident in her gift. But somehow, she said, "Yes, sir, Dr. Graham."

Then he said the most amazing thing. "Well, would you sing me a song?"

Gretchen turned white as a sheet. She was terrified. She's also super shy. I was thinking, *Woman, you better get up and sing. Billy says sing, you better sing.*

And in one of the most beautiful things I've ever seen, she stepped around me and kneeled down between Dr. Graham's good ear and me. And when she knelt, he leaned toward her and she started singing that Bethel song, "Closer."

And when she got to the chorus—"So pull me a little closer"—Dr. Graham just closed his eyes and lifted his hands. I was awestruck. My wife was leading my—and almost every pastor's—spiritual hero in worship. "Take me a little deeper..." I was blown away.

Finally, she wrapped it up and he opened his eyes. Straight up, he said, "I believe that's the most beautiful song I've ever heard."

I was thinking, *Baby, if Dr. Graham says you can sing, then you can sing. And trust me, this man's heard some people. Like, the best ever.*

As long as I live, I'll never forget Dr. Graham affirming my wife when she needed it most.

Then I said, "Dr. Graham, would you pray for us and our ministry?"

He never hesitated. He reached out, held our hands, and I remember he said, "Dear God, please protect this man from himself."

I sort of cracked one eye and I remember thinking, *Have you been talking to my wife?*

But he prayed over and for us. Amazingly, he never mentioned the ministry. He just prayed for our marriage. For us. When he said, "Amen," he looked at me and said, "You make disciples; you love your wife; Jesus will build His church."

To me, Dr. Graham was speaking Matthew 16:18: "On this rock I will build my church." And for some reason in that moment, it just got real simple for me. It's not my job to build His church. That's Jesus' job. My job is to tell everyone who He is—THE Christ—and walk in obedience. It was just a mind-blowingly simple moment of clarity for me.

The last thing I asked him at dinner was this: "If you could preach one more crusade, what would it be?"

Without hesitating, he said, "Oh, that's easy. I'd preach Galatians 6:14." Then he just stopped.

I smiled and sat back, nodding. "Mm-hmm." Actually, I made a prolonged mooing noise. I hear it at church often. It's sort of a grunted "amen" and it sounds spiritual.

Truth be told, I had no idea what that verse said. But he was pretty old and couldn't see too well, so off to one side, I pulled out my phone. All the while, I'm mooing in agreement. "Oh yeah. Glory."

So I punch my Bible app and bring up Galatians 6:14: "But far be it from me to boast except in the cross of our Lord Jesus Christ, by which the world has been crucified to me, and I to the world."

And I was sitting there thinking to myself that if anybody ever had the right to think to themselves that they'd done some things, it would be this man. Galatians 6:14—he didn't hesitate. And then in what I like to think was his last crusade, he went on to share the gospel with us, at the table. The Word of God spoke through that man to us. To just remind us.

I grew up Baptist. I like to say I'm a recovering Baptist. Meaning, I haven't been around too many charismatic events. Just not my history. But something shifted in the atmosphere in that moment for us. Gretchen walked out of that house without the fear and insecurity and trepidation that had been hounding her. Something in our lives shifted in that moment.

Shortly thereafter was when my boss and pastor, Jerry Sweat, came to us and said, "We know God has called you to lead a church. We think it's time." So, with his blessing and encouragement, we launched The Church of Eleven22.

Since we started, some ten thousand people have been saved. We've baptized over three thousand. And today, between Sunday services and online downloads, more than three hundred thousand people a week are listening to or watching the sermons. I'm not saying that to make it all about me. It's not. I'm a country preacher from Dillon, South Carolina. I love my King and I love His Word. And I say this a lot and I'm not kidding—my sermons are moderately delivered and exceptionally received. The Holy Spirit does that. Not me.

You can trace everything that has happened to us back to that day. In unbridled humility, Dr. Graham did something to us, for us, and in us that gave us a confidence and a courage where there had been timidity before. I never thought I'd lead a church like Eleven22. What God does in us and to us and through us exceeds my hopes. I also never thought I'd meet Dr. Graham, much less have dinner with him. I want to be careful that I don't make more of this than I should, but something was transferred or deposited not by him but by the Holy Spirit in that moment.

And I thank God for it.

God the Father, through the Spirit, raised the Son to life. Our faith is based on an event. He was dead. He's not now. What is impossible with man is possible with God.

We started this journey staring out across Jerusalem. THE mountain of God. The place where He has written His name forever. Literally. The shape of the mountains spells His name. And the reason this mountain matters is because after Jesus shed His blood,

His friends pulled down His cold, dead, lifeless body and placed Him in an unused tomb. In the prologue, I said, "This is where, three days later, He rose from the dead and walked out shining like the sun. Tomb empty. The keys of death and hell hanging from His belt. On this mountain, the tomb is empty. Which changes everything. For everyone who would believe it. Forever."

The reason we're talking about this mountain is because the tomb that it holds is empty.

The mountain may hold the tomb, but the tomb couldn't hold Him.

Let me say that again because it's the point: the mountain may hold the tomb, but the tomb couldn't hold Him.

Jesus is alive. Right this moment. Reigning.

And because He's alive, everything He said is true. And we can trust Him. We can believe *in* Him. Put our faith in Him. Surrender to Him.

I started this book with seven questions. Let me circle back around. When push comes to shove:

1. Do you live as though you can save yourself? Do you believe His promise to you?
2. Who tells you who you are? You or Jesus?
3. Do you still worship your idol? How long will you limp between two opinions?
4. Do you really want to be blessed?
5. How will you stand against the enemy?
6. Do you want to be healed? How about delivered?
7. Do you understand what was finished? Do you even care?

Bottom line, how do you live? Like, really? Is the cold, dead body of Jesus still lying in that tomb?

Or…is He alive? Ruling and reigning, right now?

What would happen if you, like Paul, knew Christ and the power of His resurrection?

If you believe that the tomb is empty, and you are following Christ, then by definition, you follow Him out of the tomb.

The empty tomb means that you don't have to continuously walk in the weight and consequence of your sin. That Jesus alone saves us. That Jesus alone tells us who we are. That Jesus alone is worthy of our worship. That Jesus alone blesses us. That Jesus alone has empowered us to both fight and defeat the enemy. That Jesus alone delivers us. And that Jesus wasn't kidding when He said, "It is finished."

The empty tomb means you no longer have to walk in shame and condemnation. You don't have to walk in addiction and habits that kill you. You don't have to walk in unforgiveness and bitterness. You don't have to walk in a scorecard or under some measuring stick of all the things you've done wrong in your life. You don't have to walk in a world that is allowed to label and identify you and tell you who you are because of your past.

I love that Bethel song—especially when Ricky Skaggs's daughter sings it—that says, "If you walked out of the grave, I'm walking too…" When I'm alone in my truck, I crank that thing and sing it at the top of my lungs.

What's the first thing that Jesus tells Lazarus when he walks out of the tomb? "Take off your grave clothes." Why? Because he's alive, and living people don't wear dead people's clothes. A lot of people believe in Jesus for their salvation but continue walking as if He's still lying behind that stone. Nothing but dust and bones. How ridiculous would it be if, three or four weeks after Jesus brought Lazarus back to life, he was still walking around with his old, stinky, spiced, and embalmed grave clothes? Would that make sense to anyone? You'd be like, "Bro, what are you doing? You don't need to wear those things anymore. You're not him. He's dead. And the dead you is gone. The new you is alive. Besides, those things stink..."

What does Jesus tell the paralytic? "Take up your mat and walk." Why? Because pain can be a platform for the glory of God. But if three or four weeks later you saw this man lying back on his filthy, nasty mat, you'd say, "Bro, what're you doing? You are not crippled anymore. And you're not an invalid. Get up out of your own mess and walk." When we return to the habits and addictions and the old pathways of the old self, we're just a living man who put a dead man's clothes back on. This is a man who has been set free from the prison of being a cripple. He can now run, walk, jump, praise, and, to top it off, he has been granted access into the temple. Mind you, because of his crippling ailment, he has been excluded from the temple his whole life, by the law. Now he can run in and out the doors at will. Why would that man choose to return to his mat and lie in the cesspool of an invalid's waste when freedom lies before him?

Before Saint Augustine got saved, he was quite a womanizer. Following his conversion, he returns past a woman in the street. A former mistress. She sees him and says, "It is I, sir. It is I." Just judging from her language, maybe she's expecting the party to continue where it left off. Augustine ignores her. One account reads that he "ran the other way." But she's relentless, like sin, so she tracks him down again. "It is I. It is I." Augustine is trying to be obedient to Scripture. He's "fleeing sexual immorality." But she's not having it. Finally, she faces him. "Sir, it is I." To which Augustine responds, "But it is no longer I." A beautiful summation of Paul: "I have been crucified with Christ. It is no longer I who live, but Christ who lives in me" (Gal. 2:20).

Let me ask this: If Jesus walked out of the grave, why are you still crouched in the corner? Chained to the wall? Why are you making your bed in there? If the prison doors have been flung wide, ripped off the hinges, and the stone has been rolled away, then why have you made the tomb your home? If you've been crucified with Christ and it is no longer you who live but He who lives in you, and the life you now live you live by faith in the Son of God who loved you and gave Himself for you, then why are you still wearing grave clothes?

Maybe this is what Paul means when he says in Philippians, *Walk in a manner worthy of the gospel of Jesus Christ.* The Joby Martin translation reads like this: Rip off the grave clothes, burn them, and let Jesus wrap you in His robe of righteousness. Then run out of the tomb and into the arms of the Father. Why? Because it is finished, and when He said this, He wasn't kidding.

Jesus left behind sin and death and condemnation and the penalty of sin. All of it. Why? For the joy set before Him. Who is that joy? You are. I am. So, tell me, why on earth would we ever do anything to identify with the grave or allow ourselves to be identified with the grave? The grave has no power. It couldn't hold Him and because we are in Him, it can't hold us.

Look, I don't have a monopoly on this walking-out-of-the-grave thing. One of the things about me that frustrates me most is how I still struggle with the same things I struggled with as a sixteen-year-old boy. Seems like at forty-seven, I would have outgrown some of those things.

But I haven't. You can ask Gretchen.

But thanks be to God, the only hope is not me and my ability to white-knuckle out of this and willpower through it. Turns out the only hope is this:

If the tomb is empty, anything is possible.

Including me walking out of the grave because He did.

Including me walking in a manner worthy of the gospel of Jesus Christ.

This message is way different than "Try harder." This message is way different than "God's good. You're bad. Try harder. See you next week." If God breathed the *ruach* of life into His dead Son, then surely He has breathed that life into me. And into you.

And...if He walked out of the grave, I'm walking too.

In truth, it changes everything. It changes the way we go to work. It changes what we do with our money. It changes the way we love our spouses. It changes the way we parent our children. We don't have to do it the way the world tells us to do it. Everything the world worships is temporary, but the One that we worship walked out of the grave and ascended to the right hand of God the Father—who is eternal. Jesus is seated at His right hand, tapping His toe, waiting to step foot back down on this mountain and make all things new.

The empty tomb changes everything. About everything. For everyone who would believe.

Forever.

A lot of people in my position get really focused on how to grow a church. How to put butts in seats. Counting the offering. Salvations. Baptisms. Online views. Followers. Ad nauseam. And I'm not immune to hoping for those things, but I often remember what Billy Graham told me at dinner: "Love your wife. Make disciples. And Jesus will take care of His church."

As a man, father, friend, and pastor, there are four things I cannot do: I can't make anyone repent, forgive, worship, or love. And a disciple repents continuously, forgives those who don't deserve it, worships relentlessly, and loves the unlovable.

Our church has opened campuses in prisons. Legit campuses. We meet every week. And the prisoners all wear the same clothes because the state gives those to them when they walk in. Some of those men and women have been released and they now attend one of our other campuses. But when they walk in, they don't wear their prison clothes. And yet some of you have been set free from prison but walk into your day wearing pants with stripes and a shirt with a number that no longer identifies you.

That cell is not your life. You're free. At nighttime, you don't knock on the warden's door and ask to sleep in your old cell. Would any prisoner anywhere ever do that? Of course not. I've met many of the guys in prison. And truth be told, many of those men in prison, eating and sleeping behind bars, are freer than those of us on the outside—because they have found freedom in Christ. They understand, maybe better than most of us, what *tetelestai* really means.

Have any of you spent any time in a hospital? A night? Week? Month? What's the first thing they give you? One of those stupid gowns that's open in the back so every time you walk down the hall, everybody can see your backside. But here you are. Out of the hospital. Are any of you still wearing that robe? How about the armband? Of course not. Consider how ridiculous it would be to walk into a steak house wearing that robe.

"Hi, I have a reservation for seven."

The receptionist would shake her head. "Um, no you don't. You need to be in a hospital."

You laugh. "No, I'm good. They discharged me."

The receptionist scratches her head. "Then why are you wearing those clothes?"

Like Peter after he denied Jesus, we return to our old ways of life. We cease "following Him" for a whole host of reasons. Shame is a big one. But what shame can stand up to *tetelestai*? Who can argue with the King of all kings, who upholds all things by the Word of His power and through whom all things were made? We go back to these old habits and just fall into a rut of, "Well, this is who I am." We suffer gospel amnesia and forget who we are.

Paul proclaimed his desire was *to know Christ and the power of His resurrection.* But why? I mean, really. What's the big deal? So, some guy beat death. Good for him. What's that got to do with me? I think if we really knew this, like, in our core, it'd make our fuzzy little heads explode.

The big deal is this—if Jesus walked out of the grave, and you have been crucified with Christ, that means you've been raised with Him. Born again. All things new. When the Father looks at you, He sees His Son. So, why are you still wrapped in your grave clothes?

One last time: If the tomb is empty, and "it is finished," why do you live your life as if it's not and it isn't?

I've wrestled with including this story about Dr. Graham. Maybe I should have kept it to myself. Maybe you think I'm trying to make it all about me or let you see how cool I am. Trust me—I am far more amazed by this event than any of you. I'm a redneck from Dillon and he's Dr. Graham. I mean, come on. Who am I that God would allow it, much less invite us into it?

That said, He did. So, I've included it for two reasons: One, if I'm honest, I never thought it possible. And two, something was transferred into and through us that night. Not because of anything we did, but because God wanted to do a thing. And it made a difference. We left dinner different than when we arrived. And we lived differently afterward.

And I want that for you.

If I could transfer something into and through you, right now, by the power of the Holy Spirit, I would. So, in the same way Dr. Graham prayed for Gretchen and me, would you let me pray over you? Maybe we should do this on our knees. I'd invite you to join me on the floor. Facedown.

Pray with Me—and Let's Walk Out of the Grave

Our good and gracious heavenly Father, we thank You for the empty tomb and the power that dwells in anyone who has put their faith in Jesus. Lord, I pray that through that same power that brought Jesus out of the grave, we too would walk in a manner worthy of the gospel of Jesus Christ. Lord, I pray for every man, woman, and student who reads these words. May they take off the grave clothes of the past. May they put off addictions and habits and false thinking and ego and insecurity and that old way of life. May they instead walk in a newness of life. Lord, I pray that You would give us eyes to see as You see, that we would be able to do as You say. Lord, I pray that the gospel would take such root in our hearts that we would boast in nothing but the cross of our Lord and Savior, Jesus Christ. May this world be crucified to us, and us to it. May we no longer live but may Christ live in us and through us. And for any believer who has not taken up their mat and walked, but instead has decided to lie back down in the filth, would You please bring conviction to walk in a newness of life? I thank You for the abundant life that You have called us to. I pray that we would find rest and reward in the fact that it is finished. Therefore, the performing and pretending are over. Thank You that if the tomb is empty, anything is possible. In Jesus' name. Amen.

Acknowledgments

To the One True God. Father. Son. Holy Spirit. I know that this entire book is all about you, but I must acknowledge you every opportunity that I get. Father, thank you for choosing me based on your own grace and goodness. Holy Spirit, thank you for making your home inside of me. What the enemy whispers is unfit for use, you have made your temple. Jesus, thank you for not only taking my place, which I will never be able to get over, but also for calling me your friend.

To G. You are simply the best. I would not be me without you. When I wanted to quit ministry two decades ago, you talked me into giving it one more chance. When I was afraid to launch The Church of Eleven22, you were the one who spoke courage into me. When my sermons are not very good, you always tell me they are the best. Many pastors marry their lid. I have married a launchpad. Ah do.

To JP and RC. I'm so proud of you both. I know it cost you a lot for me to be your dad. I thank you both for role you play in our family for us to play our part in the great commission. Of all the things I get to do, which are incredible, nothing brings me more joy and honor than getting to be your dad. Our church will have dozens of lead pastors. This world has had countless ministers and ministries. I am proud to be your one and only dad. I love you both all the way.

To The Church of Eleven22. I really do love you like crazy.

To the elders. Thank you for your love and devotion. Thank you for your willingness to tell me no. Thank you for your faith in God's call on my life. Thank you for going to war on behalf of me and my family. Thank you for taking on the fiery darts of the enemy for over a decade now. Every blessing outside of my family that I have in my life has come through your hands. I will forever be indebted to each of you. Thank you for not being ruled by fear but for faithfully pressing on.

To the deacons. Thank you for your tireless service. Thank you for being on the frontlines of ministry day in and day out. Because you are faithful to what God has called you to do, I am able to do the same.

To our pastors and staff. It is such a privilege to co-labor with you for the sake of the gospel. Never forget that God does not give churches to pastors. He gives pastors to churches. It encourages me to see the way you care for the flock and love His bride. Thank you for your humility to "follow me as I follow Christ." We are family. Thank you for that.

To anyone who considers Eleven22 their church. You are simply the greatest gathering of people I have ever encountered. Thank you for leaning into God's Word being preached. Thank you for your hunger for sound doctrine and God's Word for real life. Thank you for not faking it and for allowing me to do what I do.

To Keith Darnell, Lynn Turner, DR, Bill Ross, Pastor Jerry Sweat. Each of you hired me at different seasons of my life in ministry. Thank you for seeing in me what I often didn't see in myself. Thank you for believing that God could use even someone like me. Thanks for taking a chance. I am thankful that God put each of you in my life at just the right time.

To Charles Martin. I thank God for you, brother. I thank Him for your friendship and brotherhood. I am so glad He put you into my life at just the right time. I am thankful for the way God has connected your heart, soul, mind, and pen. Thank you for helping me take what I believe are God-inspired thoughts and ideas from the stage to the page. I hope we get to do this for decades to come.

To my mamma, Linda. I learned the tenderness of God from you. Thank you for that. Thank you for believing in me. I am proud to be your son. If I have any ability to articulate the gospel in such a way that people can understand, I learned that from you.

To my daddy, Joseph Perry Martin Jr. The reality that God is our Father was always an easy thing to grab onto because of the kind of dad you have been to me. Thank you for always being there. Thank you for pushing me to do hard things when I didn't want to. Thank you for putting your faith in Jesus and for allowing me to follow His call on my life. I know that you are proud of me in all the right ways, and that means more than you will ever know.

About the Authors

Joby Martin is the founder and lead pastor of The Church of Eleven22 in Jacksonville, Florida. Since launching the church in 2012, he has led a movement for all people to discover and deepen a relationship with Jesus Christ. In addition to providing The Church of Eleven22 with vision and leadership, Pastor Joby is a national and international preacher and teacher. He has been married to his wife, Gretchen, for over twenty years and they have a son, JP, and a daughter, Reagan Capri.

Charles Martin is a *New York Times* bestselling author of sixteen novels, including his most recent, *The Letter Keeper*. He has also recently authored two nonfiction books: *What If It's True?* and *They Turned the World Upside Down*. His work has been translated into more than thirty-five languages in forty-plus countries around the world.